28
SECONDS

MICHAEL BRYANT

28
SECONDS

A TRUE STORY
OF ADDICTION,
TRAGEDY,
AND HOPE

VIKING

VIKING
an imprint of Penguin Canada

Published by the Penguin Group
Penguin Group (Canada), 90 Eglinton Avenue East, Suite 700, Toronto, Ontario, Canada M4P 2Y3

Penguin Group (USA) Inc., 375 Hudson Street, New York, New York 10014, U.S.A.
Penguin Books Ltd, 80 Strand, London WC2R 0RL, England
Penguin Ireland, 25 St Stephen's Green, Dublin 2, Ireland (a division of Penguin Books Ltd)
Penguin Group (Australia), 250 Camberwell Road, Camberwell, Victoria 3124, Australia
(a division of Pearson Australia Group Pty Ltd)
Penguin Books India Pvt Ltd, 11 Community Centre, Panchsheel Park, New Delhi – 110 017, India
Penguin Group (NZ), 67 Apollo Drive, Rosedale, Auckland 0632, New Zealand
(a division of Pearson New Zealand Ltd)
Penguin Books (South Africa) (Pty) Ltd, 24 Sturdee Avenue, Rosebank,
Johannesburg 2196, South Africa

Penguin Books Ltd, Registered Offices: 80 Strand, London WC2R 0RL, England

First published 2012

1 2 3 4 5 6 7 8 9 10 (RRD)

Copyright © Michael Bryant, 2012

The David Foster Wallace quotation on page v is taken from *Infinite Jest*,
published by Little, Brown in 1996.

A portion of the proceeds from the book will be donated to the Pine River Foundation.

Manufactured in the U.S.A.

LIBRARY AND ARCHIVES CANADA CATALOGUING IN PUBLICATION

Bryant, Michael J. (Michael James), 1966–
28 seconds : a true story of addiction, tragedy,
and hope / Michael Bryant.

Includes index.
ISBN 978-0-670-06644-5

1. Bryant, Michael J. (Michael James), 1966– —Trials, litigation, etc.
2. Lawyers—Ontario—Biography. 3. Politicians—Ontario—Biography.
4. Sheppard, Darcy, d. 2009—Death and burial. 5. Cycling accidents—Ontario—Case studies.
6. Law reform—Ontario. I. Title. II. Title: Twenty-eight seconds.

KE416.B79A3 2012   340.092   C2012-903280-8
KF345.Z9B79 2012

Visit the Penguin Canada website at **www.penguin.ca**

Special and corporate bulk purchase rates available; please see
www.penguin.ca/corporatesales or call 1-800-810-3104, ext. 2477.

ALWAYS LEARNING   **PEARSON**

TO MY BROTHER
ALAN THOMAS BRYANT (1972–2011),
AND TO SUSAN ABRAMOVITCH

"Both destiny's kisses and its dope-slaps illustrate
an individual person's basic personal powerlessness
over the really meaningful events in his life:
i.e., almost nothing important that ever happens to you
happens because you engineer it."

—*David Foster Wallace*, Infinite Jest *(1996)*

"A pedestal may be a very unreal thing.
A pillory is a terrific reality."

—*Oscar Wilde*, De Profundis *(1897)*

CONTENTS

Top Down

At dusk on the night that everything changed, my life was almost embarrassingly triumphant. I had an impressive new job. I had two glorious children. I was celebrating the 12th anniversary of the marriage that produced them. My parents and siblings were alive and well. At age 43, my future was featured favourably and often in glossy media.

Any day now, *Hello!* magazine was due to run its series on the perfect couple with the perfect kids, the perfect home, the perfect careers: he a political force shrewdly biding time, building connections and influence away from elected office; she an entertainment lawyer to the stars; the children enrolled and thriving in French immersion at Toronto's toniest public school.

Fast forward, however, and you might think I'd become Job's apprentice.

On August 31, 2009, on a strip of Toronto known as the Mink Mile—the ritziest stretch of high-end retail shops in Canada—I was involved in the death of a man. Later, I was charged with killing him.

In 2010, those charges were dropped and the legal ordeal ended. But so did my marriage. In 2011, my younger brother died suddenly in his thirties of a rare heart condition. We were holding hands when he passed away.

Until the night that everything changed, I was one of fortune's favoured sons, and the inside of a jail cell seemed as unlikely a destination for me as the far side of the moon. Until then, by almost any measure, I was on a roll. Everything I'd ever sought out, ever dreamed of, ever imagined had become true in my life.

I had met and married a great and brilliant woman, Susan Abramovitch. I had decided that clerking at the Supreme Court of Canada was the best legal launching pad, that Harvard was the best graduate law school, and that Wall Street's Sullivan & Cromwell was the best law firm. I had sought, and obtained, a place at them all.

And my pride swelled further as I piled up the accomplishments: elected to the Ontario Legislature at age 33, the province's youngest-ever Attorney General by age 37, Government House Leader at 41, and then, in my final months in office, participating in the auto industry rescue of 2009. Then I exited from politics under my terms, voluntarily, and into my brand-new job as Toronto's top investment booster.

By the night it all changed, I had created a monster of a media darling, and harboured a titanic ego—in every sense of the word. "Michael Bryant is content to strut towards a window table," a newspaper journalist wrote around that time, "and do what he does best—be the centre of attention, without even trying."

And this particular night, our wedding anniversary, was surely destined, just like everything else I touched, to turn out golden. The night began, as it would famously end, in my black 1995 Saab 9000 convertible, a spruced-up beater that had cost me a little over $6000.

In that car, everything changed. For ten years, in the unrelenting crucible of politics and high office, some of it as the Chief Law Officer of Ontario, I had avoided personal scandal and public defeat. Then, because of what happened in just 28 seconds, I had more scandal and defeat than most people are likely to know.

I'd once sat atop the Ontario justice system. For four years, I'd been accountable for 900 criminal prosecutors, many of whom I'd hired or promoted. I'd appointed more than half the judges for the main criminal court, plus the chief justice, all her associate chief justices, and more than a hundred Justices of the Peace. I was friends with dozens of judges on the Ontario Superior Court and Court of Appeal, and a number of the justices on the Supreme Court of Canada. Like any Ontario Attorney General, I'd been accountable for about a half-million prosecutions a year.

Suddenly, I was the one being prosecuted.

I ended that anniversary night sitting in a Toronto jail cell, charged with causing the death of a man I'd never met, but a man I probably knew better than he, or anyone else, might have imagined.

On the night that everything changed, well ... everything changed.

Most importantly, a man named Darcy Allan Sheppard lost his life. Twenty-eight seconds was all it took, from the time he stopped his bicycle in front of my old Saab convertible, to the moment of impact, skull to concrete, and then his death. It was an irremediable horror, and the greatest tragedy to which I'd ever been party.

For me, it began a period of unimaginable sorrow and anguish. For, just as tragedy, death, and loss were unexpected visitors to my world, the grief, self-doubt, and humility that accompanied them were equally unfamiliar emotions.

I would immediately lose the job I had once thought so very impressive and important. I would lose the marriage I was celebrating the night that tragedy visited, a marriage that had blessed me with my children and carried me through the worst of times. I would lose my younger brother—my only brother—the brother whose name I'd chosen, the brother who had stood beside me as the best man at my wedding.

I would lose, it was taken for granted, any prospect of a future in public life. The news media, after all, had instantly declared the accident, those 28 seconds, to be Canada's *Bonfire of the Vanities*. It was, to some quick-to-judge commentators, Michael Bryant's very own Chappaquiddick.

Still, there were other losses. Some of those were necessary; some were even healthy. All were difficult.

I began to shed my prideful aspirations, my hubris, my delusions of control and invincibility, my cocksure notions of what mattered in a life. I began to benefit from a downsized ego, a more generous perspective, a capacity to see the joy of small blessings.

This is the story of how, in a matter of seconds on a summer evening, lives from opposite ends of society, from different poles of privilege and possibility, intersected and collided, and how, for me, everything changed.

It is a story of tragic flaws and human foible, of obsessions and compulsions—the kind society encourages and applauds; the kind it reviles.

It's a story of our justice system, and our health-care system; how some of it works well but some of it doesn't.

It's a story of success, and the skewed way we sometimes define it; a story of shattering personal crisis, and how crisis is not always the worst thing that can happen in a life.

It's a story of relationships, of the redemptive power of love, of the sometimes unexpected places love is found.

It's the story of how, starting slowly, in fits and starts, with love and help and willingness and hard work, and while facing the biggest challenges I would ever know, something happened.

I came back. I came back changed.

ONE

Happy Anniversary

It was at the end of a draining three-hour interrogation, on March 23, 2010, that the prosecutor asked me a question. "Would you have done anything differently that night," he said, "knowing what you now know?"

Before I could answer, my lawyer, Marie Henein, began yelling at him. This served two purposes: it shut me up, and it made her objection crystal clear to all in earshot. The question, after all, was speculative and hypothetical. Witnesses, it is axiomatic, should never, ever answer those. Marie made her point emphatically, as is her custom, and the prosecutor half-grinned as he quickly backtracked. Almost in spite of myself, when things fizzled into a brief silence, I answered:

"I never would have left the house," I said quietly.

But I did leave the house.

IT WAS AUGUST 31, 2009. It was the 12th anniversary of my marriage to Susan Abramovitch. It was a lovely, late-summer day in Toronto. It was the morning of the night that everything changed.

"Happy anniversary," she said, stirring beside me. And we hugged. No kiss. Twelve years of marriage, 17 years together, two kids. *And* morning breath. No kiss.

"So what *are* we doing?"

My voice croaked to life. "Well, I thought that ..."

This wasn't actually true. I hadn't thought anything. I remembered it was our anniversary because, a few seconds ago, she'd said so.

I had no gift, no plan, even though I'd been responsible for arranging something in the way of celebration. That was my job, probably because I was in the doghouse.

I was usually in the doghouse that summer. Somehow, I wasn't engaged with the same human race of which my wife was a member. I was a distracted presence in my own marriage, my mind usually somewhere else. I was going through the pressure of a career change, a significant reorientation, maybe even something of a small mid-life crisis.

Even if I weren't in the doghouse, we were a couple waist-deep in that phase of kid-driven living and domestic routine in which attention to one another is often a fleeting afterthought.

So I tried to set things right, making it up on the fly. For me, this was not an unusual state of affairs.

"I am currently thinking as I speak that …"

I suggested Middle Eastern fare at a place on College Street run by a colourful, one-eyed character from our past.

"Sounds good. So what time?" she said.

"What time works for you?" My inability to actually forge a plan was maddening. The eggshell crunches were deafening as we tiptoed around each other toward an arrangement.

I'll pick her up at work, and we'll drive to dinner in my car, it's decided.

We're moving now, out of the bedroom. The morning rituals were underway. Wake the kids—Sadie, age 7, and Louie, 5. Down the hardwood stairs, carpeted down the centre, to the kitchen of the house in which we intended to grow old. That was the plan.

We'd bought the place in 2004 from a home builder who'd gutted and renovated it. It was turn-key perfection in a tony neighbourhood. It also had slippery hardwood at the bottom of the stairs. "Take off your socks, Louie!" I hollered. Louie liked sleeping with his socks on.

Next: turn on the Sirius Satellite Radio atop a tall speaker. On went the Sony receiver and NPR started playing on the living room and dining room speakers, adjoining the open kitchen. The morning ritual continued. Viking Professional Series gas stove. Rancilio Rocky coffee grinder. Gaggia espresso machine. Scandinavian-designed dishwasher that blended in like a cupboard. You get the picture.

Next: heat milk for the kids' cereal. They liked warm milk. Susan moved past me in a blur. She got the bowls, spoons, cereal box. It was the typical choreography as our family stirred to our usual morning soundtrack. The espresso grinder grinding, the microwave beeping, then a loud click from the basement entrance. Our nanny, Sarah, had arrived. I opened the front door to get the newspapers: *The Globe and Mail*, the *Toronto Star*, the *National Post*.

"Sarah's here!"

So we stopped tending to our kids and started grooming ourselves for work. The shower built for two, a pair of enormous shower heads almost a foot in diameter extending down from the ceiling. In Mexico, they'd call it a car wash.

Minutes pass.

Susan's water was scorching. Mine was not. I needed to be shocked by cooler water to wake up. In the old days, I'd all but take up residence in the shower, trying to wash away the hangovers. But that was three years ago.

"So," called Susan from the walk-in closet, "meet outside my work at 6:30?" By her reckoning, that should make sure I was there by 6:45.

"Limit on the presents, right?" (Meaning: not too expensive.)

"Right."

I read the newspapers while breakfasting on microwaved oatmeal. The kids heaved their backpacks on at the door, the packs huge on their little frames. Dad's 5'8", Mom 5'3". Sadie and Louie are unlikely, the paediatrician says, to have lankiness in their future.

Kissed and hugged, the kids headed down the front steps with Sarah for school. A little later came Susan's goodbye, shouted in the direction of upstairs where I was leisurely getting dressed, staring at fuchsia socks and peppermint ties.

I left the house a few minutes after 9 a.m., taking for granted the ordinary blessings of my life, not guessing that mornings would never be routine in our house in just this way again.

IT'S A SUNNY DAY, heading toward 20°C. That means my convertible top will be down, folded back, all day, all night. I'm happy when the top's down. Otherwise, I'm claustrophobic. I need sun.

I've been driving the 1995 Saab for just over a year. It has some iffy bodywork, but a decent paint job. I bought it from a small, private dealership that seems to specialize in refurbishing junkyard dogs. I keep it washed and waxed pretty well. With the top down, it looks nice. There's a subwoofer installed in the scrunched back seat, speakers in the doors, a deck connected to my iPod. The Saab rocks, its clunker lineage notwithstanding.

Even so, it doesn't start so well this morning. (Let's just say the CAA truck has visited this address more than once.) The Saab turns over a few times before it starts. It doesn't idle without some gas. It stalls. I start it again, rev it for about ten seconds. Now it's okay. But backing up is always a little tricky because the transmission is balky.

Now I'm off, driving west to Avenue Road, ready to take an illegal left en route downtown to Invest Toronto, my new workplace, where I'm the freshly appointed president and CEO, charged with selling the city to the world. Invest Toronto was tasked with making new employers magically appear, and with expanding the existing ones. I was the proud new CEO of a proud new city agency with a budget that paid for a few people's salaries and a flight to Shanghai.

At my office in Metro Hall, my vice-president and perennial woman-Friday, Nikki Holland, runs down the schedule of people I'm to meet. But I'm restless, looking through a window at the sun, wishing I was out in it. By the end of August, Canadians know that summer is checking its watch and we're loath to waste an hour of it.

I have lunch in an underground food court with the city's senior bureaucrat on economic development.

At 1 p.m., I decide it's time for a drive with the top down and a cigar. I started smoking cigars the same week in 2006 that I stopped drinking. Now, they're an expensive and regular habit—Cuban, Nicaraguan, the occasional Honduran.

I'm driving nowhere in particular, but thinking I might pick up some cigars, when I remember I have to buy an anniversary present for Susan. On Queen Street West I notice a shop that sells Japanese paper and fancy notebooks. Susan likes notebooks, little ones, to make to-do lists and collect phone numbers for household fixers.

I spend a half-hour browsing, finding the right notebook and the right pen. A chiyogami-covered journal and a Micron art pen. I buy a fancy origami bag and tissue to put it in. It will fit nicely into our self-imposed anniversary budget. I do not imagine that the first entry in the notebook, some hours hence, will be the telephone number of a criminal lawyer.

On the trip back to the office, I try not to check my BlackBerry while I'm driving because it's dangerous, illegal, and I voted for the legislation that made it a Provincial Offences Act violation. But at stoplights I do it anyway. There are messages.

My friend Andy wants to meet for a cigar later in the week. Answer: Great!

Nikki wants to know when I'll be back in the office. Answer: Two minutes.

Susan says she's arranged for Sarah to stay late and babysit tonight. Answer: Yay! (Was I supposed to do that?)

Back at the office, I have more meetings. When my mind wanders, I worry whether the gift I bought Susan is too practical and unromantic. She *is* practical, but getting the balance right matters.

Our marriage is in trouble. We know it. We've been in counselling since the spring. It's our second counsellor. A gift that strikes the wrong note could wreck the night. And what about the card? Too gushy and it would sound insincere. Too close to the mark and there'd be no respite, even for a few hours this evening, from the tension that's become the new normal. So I choose one of those little tags, enough to write her name and "Happy Anniversary" and "Love, Michael" and "xoxox."

Time for a jog. Running has become an obsession. And the clothes! Yes, obsessive about those, too—Jacflash, Great Stuff, Boomer, eBay, Cabaret. The *National Post* had recently done a story on Invest Toronto's new CEO "on the town" shopping for clothes. Cringeworthy. Still, this deep dive to shallowness seemed appropriate for someone—me—who appeared fit, but whose self-esteem was growing obese.

I shower at home after my run, and put on cologne Susan had given me for an earlier birthday present. Smelling like a Parisian cabinet minister, I linger outside with a cigar.

Then I remember that I was to pick Susan up at her office. *Shit!* I'm about to be late for our anniversary. I jump in the Saab and drive down Avenue Road, left on Adelaide. I'm lucky with traffic— all the streetlights go my way, no unexpected obstructions, no speed traps. I stop outside First Canadian Place, Susan's building.

It's about 6:45 p.m., right on schedule, when she appears, opens the passenger door, and falls into the low-running convertible. We transfer the gift she's carrying to the trunk, settle into the car, and, top down, head north and west toward College Street, talking about …

"My mom's train arrives at—"

"Did you transfer the $500 into the joint account—"

"When do you want to close the cottage—"

"Brenda called, looking for the cheque—"

… *married stuff.*

Looping around Queen's Park, I go quiet. I'd resigned as Member of Provincial Parliament for St. Paul's less than three months earlier. I'd been there for a decade. It was over. Except it wasn't.

West down College Street, west past Spadina, an illegal U-turn around Grace Street before Bathurst. We score a parking spot about 70 feet from the restaurant. Pay for parking. Put the ticket on the windshield. Leave the top down. Walk to the resto.

And our anniversary celebration begins.

THE RESTAURANT, Ghazale Middle Eastern & Vegetarian Foods, was a Lebanese spot that served our favourite shawarma in Toronto. It was a modest place—less than a restaurant, perhaps, but more than a fast-food joint. It had wobbly white plastic tables and chairs on the sidewalk, seating a half-dozen people tops. Inside were stools and a counter.

Actually, Ghazale was our favourite shawarma place, transplanted. The original establishment was on Bloor Street West, beside the local retro movie theatre in a neighbourhood called the Annex. The Lebanese owner was unforgettable for having only one eye, the other socket empty, with no glass eye replacing or patch covering where the left eyeball should have been.

We had lived in that neighbourhood, on Palmerston Avenue, beside a children's library. Until Louie was born the little two-bedroom red-brick house, our first, had accommodated the three of us without feeling cramped. Those days on Palmerston were fun—lots of fun.

Neither of us had grown up in Toronto. Susan was from Montreal, by way of Ottawa, New York, and Paris; I came from Victoria, B.C., by way of Vancouver, Ottawa, Boston, and London, England.

On Palmerston, we were steps from the subway and every cuisine imaginable. The Lebanese joint was a regular takeout for us. Then the one-eyed owner moved his restaurant south a few blocks, to College Street.

At $6.99, the most expensive item on the menu was the Shawarma Platter, which we each ordered. I ordered Nestea in a can. Susan had water. We collected our dinners, pita wrapped in tin foil with vegetables in a moulded Styrofoam takeout container, all placed on a faded brown plastic tray. I dropped the Nestea while trying to balance the gourmet anniversary meal. We ate outside.

"Happy anniversary." And we toasted ourselves, Nestea can to water bottle, the eye contact brief, her smile forced, air blown through her teeth. Happy Nervous Anniversary.

I ate too fast. Susan talked about her work, me mine. We tried to remember anniversaries past, which scared me. To begin with, I can't remember many. They are lost, for now, to bourbon-pickled brain cells. But what scared me most was the absence of heartfelt *anything* at that moment, apparently for both of us.

We were perfectly aware that no relationship is effortless, that few romances remain unaltered, that ardour invariably is cooled by time's tide. Sandcastles are built, then washed away. At first, you think things are just hidden, buried under there somewhere, in the sand. The realization that a moment has come and gone can be dispiriting. But then a couple needs to want to build another sandcastle, together. And another. And another. It takes a lot more than just conjuring wistful memories of the original castle, effort-lessly refashioned into being on some perfect, long-ago afternoon.

We were trying, both of us. But to me, we sounded more weary than anything else.

It took us just over half an hour to finish our meal.

"Walk on the beach?"

"Let's do it."

So at about 8 p.m., with the sun dropping, we drove along Lakeshore Boulevard to the Beach—or Beaches—at Lake Ontario in Toronto's east end. (It tells you everything you need to know about the relatively charmed status of that self-consciously Bohemian neighbourhood that the locals have time and energy enough to argue about its name.)

We parked. We took the tissue-stuffed gift bags out of the trunk of the car. I'd also packed some casual clothes for Susan. It was an effort to seem "thoughtful," not my usual forte. But she decided not to change.

Twilight now, barely, and we walked to a bench beside the boardwalk and sat down to exchange gifts. Susan gave me a smallish cigar humidor, the kind you can travel with, with two Cuban cigars inside to humour my newest obsession. The gift was thoughtful and smart, like Susan. I gave her the pen and notebook.

Then, we went walking. Susan, still in business uniform, had heels on. One got snagged between the planks of the boardwalk as we crossed, so she pulled them off and barefooted it—shoes held aloft on a finger—toward the shoreline.

We talked about our marriage—part debate, part monologue, part argument. Then, at about 8:30 p.m., we walked back to the car.

I've often mused since that if Susan had maybe been stuck in the boardwalk a bit longer—only half a minute or so—delaying our departure, or if I hadn't dropped the Nestea can back at the restaurant, or if we'd just moved through the evening more quickly, it all might have unfolded differently. But life doesn't work that way.

Instead, we continued our evening.

"Wanna sweet? Maybe a baklava?" I asked.

"Brilliant," she said.

So we drove north to the Danforth, as it's known in Toronto, then west along the Greektown strip. We had no particular place in mind. We did that maddening, stop-and-start drive of people not quite sure where to go or park. For blocks, we drove past closed bakeries and loud restaurants, until we came upon the perfect place, Akropolis Pastries & Pies, east of Pape Avenue.

Inside was a counter with the desserts displayed. A few people were eating outside. There on the sidewalk was the second wobbly plastic table and chair set we'd sit upon that night. The proprietor shooed some regulars away from the table for us. This was a table for lovers, it seemed.

I had mint tea and Susan did too, and we shared some baklava. The proprietor insisted on serving us on a polished silver tray, with china cups and saucers. I paid the $10 bill while Susan slid a tip under her saucer.

The receipt said it was 9:36 p.m. when we left Akropolis—or so the newspapers reported that week. Susan mentioned wanting a travel book for Brazil. She was to travel there on business to the Rio Film Festival, and was taking her mother along. The trip wasn't until October, but she liked to plan ahead.

I kicked myself for not thinking of adding the travel book to her anniversary present. I suggested that, if we hurried, we could make the Indigo book store at Bay and Bloor, near Yorkville, on the way home. One of us called to find out that they closed at 10 p.m.

The evening was still warm. I loved driving with the top down on the Saab. After we crossed the Bloor Viaduct, we decided we wouldn't make it in time to get the book at Indigo, or at least we'd be too rushed. So we never did make the left turn on Bay that might have rerouted our fate.

Approaching Yonge Street, westbound about 50 yards east of Yonge and Bloor, the traffic slowed; I assumed it was because of construction. We were bumper to bumper, sometimes at a standstill. So I undid my seatbelt and rose up in the seat, looking to see what was holding us up.

I saw large orange-and-black traffic pylons, maybe four feet high, placed randomly across the road, blocking traffic. I saw a man on the southeast corner of Yonge and Bloor, behaving like a Tasmanian devil—presumably the man, I surmised, who had strewn the pylons across one of the busiest intersections on the continent—screaming at a white SUV, spit spraying the windshield. Then, he began tossing garbage into the traffic.

He was pretty clearly under the influence of something. My first thought was, "Hello, brother. You're one of us, aren't you?"

I yanked up the emergency brake, opened the door and, with the presence of a peacock, got out to move a pylon. I talked to a pedestrian standing by the road.

"That guy's trouble," the man said. "He's trouble," nodding toward Yonge and Bloor.

I have no idea if the "trouble" in question saw me leave the car and undo his handiwork. Maybe he did. Maybe it was the provocation that prompted what followed.

I got back in the car and continued west along Bloor Street. What I didn't do was what, under the circumstances, any prudent urbanite might have. I didn't raise the convertible top. I didn't crank up the windows. I didn't lock the door.

As we moved on, I saw the man on a bicycle, doing figure eights in front of another car, taunting the driver to pass, then blocking his way, laughing. He was yelling and laughing incoherently, making a lot of noise.

We must have passed him at some point. I passed Bay Street, still heading west on Bloor. This is where, had we been going to the bookstore, we would have turned left, onto a different course, in every sense of the term. But we didn't. I came to a red light at a pedestrian crossing between Bay and Avenue Road.

Just past the crossing, construction vehicles took up the lanes adjacent to the centre line in both directions. Westbound traffic was funnelled into one lane near the curb, as was eastbound traffic on the other side.

We were stopped across from the Chanel store on the Mink Mile. Susan was chatting away, but I wasn't listening. Something was wrong. I had no idea where that crazy cyclist had gone but I feared his return. I was peering past Susan at the mirror on her side, the curb side, where I expected he might appear.

The light turned green. I started to drive forward. Something entered my peripheral vision on the left.

The man on the bicycle breezed by, swung at my face, then swerved in front of our car and stopped. I hit the brakes. The old Saab stopped and stalled.

The man pivoted around to confront me. He growled and glared. Soon he would throw his heavy Kryptonite bicycle lock and bag at me (and miss).

"Now what're ya gonna do?"

The 28 seconds had begun.

I kept him in my sight as much as possible, flickering my eyes up to the rearview mirror, ready to back up the Saab, looking to drive around him and escape.

I don't know what drew him to me, made me the lightning rod for the erratic lightning he personified. Maybe my crime was simply leaving the top down and making us an inviting target.

Maybe it was that I had failed to stay put during his staredown. Maybe if I'd done nothing, he would have spent his fury, grown bored, gone away.

Whatever it was, the man seemed to grow larger as he approached, looming over Susan and me, growling and cackling.

I didn't ask Susan what I should do. I just decided, myself, how to escape this nightmare, to *will*—as I almost always had been able to before—the result I wanted, to get away, to continue my long winning streak, to sustain my sense of invincibility.

What had brought Darcy Allan Sheppard to Bloor Street that night was a lifetime of misfortune and bad decisions I wouldn't learn about until much later.

What had brought me to that intersection was a dizzying run of good luck that was about to end.

TWO

Made in B.C.

I was pretty much born into politics.

My arrival in the world in 1966, as the second child and first son of Ray and Margaret Bryant, came the same year my father became Mayor of Esquimalt, B.C. He was, at 29, the youngest mayor in Canada at the time. And just as I would follow my dad into politics, he had followed his.

My grandfather, Jimmie Bryant, was born in Cornwall, England, and arrived in Canada at age six with my great-grandmother. My great-grandfather, Thomas, had come out ahead, in the immigrant custom, to earn passage for his family and was working at the Esquimalt navy dockyards, the No. 1 employer in town.

The dockyards dated back to 1837 and were commanded by the British Royal Navy until 1905. The Canadian Navy was born five years later, and the Esquimalt Dockyard was formally transferred to Canada in late 1910. This was where Jimmie Bryant would work as a machinist, as his father had before him.

My grandfather had polio as a boy and had a bum leg, having ditched his leg braces every morning behind the house in St. Ives, Cornwall, in order to play goalie in the soccer games. As a result, in adulthood he wore a special shoe that weighed 100 pounds—or so it seemed to me as a boy when I tried to pick it up. He walked with a heavy limp and used a cane. But he refused to let it affect his life or slow his pace. He was a man about town in Esquimalt, a union organizer and an alderman. My dad tells me how, when the film projector at the movie theatre would go on the blink, his father would get up on stage and lead the audience in song.

Legend has it that my grandfather founded Saxe Point Park, which once had been Hudson Bay Company land used as a funeral pyre by the East Indian community and became a garbage dump in the 1920s. There was a small pond in the area that the Esquimalt municipality started filling with refuse. Then, in 1934, the municipality purchased the land from HBC in a tax sale. A municipal by-law written that year set Saxe Point aside as parkland.

I'm told Jimmie would hobble and hack his way through forest to study the site. He was going to turn the garbage dump into a park. And he did. It's now 15 acres of peninsula seafront, with magnificent views of Juan de Fuca Strait and the Olympic Mountains, a place of exposed rock, craggy cliffs, gardens, woods, trails, picnic benches on green lawns, a sheltered beach. This was where his—and later his wife's—ashes were scattered. It's where I go to visit them when I'm in town. And it's where I proposed marriage to Susan.

There was also a big empty field where Jimmie imagined a recreation centre. So the town built the hockey rink and rec centre on Esquimalt Road. Many also credit Jimmie Bryant for transforming the Gorge Park from its 1950 vandalized drabness to its current splendour. He was a visionary, an organizer, and a showman. And he got stuff done.

He's my political idol, I guess. Not Pierre Trudeau or John F. Kennedy or anyone like that. Him, my Papa Bryant. He was a councillor for 15 years and he greatly improved the community. My first taste of overwhelming, heart-scalding grief was when, in

1977, my mom put down a laundry basket she was carrying, red plastic and oval, and told me my grandfather had died.

About a year before I was born, the mayor's chair opened up and everybody assumed Jimmie was going to run for mayor. But he didn't have any post-secondary education, as he thought a mayor should. Instead, he urged my father to run. By then, Dad had a commerce degree and had graduated from law school. So my father ran for mayor, and my grandfather ran for council. Everybody voted for Bryant and Bryant and Dad was elected mayor at 29. Father and son served on council together.

But it lasted only one term. In 1968, my dad got re-elected as mayor, but Jimmie didn't campaign. He thought it was immodest and that his record spoke for itself. It didn't turn out to be a good strategy; he lost by a few votes. And that lesson stuck with me. No matter how good you are or how well you serve, the day could come when you would be given the boot.

Esquimalt was a great place to grow up in, but we made our own entertainment. At the end of our street there was forest you could get lost in and giant rocks for climbing. My cousin Tanya was the same age as me and lived right next door. We'd often get into trouble together. She'd urge experiments—like testing a window's breakability—and I'd execute her plans.

Once, when I was about 4, Tanya and I scrubbed the driveway of our house with beer. I remember it was a case of Labatt's Blue, stubbies. We must have found a bottle opener. We'd each take a sip of the beer, then pour it on the driveway and it would suds up like soap and we'd mop it. My parents, on their return, were unimpressed. It wasn't the last time I'd be in trouble over alcohol.

In Esquimalt, such religious education as I received occurred at a place called The Truth Centre. It was a new-thought church, sort of a combination of Unitarian and Christian Science. It was headed up by a lady named Dr. Emma Smiley. Essentially, it made a religion out of optimism. I don't remember any talk about Jesus. I just remember being told that God was everywhere and good, and that if I nurtured positive thoughts they would come to pass.

As much as I'm proud of my father's precocious political achievements, my mom might have been more impressive still when I was growing up.

Between the birth of my older sister, Janine, in 1962 and my arrival four years later, my mother had a stillborn child and almost died. It was then that she sought counselling from Dr. Smiley. And it was around that time, we think, that her multiple sclerosis began to manifest itself.

She was diagnosed with MS when I was a newborn. One morning, she woke up cross-eyed and stayed that way for a month. At other times, her knees would buckle and she'd collapse. Or she could hear out of one ear and not the other. She was easily exhausted.

Her obstetrician was my godfather, Dr. Robert Morgan. Dr. Bob would later leave Victoria and his college friendships to head up the medical school at the University of Toronto, to teach at Stanford, and eventually to make some serious money as an expert witness on environmental matters. He would reappear in my life when I graduated from law school. By then, he had a place in the Bahamas, which I showed up at about a year later. We went fly-fishing in the knee-deep waters for bonefish and barracuda. (All godfathers are allowed a little hiatus, as long as they come back with a place in the Bahamas where you go bonefishing.)

Two memories from my visits stand out. First, Dr. Bob introduced me to what became my favourite drink—Manhattans—and to my favourite bourbon, Maker's Mark. Second, he told the tale of my mother's diagnosis.

My parents had insisted that he diagnose her suspected ailments, as they didn't trust doctors at the time. Only him. After doing the tests, he sat down with my dad outside our house in Esquimalt.

"She won't live to age 50," Dr. Bob said. "And she'll likely be in a wheelchair in a few years."

My father refused to believe it. And my mother, still in her twenties, refused to cooperate with her prescribed decline. Over the years she would have flare-ups—"relapses," she called them. But sometimes her MS would go into remission for long periods. She walks with a cane. She naps a lot. But she is positive and happy all of the time. Far from expiring by 50, she's kickin' MS's butt well into her 70s, thank you very much.

For some time, my dad had wanted to move the family from Esquimalt. He was one of a few kids in his high school who went to university. Most got jobs as soon as they could and thought there was something wrong with anyone who wanted to go to school any longer than was required. My dad wanted us to grow up where the culture encouraged larger dreams.

Family legend has it that the moment of truth came when I was about 3. Dad was late for a council meeting because he'd been playing with me. He was my hero. As he was pulling out of the driveway, I ran after him, yelling, "Daddy! Daddy!" not wanting him to go. He looked in the rearview mirror at me, crying in the driveway, until he couldn't stand it anymore. Then he adjusted the mirror so he couldn't see. The story is that he arrived at the council meeting that day and announced he wasn't running for re-election.

He was only 32. There was lots of speculation that he'd end up running provincially or federally. But he never held elected office again. He went back to practising law in downtown Victoria on Fort Street, mostly handling estates, public works, real estate—a solicitor's practice. He'd become the founding general counsel of B.C.'s Municipal Finance Authority, a bank made up of and for the treasuries of towns and cities. Smart.

Then, when I was 6, two big changes happened in our family almost simultaneously. We moved to Longview Drive on Gordon

Head in Greater Victoria, near the university. And my parents adopted my brother, Alan.

I don't know how they did it, but I swear they timed it so we moved the same day we picked up the infant Alan. I got to name him, after my best friend. Alan Thomas Bryant was a redhead. He would grow to 6'1", towering over the diminutive Bryant clan. For the first years of my life, I'd worshipped my older sister, Janine. But as Alan grew, we did more and more together. When I was 10 and he was 4, we'd take the bus to the first McDonald's in Victoria for breakfast every Saturday morning. It was about a 40-minute bus ride and it was the highlight of our week. Egg McMuffins for me, pancakes for him, then we'd turn around and go home.

In Victoria, I started at Fairburn Elementary School in 1972, then later went to Arbutus Junior High School (where NBA basketball star Steve Nash would soon walk the halls with Alan). They don't call them the formative years for nothing. As with every other child, things happened that, unbeknownst to me at the time, were shaping me in ways large and small.

I was the shortest kid in my class, always trying out for the teams and never making them. Along with that disappointment, I didn't escape the fate common to many small boys. Doug D. was two years older than me. And a two-year age difference, especially when the younger kid is small for his age, amounts to the difference between David and Goliath.

Doug D. had what these days would be called a posse. And, once, on the way home, I became the day's prey. I was cutting through an overgrown vacant lot with well-worn trails when the chase began. I had no clue what I'd done to earn their wrath, but I began running toward the edge of the field. If I could get there, I'd be in view of my house. In my house was a large German shepherd named Trixy. I grew up with German shepherds. First Trixy, later joined by Alan's very own Kimo and Marley. I loved those dogs.

Anyway, Trixy had a bark so loud she could scare a pit bull. Maybe my mom would come to the window, see what was happening, and let Trixy out the front door and the mass of muscle and teeth that was my dog would race to my rescue.

But it soon became clear I wasn't going to make it to the edge of the field. I stopped and turned to face my pursuers. Doug just started laughing at my foolhardiness. I remember the sneer. I remember the string of saliva that travelled from his mouth to my face. I remember it stringing across my forehead and eyeball and cheek, hot, before I wiped it and retched. Then, I remember being on the ground, my face pushed hard into the dirt. I remember the smell of the earth being salty and the odour of cement and metal and pain. I don't remember how long the beating went on. I only remember walking home defeated, then wailing on the sofa, my mom sitting next to me, ignoring the curse words I spat out. I railed against God, and against Trixy, for allowing this to happen.

"Oh, Michael," said my mom. "I don't know what to do."

It wasn't the first time I'd known such pain and shame. It was hard at first to convince my mother, but sometime that year I started boxing. And I made it my sport.

I started, of course, at the London Boxing Club, Victoria being more British than Great Britain itself. The gym was downtown, in the basement of a Nelson's Music Store. It had two heavy bags and two rings. I started going with a buddy named Kelly, whose dad was a police officer. Eventually, Kelly stopped going. But I didn't.

There were about 40 kids split into two groups, the experienced (which is to say talented boxers) and the beginners (or others). I stayed in the latter group the entire time. The coach of my group was Mr. Ballantyne. His son was Clifford Ballantyne, who ended up fighting professionally.

Once, I boxed the smallest kid in the talented group. It was the first time I saw stars, but I loved it. I loved hitting the heavy bag. I loved jumping rope. I loved all those calisthenics, the runs we'd go on. I loved putting on the hand-wraps and snorting with a well-landed punch.

Boxing was rational. It was broken up into weight classes, so I would be fighting someone almost exactly my weight. It would be an equal contest—in theory, anyway. I was not only small, but compact and heavy for my stature. The flyweights I'd compete against almost always had longer arms, which presented problems.

I was never a great boxer, especially outside the ring. Once, in the schoolyard, I took on a kid who was blind in one eye. He was a southpaw. His right eye didn't work. This should have made him susceptible to a right lead—throwing a right cross to the right side of his face, across his right front leg. To make matters even easier, he started out throwing a roundhouse left hook, leaving himself laughably defenceless to a right lead.

But for some reason I froze solid, stood there flat-footed, and—after he let me have it—ended up gasping for air on one knee when the bell rang to end the lunch-hour. It seemed I was a fighter in all things except the fights.

Still, it was the concept of being a boxer that benefited me. It created a sense of confidence, but more importantly an aura around me that played well with the other kids at school. Even though I wasn't likely to become a legend of the ring, I was still the only boxer known to Fairburn Elementary and Arbutus Junior High. I spun exaggerated stories of my prowess. Muhammad Ali became my hero, and his cockiness was the kind of armour I adopted too. Boys stopped wanting to fight me. And I stayed at the London Boxing Club almost until I finished high school.

In high school, things were better for me. I wasn't a jock. I played basketball on the B team and that was it. I also wasn't much of a bookworm, but I must have done something right because I sneaked onto the Honour Roll. Mostly, I partied and had my heart broken.

I started playing the trumpet (my dad had played it) at about the same time I started boxing, and it too helped build my confidence. (When I met Susan I was playing in an amateur jazz band, and as an MPP in Toronto I would play "The Last Post" at high school Remembrance Day services.) I played in the junior high school band. We finished second in the nationals in Calgary when I was about 13; it was my first time east of Vancouver. Our world had been one of West Coast sensibilities. We travelled to Seattle, to Disneyland, and to Hawaii after my dad started making some money.

My life back then was basketball, music, and parties. I got my first girlfriend at Mt. Douglas High School, and we went out for about a year and a half. I'd been crazy about Michele since Grade 8, but it had taken her a few years to see the appeal in my attentions.

When I graduated, my marks were not top-notch but good enough to get into the University of Victoria. The plan was that I'd go there for a year, as my dad did, then go to UBC, as he had, and eventually become a lawyer, as he was. If my dad's was the path I was vaguely following as I headed off to university in 1984, it was around this time that that my mother and my sister stepped in to put a little focus and direction in my life. In truth, there were probably few people on the planet, certainly few on Vancouver Island, better qualified for that task.

When I was 15, my mother, who'd been a teacher, went back to UVic herself to get her Bachelor of Education degree. Life being a curious thing, she became a full-time university student the same year that my sister did. The first consequence of Mom's decision was that everyone in the family had to take on some tasks around the house. That included dinners. Everyone had to cook dinner one night a week. That included me. And with the lack of culinary imagination typical of the teenage male, I almost always made the same thing: tuna tetrazzini, a fancy name for tuna casserole from a box. Think Hamburger Helper, except you've got to open a can of tuna (or cat food, accidentally, but I never made that mistake again).

Another consequence was that the Bryant household became something of a hothouse of learning. I remember cue cards everywhere. And I remember our hallway being lined with books my mother and sister had borrowed from the Faculty of Education library. There must have been 100 or more. It seemed to me there was no way they could have read them all. I convinced myself that what they'd done was basically take the school library hostage in the name of scholastic victory.

As I recall, they placed first and second in their graduating class. I got the impression they were extremely competitive—not with each other, but with the rest of the world. This helped nurture my already growing sense that ours was a Hobbesian realm in which competitors must be not only defeated but destroyed. It merely built on a message I'd already got from my dad that if I didn't scratch and fight like hell to achieve success, the world would have me for breakfast.

My mom, I think, just wanted me to fulfill my potential. She and my sister had both finished university not long before I started. They were both superb students and teachers, great with the mechanics of academic learning. They basically taught me how to study, how to write an essay, how to be a student.

During my year at UVic, I lived like a Jesuit. The priority was books and marks. I took a typical first-year course load—history, political science, philosophy, English. In my spare time, I read a lot and was very big on John Irving's novels. *The World According to Garp, The Hotel New Hampshire*, and later, *A Prayer for Owen*

Meany—I read them all. Maybe it was because Irving had been a wrestler, while I was a boxer, and wrestling was threaded through his work. Maybe his was a sensibility with which I could identify.

After a year at UVic, I was accepted into the honours English program at UBC. I'm embarrassed now to say that, though I obtained both a B.A. in English literature and an M.A. in political science, I was extremely strategic in my studies. I was very competitive and obsessed with achievement, focused more on marks than on learning. I was a heavy consumer of Coles Notes, figuring it was more efficient to read the condensed version and write on that than it was to actually read the book. But two things happened while I was in university that made an impact on me.

I read a book titled *W.A.C. Bennett and the Rise of British Columbia* by David Mitchell. Bennett's populism made a lot of sense to me. He was, like my grandfather, a builder. He built bridges and dams and highways and infrastructure. He was on the cover of *TIME* magazine in 1966; the cover story ran under the headline, "Canada: Surging to Nationhood." It was Bennett's inspiration that gave some energy to the pull that politics already had on me from the example of my dad and grandfather: I decided that (a) I wanted to be in politics, and (b) I wanted to be the Attorney General and maybe Premier of British Columbia.

During my last year as an undergrad at UBC, I also took a course that had a profound effect on my thinking and my life. I'd already taken a class or two from Professor Paul Tennant in municipal law and provincial politics. I liked him as a professor. He also taught aboriginal rights.

Now, I was born and raised in a province whose government denied that there was such a thing as "aboriginal rights," even after they'd been entrenched in 1982 by the repatriated Constitution of Canada. My education had taught me the fairly common view that Canadian history began in 1867, not at the time of the first European contact with First Nations; that segregation was bad, assimilation was good; that this impoverished culture would have a better life if it abandoned ways that weren't working and did things the mainstream (Caucasian) way.

So I took the class mainly to disprove Prof. Tennant's explication of aboriginal rights as requiring special constitutional protections. Another modest undertaking by Michael J. Bryant. What I came away with was something entirely different. I *got* what Paul Tennant was saying. I was awakened to the shameful history of Canada's treatment of aboriginal people. And it changed everything about my outlook.

Essentially, I started becoming a liberal and a Liberal. That is, I began to depart from the anti-statist tendencies of my political lineage, and the anti-NDP ideology that polarized B.C. politics (truly a two-party province, throughout its history, the right being represented by Conservatives, then by the Social Credit Party, then, believe it or not, the B.C. Liberal Party; the left being represented by Liberals, then CCF, then the NDP). This made me a liberal thinker, and a Liberal Party supporter.

The injustice of Canada's treatment of aboriginal peoples was more than disturbing to me. It became a lifelong cause to address the injustices, past and present. As a student, I would go on to complete two graduate degrees on the subject. As a lawyer, my focus was always on aboriginal rights. As a politician, I'd do my best work with aboriginal leaders. Most important, I have enjoyed loyalty, generosity, friendship, and even spiritual bonds with men and women of aboriginal descent.

It's for this reason that when Darcy Sheppard, the man on the bicycle as those 28 seconds began, would turn out to have First Nations blood and be recognized as Métis, it would strike me as a twist of fate cruel beyond reckoning.

THREE

Law, Love, Luck

With two university degrees to my name, I left British Columbia in 1989 to study aboriginal rights. I was bound for Toronto's Osgoode Law School, because that's where the gurus were.

But if Paul Tennant had helped ensure my mind was newly open on that issue, my attitude and outlook about education otherwise hadn't much changed. At Osgoode, my competitive and ruthless approach to school grew even more intense. I was convinced that the students I was competing against were out to get me.

Not surprisingly, I didn't make many friends, at least at first. I had a lot of free nights in my basement suite in the High Park area. I spent a good chunk of that fall drinking alone with a black-and-white TV, feeling misunderstood, unloved, and sorry for myself. I was homesick and feeling guilty. I had just ended a year-long relationship, and not very graciously at that. Basically, I just left the province. I didn't tell her I was going to law school or Toronto. I just left.

If there was an upside to my social isolation, it was that I actually went back and read all those books on the English curriculum that I'd never read at UBC. It also enabled me to focus like a laser when I had to.

It was at law school, as a result, that I became a top student for the first time. And, once again, it was Bryant family experience that helped build my success. This time it was my dad who taught me what turned out to be the best scholastic trick I ever learned.

Law school is all about exams. Typically, the final exams were worth 100 percent of the final mark. So, above all, you'd better learn how to write them. My dad said that most people go into exams with ten hours of material in their head and only two or three hours of writing time to cram it all in. In effect, they know too much and don't finish all the questions. He maintained that exam writing was a skill and, like any other skill, was something you had to practise. So that's what I did. I tried to write three practice exams for every exam I actually wrote. This meant that I would usually go into exams with about three and a half hours worth of content for a three-hour exam. My margin of error was smaller, but the payoff was great. I almost always did better than the other students who went in there with too much knowledge and not enough exam-writing experience. I succeeded because, by then, I was a veteran exam writer. Again, it was very strategic.

Looking back, it also helped me develop skills that were wholly transferable to politics. I was a quick study and knew when I had enough information to speak to an issue. A decade or so later, as Attorney General in Ontario, I might not be an expert on, say, organized crime, but I could sure sound like one for a short press conference.

The cure for my isolation turned out to be this formula for exam-writing success. After getting A's the first semester, I realized that there wasn't much to do between a term's beginning and the exam study period. While many were burning themselves out, reading everything for every class, I was free to party with the more social set—a handful of hardcore revellers, mostly guys, who vacillated between being leaders and outcasts. I was less a member of this gang than a fellow reveller, never quite fitting in, I thought.

In my mind, I continued imagining myself as tragically alone and unloved at law school (more on that disease of misperception later). The reality was different. In fact, slowly but steadily, I made more friends over the course of the three years leading to our graduation in 1992. To most, I appeared bombastic, overconfident, occasionally humorous, and often inebriated.

When we graduated, some of my fellow students were startled to see me finish second in our class of more than 300. Some of them saw me primarily at the Thursday-night pub, where I often could be found on my knees—either because that's how I was dancing after midnight, or because I couldn't stand up. (I distinctly remember taking a nap on the dance floor, sticky with beer and rum and Coke, with people stepping over me, after last call at 1 a.m.) At graduation, the gold, silver, and bronze medallists were called up on stage. One friend, who later became general counsel to a major corporation, told me that when she saw me go up there her jaw dropped— because she'd been wondering whether I would even graduate.

If the recurring themes of this phase of my life were luck and chutzpah, probably nothing illustrates it so much as the letter I wrote in my first year at Osgoode to Ontario Premier David Peterson.

It was around the time of the Meech Lake constitutional accord. The First Ministers had reached an agreement that year to salvage the deal that Prime Minister Brian Mulroney intended as his great legacy of nation-building. Also, the federal Liberal leadership campaign was in the midst of picking a successor to John Turner, who—though performing much better than he had four years earlier—in 1988 had suffered his second straight majority defeat at Mulroney's hands.

So I wrote Peterson a three-page letter, entirely unsolicited, praising his tenure as premier and urging him to run for the federal Liberal leadership. To my astonishment, I got a phone call from his office, inviting me to come to Queen's Park and meet the Premier. I remember thinking, "What a great country this is. You just write a letter to the Premier and he invites you to his office to chat about it!"

On my very first visit to the Ontario Legislature, I ended up sitting in the Office of the Premier. We spent about 30 minutes together. Crisp white shirt sleeves rolled up to his elbows, top button undone, Peterson had been smiling and laughing throughout our visit. He asked me what I wanted to do with my Osgoode Hall law degree. I told him, "I'd like your job one day." Then he got this look on his face. It was the first time I saw that party leaders don't much like to be told that someone else wants their job one day.

I also said I'd like a summer job in his office. Eventually, his staff did offer me a coveted position in Attorney General Ian Scott's ministry. New to Ontario, though, I'd barely heard of Ian Scott, so I decided to go to Borden & Elliott and work for one of Toronto's finest barristers, Dennis O'Connor, that summer. (I'd make up for it by naming the Ministry of the Attorney General's building after Ian Scott, and his great predecessor Roy McMurtry, when I eventually got that Attorney General job myself.)

The job working for O'Connor was a plum. He would one day head Ontario's public inquiry into the water contamination in Walkerton, Ontario, that resulted in the tragic deaths of seven and made thousands more sick. O'Connor is now Ontario's Associate Chief Justice. But I left after a month because my father had decided to run for the provincial Social Credit nomination in the riding of Saanich South, and I went home to help run his campaign. He won the nomination, but the next election was an NDP sweep. Andrew Petter, who'd become B.C.'s Attorney General, finance minister, and a university president, became the Member of the Legislative Assembly for Saanich South, in Greater Victoria.

The next year, the summer of 1991, I was working at Blake,

Cassels & Graydon in Vancouver for Marvin Storrow, an old classmate of my father. He was a pioneer litigator in aboriginal rights;
he successfully argued all the major Supreme Court of Canada
cases of the 1980s and '90s. I assumed that I'd eventually be back
in Vancouver after law school, working for Storrow, once I finished
my clerkship in 1993.

The prized post for law school graduates is clerking at the
Supreme Court of Canada. Each of the nine justices chooses three
clerks, so only 27 of the top graduates from across the country make
the grade. Interviews are held at the end of second year. Then the
judges choose, sort of like a hockey pool, picking in three rounds
according to seniority.

I interviewed with the late John Sopinka, a highly competitive
former CFL football player who liked me because I boxed; with
Frank Iacobucci, who was one of my father's best friends at law
school; and with Beverley McLachlin, who was named to the court
from British Columbia and whom I saw as my best shot because
she always picked a clerk from B.C.

I didn't show up for my interview with her wrapped in B.C.'s
provincial flag, but it was close.

True to form, I again tried to manipulate the process as best I
could. When I heard McLachlin was speaking at Phi Delta Phi, the
legal fraternity at Osgoode, I immediately joined the fraternity in
order to attend—and, because I knew the president, also managed
to wangle the chance to introduce her. Whatever friends I had at
Osgoode, every one of them had found his way into the legal fraternity (and its free beer). I'd been the last of that crowd to join, and
only did so because McLachlin was speaking. So—and I suppose
this could have backfired—I arranged for a few of my friends to
approach her while I was making the introduction and tell her
that "Michael's a wonderful, fantastic leader within Osgoode." Or
words to that effect.

Astonishingly, it seemed to work, because when she called me in the spring of 1991, she said she had been quite struck by that night, by how I seemed to be a leader within the school, by the fact I seemed to have the respect of my peers. Well, I had the respect of a couple of drinking buddies, anyway.

When McLachlin offered me a clerking position, I said yes, hung up, jumped into the air, and smashed my hand on the low ceiling of my basement apartment. I was a Supreme Court of Canada law clerk!

IN AUGUST 1992, I arrived in Ottawa and took an apartment in the capital's Chinatown at MacLaren and Bronson. If my lodgings were modest, my workplace could hardly have been grander or more imposing.

The Supreme Court of Canada, all marble and granite blocks, sits just west of Parliament Hill, on the bluff overlooking the Ottawa River. It's set well back from the main thoroughfare of Wellington Street, the better to establish an air of aloof authority. It was designed by Montreal architect Ernest Cormier, the corner-stone laid by Queen Elizabeth during her visit in 1939, and the building was completed in 1941. Its first few years were spent more in the service of Canada's war effort than its justice system.

Twenty of the 27 clerks worked in a maze of cubicles in a massive third-floor room with large windows overlooking the front lawns and the approach to the Supreme Court's main entrance and the building's huge and humbling foyer.

At the Court, our job was primarily research and writing. Clerks produced three products. The first were "bench memos" to be read by the justice along with factums (the written legal arguments made by each of the parties before the Court). I always thought of bench memos as a pre-judgment judgment. Might as well tell Justice McLachlin what I thought she should do. We also helped draft judgments and recommendations for leaves to appeal (i.e., which cases should be heard by the Court).

If being the Attorney General of Ontario was the best job I ever had, clerking at the Supreme Court was a close second. I loved it. I was extremely confident in my own capacity to make judgments. I didn't have a lot of second thoughts about anything. Most of the other clerks were overwhelmed by the responsibility and under-standably wanted to research exhaustively and consider what they were recommending in their bench memos to the judges or in their draft judgments. It was easy for me. I had delusions of grandeur.

Madam Justice McLachlin and I worked well together because she's prolific and decisive. She makes a decision and she sticks with it. She wants clerks just to cut through the material and get right to the point. "Here's the problem; here's the solution." That's more or less how I got through law school, so it worked out well.

In addition, McLachlin had been appointed to the Supreme Court only three years earlier. She had been spotted as a star while a law professor at UBC, where she counted former Prime Minister Kim Campbell among her students. Then she went from county court judge to the Supreme Court in less than a decade.

The speed of her ascent was unprecedented and is unlikely to be repeated. But because of it, she hadn't decided that many issues as a trial or appellate court judge. So we worked on most of the issues from first principles. Normally, she would do the first draft and we clerks would edit and fill in the blanks on her work. Other clerks assigned to more experienced justices said they sometimes felt more like librarians than lawyers, fetching previous opinions on a given issue written by that judge. In the McLachlin chambers, we felt that we were creating her library in real time.

Working for her, I had a memorable year. For the first time in my life I felt popular among my peers. Up in our work room, I had sort of a captive audience: my fellow clerks, all working together on the top floor of the copper-topped building. I loved the work and, better still, I was good at it. Everybody else was working 15-hour days and I was working ten. Then I'd be at the pub, or dragging the clerks across the river to Hull, Quebec (now known as Gatineau). I thought Hull's drinking establishments were among the wonders of Confederation. Fellow clerks would occasionally attend these interprovincial excursions to humour me. I also loved that year because I came to think of the place I worked as *la cour d'amour*, with romances among the clerks unfolding with the passage of the seasons.

Though I started in August, most of the clerks arrived the following month. And, one day in September, we welcomed the half-dozen or so clerks from McGill University. Among this group was Susan Heather Abramovitch, the double-gold-medallist from McGill Law who would be clerking for the most experienced judge on the Court, Mr. Justice Gérard La Forest.

Actually, it wasn't the first time I'd seen Maître Abramovitch. The first was when I was crashing in Toronto that summer with my friend Lorne Sossin, who is now Dean of Osgoode Hall Law School and at the time was also preparing for a year as a Supreme Court law clerk. Lorne received the McGill University alumni magazine, and, as I leafed through a copy one day, Susan's photograph immediately caught my eye. It wasn't just her glittering credentials. I thought she was striking, alluring, pretty.

Come the day of her arrival at the court, Susan found herself one of seven clerks assigned to an office in the basement. In what must have been the first hour of her first day on the job, she visited our third-floor clerks' maze, looking for both a friend from McGill and a washroom.

In search of the latter, she came around a corner. I saw her and thought, "I'm going to marry her." This wasn't an experience I'd had before.

Susan, however, was underwhelmed. I think her first comment upon coming face to face with me was, "Where's the bathroom?"

Anyway, I quickly stepped in as if I were the host of the Supreme Court of Canada, and began making introductions. Naturally, I mispronounced her name. I threw in an extra syllable or two: "Abramon-ov-in-itch." I mean, *Abramovitch* is quite a mouthful for a boy from Victoria.

I started chasing her immediately, with almost no success. Mostly, I drove her nuts with my ability to get the work done more quickly than most of the other clerks. "Frat-boy savant" was what she called me. Not meant entirely, I assumed, as a compliment. It wasn't until late winter that year that I won her attention.

And so Susan and I had a courtship in our workplace. Not at all an uncommon experience. It's just that our workplace was the Supreme Court of Canada.

We canoodled in the judges' elevator and got caught by Tom Cromwell, then the CEO to the chief justice of Canada and later a Supreme Court justice himself. We got amorous in various nooks within the courthouse library, deserted hallways, storage rooms, and fire escapes. We even got caught, much to the entertainment of the RCMP on site, on security cameras we didn't know existed.

As it happened, we were one of several couples formed that year among the Supreme Court law clerks. My friend Lorne Sossin married fellow clerk Julia Hanigsberg, now vice-president at Ryerson University, who would become my chief of staff as Attorney General and a best friend for life. There were other marriages and common-law relationships as well. Like I said, *la cour d'amour.*

Not long after we started dating, Susan's parents—her dad a doctor, her mom a social worker—had an anniversary celebration. This Victoria WASP was the surprise that came to dinner in Montreal.

I suppose there could have been some reservations about me. Susan's parents had been raised as conservative Jews. She herself had attended Hebrew school and a conservative shul. For her, I suppose, a relationship with me was a little rebellious. Her parents likely preferred that she marry within the faith. But they were also relieved that she had found someone who wasn't intimidated by her high intelligence and abrupt, uncompromising manner. I wasn't. I was ready to have a grown-up relationship.

Neither Susan nor I could have known as our romance began and grew that one of the cases we were working on would come to figure so dramatically in our own future. That year, Madam Justice Beverley McLachlin wrote the majority judgment in a decision called *Creighton v. Regina*, the third in a trio of cases by the Supreme Court of Canada that dealt with criminal fault. One of those cases, *Hundal v. Regina*, set out the test for criminal negligence causing death and dangerous driving causing death. As McLachlin occasionally allowed, she asked one of her clerks—me—to prepare the first draft, so I wrote the early version of the Supreme Court's majority opinion.

The constitutional issue dealt with *mens rea*, or the criminal mind. The issue was whether someone could be convicted of a serious crime without being consciously aware that they were engaging in dangerous behaviour. It was a debate between the "subjectivists" (who believed that the accused had to think dangerously to be held guilty) and the "objectivists" (who believed it didn't matter what the accused was thinking so long as a reasonable person would find his or her actions to be dangerous).

At the time, I was very judgmental. I believed an objective test would suffice for conviction. We were taking rather a hard line.

Not insignificantly, to me anyway, the dissenting opinion in the *Creighton* case was written by Chief Justice Lamer, with the concurrence of Mr. Justice Frank Iacobucci, my father's old friend, a man who presumably could have changed my diapers as a baby.

It would turn out that I'd helped write a rather stringent test that, almost two decades later, I'd have plenty of cause to reflect on again while sitting in a jail cell.

A year as law clerk to the Supreme Court of Canada counts as the equivalent of articling. Afterwards, everyone goes either to Wall Street or to graduate school. It's a career trajectory generally aimed in one direction, to elite posts in corporate law or academia. From our year, nobody went to Africa to volunteer for good works. Very few people ever just go directly home.

I knew I was going to grad school; I just didn't know where. I'd applied to Stanford, Columbia, and Harvard. I'd already been accepted into graduate law programs at the first two. Columbia would even waive tuition and grant me a teaching fellowship, which would pay my way.

In the spring of 1993, I was sitting in my cubicle at the Supreme Court, holding in my hands a letter I'd read and reread about ten times. Susan and I had been going out for several months. She was clearly marriage material, in my mind. Susan was heading to New York to work at Debevoise & Plimpton, a famous Wall Street firm. She wanted to be an entertainment lawyer, but the leading firm she had her sights on told her to get some general corporate experience at one of the big Wall Street firms first. So that's what she intended to do. At Debevoise & Plimpton she'd been guaranteed a year in New York and then the next year in Paris, which was a dream come true for her. Susan became fluently bilingual at law school, studying in both languages, and earning both a civil law and a common law degree. She'd spent a summer in Paris, loved it, and wanted to live there. The obvious thing for me to do would be to go to Columbia, in New York. We could live together there. That's why the letter I kept rereading was so troubling.

It was from Harvard. I'd been accepted into the program there. No scholarships or grants, mind you. (Although within a month I would obtain both, including a Fulbright fellowship, sufficient to pay my way.) But Harvard had been a dream of mine. Who passes on a chance to go to Harvard!

Susan appeared at my cubicle and read the letter over my shoulder. I held it up. She sighed.

"What do you want to do?" she asked.

"I want to be with you," I said. "But I want to go to Harvard."

"We can always be together. Next year we'll be apart." Follow your bliss, she told me. "Go to Harvard."

There was another sigh. Was that a lump in her throat? Then she said: "Congratulations. Let's celebrate."

So Susan went to NYC to do commercial arbitration, mergers and acquisitions, and the like. And I went to Cambridge, Massachusetts. It didn't go swimmingly. The stresses of a long-distance relationship made things difficult. We split up in November for a month. My pattern continued: study and socialize, strategically. My studies went well, as did my alcohol consumption. At Harvard, I finished my master's dissertation on aboriginal rights, entitled *Legal Aspects of Intra-governmental Armed Conflict: Chiapas, Wounded Knee, and Oka*. (It would prepare me well for a future assignment with aboriginal affairs.)

When Susan and I reconciled in late 1993, about a month after we split, I made it clear I wanted to get married. She wasn't ready, but agreed we were on that path. Then she left for Paris. I tried to get a job there, but couldn't. So I got a job in London, teaching law at King's College at the University of London. The Chunnel from England to France had just opened and we considered the London–Paris commute likely to be not much worse than New York–Boston.

I was living at London House—with its subsidized pub, thank

you very much. And my drinking continued. We visited each other every second weekend, and toured much of France and England by car and train. But it was hard to be living apart. Worse, Susan was miserable at work. The American lawyers there used her more or less as a translator. The hours were absurd.

And so, in the backseat of a Paris taxi in 1995, we decided to move to Toronto. "You start your entertainment law career. And I'll begin my political career."

OUR ARRIVAL IN TORONTO in the summer of 1995 was something less than glamorous. The first place we stayed, until we could find an address of our own, was an apartment near King and Dufferin Streets, somewhat lacking in modern conveniences but fully equipped with cockroaches.

If nothing else, this amenity did create motivated house-hunters. Susan soon found a place, a house for rent near Queen and Spadina. Of course, the past almost always catches up with you. We almost didn't get it because, as a law student, I was constantly in debt and terrible at paying bills on time. My credit-card debts even became something of a joke among the other Supreme Court law clerks. Sometimes the phone would ring and it would be a credit-card company. They'd ask for me and I would say, "Sorry, no Michael Bryant here." It was an odd thing for other clerks to hear over a cubicle in the Supreme Court of Canada: Michael Bryant denying that he was Michael Bryant. It should have been humili-ating, but I thought it hilarious.

So after we found this place, the landlord called and said, "Sorry, I can't rent to you, you have the credit rating of a fraud artist." Susan was devastated, then furious. For her, debt was evil. Her father had paid cash for their family home.

Chastened, I went to the landlord and literally begged. I gave her references. I asked her to call the Honourable Beverley

McLachlin. I showed her my paycheque. Eventually, she agreed to rent to us, as long as Susan was the sole signatory.

On the career front, things rolled along. Susan had the first job. Before we returned to Toronto, Graham Henderson, husband of Margo Timmins of the Cowboy Junkies, had left McCarthy Tetrault to start his own entertainment law boutique. He asked Susan to join him. So, after we wrote the Ontario bar exams (Susan finished in the top three and got an award; I almost flunked), she started with Henderson.

Her practice—mostly music law, with a little bit of film and video gaming law—blossomed from the beginning. They built that shop up to about six or eight lawyers and she became the managing partner.

Meanwhile, I wanted to be a litigator. I thought McCarthy Tetrault was the place to be. Ian Binnie, one of the leading litigators of his generation and later a Supreme Court of Canada justice, was there at the time. They had a huge litigation department that drove that firm's profits, which was unusual for Bay Street. Most of them are transactional, mergers-and-acquisitions shops, with a litigation practice on the side. At McCarthy's, litigation was their strength.

I started there in January 1997, and that was the second best thing that happened over that New Year holiday. The first was that Susan and I got engaged.

We'd gone to Victoria for Christmas. We took a walk on the beach at Saxe Point Park, which had great meaning for me and my family. That's the park my grandfather had created, and his ashes were spread there. Susan wondered why I was proposing on a funeral pyre, and former garbage dump, but accepted nonetheless.

I had champagne cooling in the trunk of the car, confident of the outcome. And I'd booked an engagement notice advertisement in the local paper, the *Victoria Times-Colonist*, before I got the answer. It never occurred to me that she'd say no. So I proposed, she said yes, and the next day the ad was in the paper. (Everyone but Susan pointed out the risk I'd taken, but she understood me too well to affect surprise at my overconfidence.)

Almost from the beginning at McCarthy's, I was nicknamed "The Professor" by the litigation lawyers. This was not praise. They regarded me as overeducated, while they were gritty litigators. I wanted to do appeals. They liked the scholarly side of me, writing up factums and injunctions. That again turned out to be fantastic training for politics.

Injunctions require urgent action, an inhuman amount of work in a compressed period of time, and it can all end in a moment. They're often make-or-break procedures. If you win the injunction, even though it's supposed to be an interim measure, often that's the end of the case.

The lawyer often called upon to pull an injunctive rabbit out of a hat was my mentor, Tom Heintzman, Q.C. A formidable crew of litigators learned under Heintzman: Darryl Ferguson, Andy Reddon, Bill Black, Jonathan Lisus, Marguerite Ethier—all senior partners today in Toronto. From Tom and this posse of barristers, I learned how to balance the need for thoroughness with the ability to meet deadlines, the need for creativity in the moment, and the need to be prepared for everything. I learned how to anticipate what the other side might do, and to have in hand a response to the anticipated reaction. I would often have two or three appeal factums ready before we even went to court. The strategy was basically to steamroll the other side.

By now, Susan and I were both working long hours. Money was starting to flow in. But she was ensuring that we saved for a house. We were also busy trying to find a rabbi willing to marry a Jew and a Christian. There were none in Ontario. We finally found one in Montreal, Rabbi Leigh Lerner, who agreed to marry us so long as I took the conversion course. So I did. I took the course, but I didn't convert. I signed a *ketubah*, a Jewish marriage contract affirming that our children would be raised Jewish.

The rabbi had originally intended to make the ceremony quite secular and allow no Hebrew to be spoken. Susan had always envisioned that there would be some Hebrew spoken at her wedding, so she was disappointed. A few months before the wedding, I wrote Rabbi Lerner a letter and explained my own spirituality, my commitment to any children being Jewish, my affinity to Judaism even though I was unable to convert.

I told him this was not just a show for us; we wanted it to be a Jewish wedding for spiritual reasons, not for cosmetic reasons. He responded very favourably, and on the day of the wedding he said, "Okay, we're going to do the last part in Hebrew. Both of you."

It was only a line, a "repeat after me." Susan was happy. I was just as thrilled. It did, however, prompt a lot of people to assume that I'd converted.

Actually, I had discussed the possibility of converting with a rabbi at Holy Blossom Synagogue in Toronto. But he said, "I don't know how you could do it. To me, it would be like getting a sex change." I thought, yeah, I'm just not. I'm not Jewish.

At the time, my state of spirituality was pretty much what I'd gotten from my mom, a sense that there was a God, that He was everywhere, and that He looked favourably on truth, goodness, and love. I had no strong sense of Christianity and the gospels, but just to discard them seemed to be a disavowal of something fundamental to myself.

So on August 31, 1997, Susan and I were married, under a *chuppah* in Montreal's Montefiore Club by Rabbi Lerner. There with us, dancing the *Hora*, was the future chief justice of the Supreme Court of Canada, our country's first woman chief justice, the groundbreaker for whom I'd clerked. Also clapping was another Supreme Court justice, Frank Iacobucci, a man who'd gone to law school with my father and had been at my own parents' wedding.

Ours was a marriage of two people surrounded not just by love, but by headline names and top-flight success; two people who seemed ordained to succeed by gifts of intellect, education, ambition, and connection.

In addition to getting some Hebrew into our wedding, I also managed, in my usual ad hoc way, to look after the honeymoon. I was at McCarthy's late one night—actually the early hours of the morning—waiting for photocopies in the photocopy room beside a fellow first-year associate. There was an awkward silence as we waited, the machines humming in the background. I noticed a poster on the wall, advertising some tropical destination, pinned up by the photocopier staff as a substitute for a window. So, to make conversation, I said, "I don't suppose you've got an acre on the beach in Maui you could loan me for my honeymoon in September, do you?"

And he said, "As a matter of fact, I do."

His family had a massive beachfront property in Maui (beside one owned by Alice Cooper, for you shock rock fans). So, after we were married, we stayed there for three weeks.

Almost as soon as we came back from our honeymoon, we took possession of our first house, on Palmerston Avenue in the Annex neighbourhood of Toronto. So, by fall 1997, gainful employment, marriage, and home ownership were now ticked off the to-do list and my attention turned to politics.

I faxed David Peterson, who by then—thanks to the election of the NDP government of Bob Rae in Ontario in 1990, and then the drastic swing right in favour of Mike Harris's Common Sense Revolution in 1995—was long out of office and chair of Cassels Brock law firm. I reminded him of our meeting seven years earlier. He remembered. He asked what I wanted. I told him I wanted to run. He asked where. I said I didn't know. And he said, "Well, why don't you go and figure that out."

So even though I'd never been a member of any Ontario political party, never been politically active in any way except on behalf of my dad, I called the Executive Director of the Ontario Liberal Party, Guy Bethell, and asked for a meeting. When we got together, he pulled out a map and explained who were the MPPs in the area and who were the candidates for election. I didn't grasp the audacity of my inquiry, asking about electoral districts like I was choosing cold cuts from a deli counter. Bethell held back his grins, politely, assuming this was a passing fancy of mine, another vanity candidate sniffing around the Ontario Liberal Party.

The ridings had just been redistributed, as a result of Premier Harris shrinking the Legislature to 103 seats from 130, and MPPs and candidates were scrambling for places to run. Bethell told me the Liberal candidacy in St. Paul's—a riding held at the time by Progressive Conservative MPP Isabel Bassett—had just opened up. (St. Paul's was initially being held for MPP Monte Kwinter, but he had decided to run in another riding.) Our new house was just outside St. Paul's. I had no idea why it was called St. Paul's (the old parish name, it turned out). Nor did I know the names of most of the streets in the riding, having lived in Toronto a relatively short time. I was clueless as to the riding's rich history, the community leaders, the local businesses, the municipal politicians, the brewing or festering of local issues, and had only a vague recollection that the federal MP, Carolyn Bennett, had previously run as MPP but lost to Isabel Bassett. Too clueless to be daunted, I decided there and then that I would become the next MPP for St. Paul's.

By now, David Peterson had called Liberal Leader Dalton McGuinty and suggested he meet with me. So McGuinty and Rod MacDonald, one of his senior staff, agreed to a meeting, in the Opposition Leader's offices, in early 1998.

Rod was extremely charming and friendly. He glad-handed me in the waiting room and walked me into the sprawling office within which Dalton McGuinty sat, in a large leather chair in the middle of the room, facing a less comfortable, high-backed old chair at which I sat.

I'd never met him before. He was tall, his back ramrod straight; Rod sat in another chair, beside McGuinty. Rod was on the edge of his seat, literally, fidgeting with a pen, his glasses pushed up onto his forehead.

I began to speak with the cadence of a machine gun, spraying McGuinty and MacDonald with words, my hands swirling, my eyes wide with fascination at whatever I was blurting out.

Amongst other things, I told him I wanted to run in St. Paul's. I told him about the political tradition in my family and my dedication to public service.

McGuinty seemed intrigued and was amiably encouraging. He was careful with his words, however. He repeatedly paused before he spoke. Then he dropped a bombshell. McGuinty told me that if I was going to run, I couldn't be a full-time litigator at a downtown law firm.

"Yeah, I think you're right. I assumed that I'd have to campaign for the nomination full time." Of course the thought had never crossed my mind until that moment.

So, to prove my commitment, I quit my job in February 1998. (Dalton said later he was only half serious and was surprised I actually did it.) I figured I'd start up a research company and basically write factums for other law firms. And that's what I did. It was called Briefs by Bryant Inc. It paid the bills.

The Liberal nomination in St. Paul's didn't receive too much media attention, because it was assumed Bassett was going to be tough to beat. But my opponent for the nomination turned out to be formidable.

At some point that spring, Kathleen Wynne entered the race. She had made a name for herself opposing education budget cuts and as a leader of a prominent grassroots movement called Citizens for Democracy. But I had a big head start and some advantages. (Wynne would go on to serve as one of the best education ministers Ontario ever had.)

One of the first people I met when I came to Toronto was Liberal author and lobbyist John Duffy, who got me involved in the Walter Gordon Circle. There, I met the legendary Liberal David Smith, who was head of that organization and also head of the green-light committee that decided when nominations are called. He called it at a favourable time for me.

After quitting my position at McCarthy's to run for the nomination, I joined the party(!); I had no campaign organization in place, so in March 1998 I invited a bunch of my friends from law school over to my house on Palmerston Avenue. I sat on my stairs and made my first ever political speech to the 15 people in my living room, none of whom had any experience in politics. They were just drinking buddies, law school classmates, men and women and their girlfriends and boyfriends. I asked them for a cheque for $200, with no tax receipt; I asked them for nominations, to sign up as party members, and to come knock on doors with me.

I was stunned when they agreed.

I went out every night, either with Susan or one of them, or volunteers we met along the way, and slowly but surely built up a team. Carolyn Bennett, the local MP, had endorsed me, and that made all the difference. She gave me instant credibility. After that, a number of members from her riding association also signed up to help.

In September 1998, I was nominated as the Liberal candidate for St. Paul's.

Later, people asked me how I'd built the network that quickly.

Jan Innes, Les Scheininger, Joe Ragusa, John Duffy, Dr. Carolyn Bennett and her MP predecessor Barry Campbell, and former federal cabinet ministers Donald S. Macdonald and Doug Frith joined people like Sen. David Smith, former Premier David Peterson, former Premier Frank McKenna, and the late Sen. Keith Davey (the fabled "Rainmaker") as early supporters. These people were political legends. How did I do it?

I was lucky. One of my colleagues at McCarthy Tetrault was Tim Murphy, who once gave me some excellent political advice whilst I ruminated about a political career. He'd been an MPP, and would become Prime Minister Paul Martin's chief of staff. He said to me: "The only way to run, is to run."

So run I did. And running means asking a lot of people for help. All those political legends gave their limited time to me, primarily because I asked them. It was as simple as that. Once you get a couple of legends on side, more will want to join. But first you have to ask. And when you ask, you'd better be running like a winner, or else you'll just look like a talker, not a doer. Political people always admire someone who sticks their neck out, actively and often, so that's what I did.

By the time the election was called in May 1999, I'd been running for a year. Along with David Caplan's fight in Don Valley East, mine was considered a good underdog campaign for young people to join. I got endorsements from the local municipal councillors, like Joe Mihevc, who would become a good friend and local ally, notwithstanding his traditional allegiance to the NDP. Perhaps most important, Councillor Michael Walker introduced me to the politics of rent control.

At the time, rental rates in Toronto were going up because landlords were taking advantage of the Harris government's landlord-friendly statutory changes. In St. Paul's, almost 70 percent of the constituents are tenants, so my strategy was to focus on that.

I assumed the highly educated homeowners in Forest Hill would swing their vote based on what the leaders did. Like most urban areas that year, it was moving a little Liberal. What made the difference for us were tenants. I'd knock on doors and say, "Hi, I'm trying to get rid of Mike Harris and bring back rent controls." And they'd open the door and say, "Where do I sign?"

I also benefited from joining the Save Our Schools campaign mounted in reaction to the Harris education policy. The campaign was led by Mike Colle, an incumbent Liberal MPP who had represented a big chunk of St. Paul's before redistribution and was now running in the riding next door in Eglinton-Lawrence. Mike taught me a lot about retail politics, and how to be a good local politician. He remains one of the best.

A lot of the basics I knew from my dad. But, as usual, I was lucky. Mitch Frazer, a veteran Young Liberal, who was at University of Western Ontario law school at the time, ran my nomination campaign via telephone from London, and he showed me how to win an election in Toronto. When the nomination campaign started to stall in the spring of 1998, Mitch told me to hire Tom Allison, the best campaign manager around. Tom would become a great friend and work with me off and on for the next decade.

Throughout the campaign, I knocked on doors like a madman. I hadn't done any polling, but one of the local papers said I was ten points ahead of Bassett heading into the stretch. My parents came in from British Columbia for the last few days of the campaign.

On June 3, 1999, at the age of 33, just like my grandfather and my father before me, I was elected to public office. I was the new MPP for the Toronto riding of St. Paul's, part of Her Majesty's Loyal Opposition in Ontario.

FOUR

To the Palace

The Ontario Legislature building at Queen's Park was once described by historian Desmond Morton as sitting like "a huge red toad" peering gloomily at the traffic down University Avenue. By the time I arrived there in June 1999, it was more commonly known as the "Pink Palace," owing to the hue of the sandstone from which it had been built more than a century earlier.

Red toad. Pink Palace. I didn't care what anyone called it. All I knew was that I'd arrived. Election night was one of the most exciting of my life and my most exhilarating moment in politics. I guess it showed.

In my first months as MPP, I felt like I was floating, constantly, six inches off the ground. Theresa Boyle, a *Toronto Star* reporter in the Queen's Park press gallery, told me I seemed like the happiest guy in the Legislature. "You've always got a stupid grin on your face," she said with a laugh. And she was right.

Political entrances, after all, are occasions of limitless hope, nothing but the promise of the joyful unknown. And I was joyful. Once, coming down the grand staircase in the building's foyer, I literally pinched myself.

But the business of politics soon overtook my reveries.

During the campaign, our leader Dalton McGuinty had bombed in the televised leaders' debate. After the election, there spawned a small and ineffectual "Dump Dalton" movement. But the truth is that McGuinty grew a lot from the experience of his first campaign as leader. And he made it clear, in a terrific concession speech on election night, that he was staying on.

Dalton and I immediately hit it off. About that time, his Chief of Staff Monique Smith (who would later become an MPP and cabinet minister) resigned. So there was no buffer between him and his MPPs, even the rookies. I was in his office every week, on strategy, on everything.

He was trying to shore up his leadership for the review the party constitution required to be held after any election. Right away, McGuinty called that review for late November 1999, preventing dissent to ferment over time. It was also held in his hometown of Ottawa, which ensured local advantages. He was masterful that weekend, gave a stirring speech, and won an endorsement from party members that was more than strong enough to quash dissent.

As a result of his polite, reserved demeanour, a lot of people underestimate Dalton McGuinty. But there is a lot more steel there than is obvious, and a lot more competitive fire.

"I worked very, very hard to get this job," he told Robert Fisher that weekend on Global TV's *Focus Ontario* program. "I have been working very hard at this job; I am now working hard to keep this job."

No one should have doubted that for a minute. Or that he was working very, very hard to become premier.

Dalton soon asked me to chair the Ontario Liberal Caucus Niagara Conference on ideas for renewing the party, which would be held in 2001. I was gung-ho and genuinely believed in the leader. Looking back, Dalton McGuinty and I were probably as tight then as we would ever be.

ONE OF THE FIRST THINGS I did after the 1999 election was to call Charles Harnick. Charlie had been Attorney General in the government of Mike Harris. But he'd also been in opposition for a term and had been A.-G. Critic. That was important. He had exactly the kind of experience I needed. Charlie had basically been ostracized by the Harrisites after he decided not to run again in 1999 and was happy to talk to me.

Actually, I suppose I had a thing for former Progressive Conservative Attorneys General of the Red Tory persuasion. By 2000, I'd also befriended Roy McMurtry, who was then chief justice of Ontario. We started having tea in his office and had lunch together periodically. McMurtry became a confidant and sounding board to me as well. His son would run under the federal Liberal banner a few years later, confirming what many of us had assumed—the chief justice had a healthy dose of liberalism mixed into his political DNA.

He'd been known as Roy "McHeadline" in his political days. So our affinity was obvious. By now, though, his whole life was justice. Nobody was talking politics to him anymore, but he still had the bug. So I suppose I was his outlet for that. And, next to my dad, he was as good an *éminence grise* as one could find.

Charlie Harnick told me that being in opposition was going to be the most fun I would ever have in politics and that I should make the most of it. And I did. I soon figured out that if I got the visuals right—the pictures to go with any story—and if I got the timing right, I could get myself in the newspaper.

If it was a slow news day, that meant there was "dead time"— also known as a great opportunity to fill the void. In our circles, it was known as feeding the goat. The media often have no choice but to fill the void with whatever they can find; I was willing to make it easy for them. I would wake up in the morning and wonder how I was going to do it. "Okay, how are we going to embarrass the government today? How are we going to feed the media goat?"

In Opposition, we created sort of a Rat Pack II, reminiscent of the aggressive group of young Liberal MPs—Sheila Copps, Don Boudria, John Nunziata, Brian Tobin, Jean Lapierre—who took on the huge Brian Mulroney majority PC government in Ottawa in the 1980s.

In our case, it was George Smitherman, Sandra Pupatello, Steve Peters, Rick Bartolucci, Dwight Duncan, the late Dominic Agostino (who died in 2004), and me.

I had a red-letter day on my birthday in April 2000. Early that year, I found out that BB guns, pellet guns, and starter pistols could be purchased at hardware stores by anybody. There was no regulation of them whatsoever. Meanwhile, I learned that about half of the guns found at Toronto crime scenes were those phony, replica guns. So police were encountering them, and they'd been used to rob banks. We had a problem here.

I went to a Canadian Tire store and bought a phony gun—a BB gun disguised as a handgun. It was amazing. It looked just like a Glock. McGuinty's new communication director, Jim Maclean, passed me his BB gun that looked like Dirty Harry's 44 Magnum. I called a news conference outside my office. I had a placard printed up—mouth-wateringly delicious to the hungry goats of the media—to put on a podium: "Phony Guns Kill." I held a couple of these guns on my fingers and told the story.

I ended up on the front page of most of the newspapers in Ontario and got a tonne of media. It was my first blast of attention. And I discovered I had both a talent and a taste for it. Better still, when Premier Mike Harris was on a radio interview that day, the interviewer told him about my call for regulation of these guns and asked what he thought about it. Harris replied, "I think it's a good idea." So it became a huge story. Premier Backs Opposition Ban on Phony Guns.

In the next Question Period, Dalton decided that he would ask the questions about the phony guns. And Premier Harris humiliated him. The Premier applauded me over and over. He said the new member for St. Paul's—that would be me—had already done more to fight crime than McGuinty ever had. In fact, Harris said, I was "the first member of this Liberal caucus that I have seen in five years who has actually expressed an interest in this area."

It was embarrassing for Dalton. But I didn't quite get that. I thought it was funny. Harris had said my name three times, so I thought the whole thing was cool. But Dalton got this very tense look on his face, a very tense smile, and he turned back and looked at me in the back row as he sat down. That was probably the beginning of our slow unravelling.

The next day, one of McGuinty's senior staffers showed up in my office, demanding to know what other press I was trying to generate. I was told that Dalton had basically called his office onto the carpet and said, "I should be getting this kind of media." Another of McGuinty's guys I knew told me to watch my back. I said, "What? This is great. Did you see the photos? It was great!" I just didn't get it. I thought it was awesome.

In fact, it was vainglorious. Dalton McGuinty was a colleague and a friend, deserving of my support. I couldn't see it that way, and I would regret this selfishness years later. A political leader's need for support should be assumed, and unspoken, but pride disallowed me to reach out to him, in the absence of him reaching out to me. His own pride is not my business. My pride, on the other hand, would become my business soon enough.

So, between that and the fact that Dalton now had an entourage around him, my access to the leader's office all but disappeared.

About that time, I got some advice from Doug Frith, the former Liberal MP and federal cabinet minister from Sudbury whose son-in-law was a volunteer on my campaign. As was my habit, I was keen to pick the brains of anyone with political experience. Frith counselled me about relations with the leader of the

Ontario Liberals. He said, "You've got to proceed from a position of strength. Don't reach out to Dalton. Just make it *necessary* that he has to respect you."

I decided, from that time on, to get as much press as I possibly could for myself. My strategy would be to seek forgiveness, not permission, for any of my stunts. And that was the way I carried on.

Frith's advice seemed to work. In 2002, McGuinty made me Energy Critic. Again, I was lucky. It was just about the time that the entire energy system in Ontario would be scandalized by a series of events, some within the Conservative government's control, some not. But I'd play Chicken Little regardless, and lay the blame squarely at the feet of the Conservatives.

In October 2001, after the Thanksgiving weekend, Mike Harris announced his resignation as premier. He was succeeded in March 2002 by his finance minister and golfing buddy Ernie Eves, who won a second-ballot victory over neo-conservative rival Jim Flaherty. Eves had retired from the Legislature a year earlier for a senior post at Credit Suisse First Boston, but decided to return to politics when the top job became available.

Eves's first budget in June 2002 was a shrewdly generous Red Tory document that postponed proposed tax cuts and tacked away from Harris's right-wing course. We considered it a really bad day, because Eves was moving back onto more moderate turf we intended to claim.

But over the next year we caught a lot of breaks. A judicial inquiry report into the Walkerton water tragedy (involving contaminated water in a public water system, killing and injuring people)—was released, an extremely balanced but inevitably politically damaging critique of the Conservative government. A Superior Court judge ruled the Hydro One sell-off planned by Harris to be illegal and Eves cancelled it. Bizarrely, Eves decided to announce the 2003 Ontario budget at an auto-parts facility rather than in the Legislature. Historian Michael Bliss wrote that this showed contempt for Ontarians, treating them like "mindless, manipulable couch potatoes."

As if that weren't enough, August '03 brought the Great Blackout, during which the province was without electricity for days. And shortly after that, Eves called the election and turned in an awful campaign. (Ernie Eves was always gracious and polite to me over the years, even though I'd defeated his partner Isabel Bassett. But still, it was a lousy campaign.) Ontario was tired of the uproar of the Common Sense Revolution. We asked Ontarians to "Choose Change." And, on October 2, 2003, they did.

It was a landslide victory for me by more than 13,000 votes in St. Paul's. And McGuinty won a majority Liberal government.

Over the years I've observed that there are two ingredients needed to topple a government seeking re-election: the voters must first decide that the government has defeated itself, then the alternative party leader has to perform well. In 1999, Ontario voters decided to give Conservatives another term, so it didn't matter how well McGuinty performed. It mattered in 2003, however, because the people were ready to toss out the Conservatives.

In 2003, veteran Liberal MPP and cabinet minister Sean Conway sat out his first election in decades. Watching the election as a historian (as he is at Queen's University), he observed that McGuinty performed better than any leader he'd ever seen in an Ontario election. I just thought that Dalton was quite literally flawless, every single day of the campaign.

On election night, the Leader's Office brought some of the freshly elected MPPs to a central campaign party and asked us to say a few words. I didn't realize it at the time, but what they were conducting, I suspect, was a little audition for Cabinet. OK, how do they do in a crowd? Are they full of themselves? Do they talk enough about the glories of the leader?

I knew from my dad, and from watching in Opposition, what not to do on such occasions. The worst was to speculate about your own bright future and aspirations. I'd seen other MPPs go up in flames doing this. I reined it in.

In the days that followed, one of my great political godfathers, Les Scheininger, who'd been through several elections, advised me to leave town. My father agreed. They said to make sure the right people had your phone numbers, and then get away somewhere. The speculation will drive you crazy. It was good advice. Susan and I went to the cottage on Stony Lake to hide out.

On October 22, 2003, the day McGuinty's office was going to make the phone calls preceding cabinet appointments, a caucus meeting was called at Queen's Park. MPPs were all told to go home and sit by the phone from 4 o'clock on. And I did.

I was pretty confident that I was going to be in the Cabinet. Overconfident would be a better way of putting it. I had already arranged for my parents to fly in from Victoria for the swearing-in the next day. They were in the air on the way to Toronto.

By around 4:30, the phone rang. It was the first time I'd heard someone say "the Premier is on the line." And Premier Dalton McGuinty asked me to be his Attorney General, with additional portfolios: Minister Responsible for Aboriginal Affairs, and Minister Responsible for Democratic Renewal.

I couldn't have asked for more. Those were precisely the three things I was interested in. My dreams had come true. I was 37 years old and I was the Attorney General of Ontario.

When I got off the phone, I started calling people. I wanted to tell Susan face to face, so I waited until she got home from work. By 7 p.m., my parents arrived. My dad kept repeating it over and over again: "Attorney General. Attorney General. Oh, my God, Attorney General."

And I drank a bottle of Scotch.

AT THE CABINET SWEARING-IN the next day, I spotted the legendarily loquacious and colourful Ian Scott, the A.-G. in David Peterson's Liberal governments in the 1980s who had made a painstaking recovery from a debilitating stroke. I told him the gods had smiled—Ontario finally had another modest Attorney General.

Scott roared with laughter, but I wanted to pay a proper tribute to him. I decided, sitting on the government benches, amongst the MPPs to be sworn into Cabinet, that I would give a dramatic wave to Scott after I was sworn in, and then blow a kiss to my wife, who was sitting in the Visitors' Gallery with Sadie on her lap and her mom, Arlene, beside her. In the hurly-burly of the moment, I blew a stage kiss to Ian Scott, and failed to acknowledge Susan. Neither Sadie nor my mother-in-law could see to whom I was blowing a kiss, but Susan figured it out: "It must be Ian Scott," she assured them.

Any crumbs of modesty I did have, and it wasn't much, lasted about 24 hours. After the ceremony, there was a reception with the Lieutenant-Governor. That's where the deputy ministers all showed up looking like day-care supply teachers who'd reluctantly come to collect their charges.

Mark Freiman was the Deputy Attorney General. He used to be my boss at McCarthy Tetrault. So we were familiar with each other. He took me and my family to the ministry offices at 720 Bay Street, which I would later have named the McMurtry-Scott Building.

The spirit of the place was unique within the government. The professionalism and independence came, I think, from those two men. There was a robust constitutional law branch that McMurtry had created and Scott had expanded. The best constitutional lawyers in the country were all there. I knew from my days clerking at the Supreme Court of Canada that Ontario's was the first factum the judges would turn to when a constitutional issue was before them.

Mark took me up to the boardroom on the top floor of the building. At lunch, I sat down in the middle of the boardroom table. My former boss and new deputy said, "No, you've got to sit at the head of the table. You're the Attorney General." I just laughed and blushed. I couldn't do it. I was suffering from impostor syndrome.

At the end of the day, I met with Les Scheininger, my Toronto political godfather, and Jack Kay, a senior executive at a Toronto generic drug company. Jack understood large budgets, so he asked me the size of the budget for the Ministry of the Attorney General.

I had no bloody clue. But I was too insecure to admit as much to Les and Jack, so I picked the biggest number I could imagine for a department.

"I think ... I think ... it's got a budget of ... a hundred million," I said.

Jack looked surprised and confused.

"Maybe it's less!" I blurted out.

"Huh ... I would have thought it was more."

Les changed the subject, knowing full well that the budget for my ministry was more than tenfold my estimate. I was in fact accountable and responsible for a billion-dollar ministry, utterly clueless of the scope of the endeavour, at least on my first day.

That first night, officials gave me a bunch of binders and I took them home and studied them. When I came in the next day, I thought, "Someone's got to sit at the head of this table." I found it astonishing that it was me. But it was my post now. So the impostor syndrome only lasted for 24 hours.

Within about a week, I asked Julia Hanigsberg, who had been a Supreme Court law clerk with me, to be my chief of staff. She was Executive Counsel to the Cabinet Secretary at Queen's Park, on the civil service side. She had worked in the Ministry of the Attorney General for a number of years. I figured that I knew the politics; I needed someone who understood government. And she certainly knew government. She understood immediately what my offer meant—that she would basically have no life. But, after sleeping on it, she agreed to do it. For a lawyer, it's a fantastic gig. And she did a spectacular job, with everything except curbing my ego.

That week, I also hired Greg Crone to handle my media. He was a former Queen's Park press gallery reporter who had worked in McGuinty's office in opposition, but wasn't famous for adhering to a corporate message. He is, however, a genius. He was probably the best communications guy I could have had—or maybe the worst. We were kindred spirits. Probably too kindred. We had so much fun bouncing lines off each other. Crone was as entertaining as human beings get. But the two of us together, especially unsupervised, was not a recipe for understatement, although Assistant Communication Directors Sandra D'Ambrosio and Sarah Roberts did their best to balance the boys' bombast with the wishes of the Premier's Office.

Julia Hanigsberg proceeded to assemble a crack political office team. Adam Dodek, a Harvard graduate and Supreme Court clerk, left a prestigious Bay Street post to head up policy matters. Linda Shin left her elite, well-paid position at my old law firm to manage policy issues and spearhead my legislative efforts, which were ambitious. Many others, like Nikki Holland, Natasha Elkabas, Emily Bullock, and Daniel Infante, ran my life. Many more would come and go over the years, including the veteran campaign guru Tom Allison, who had run the nomination that got me started in politics, and Bay Street lawyers turned politicos Beth Hirshfeld and Alexis Levine. Perhaps most impressive was Julia's recruitment of Columbia law graduate and Cree legal theorist Douglas Sanderson.

The Ontario Attorney General's job turned out to be about half political and half legal. I got deeply involved in the files I would need to defend in public, but tried not to micromanage. The lawyers seemed to like that.

In December 2003, as my first act as A.-G., I launched the public inquiry into the death of unarmed Indian protester Dudley George at Ipperwash in 1995. Led by veteran MPP Gerry Phillips, we had demanded an inquiry for years in opposition. And I appointed former Chief Justice Sidney Linden to head it.

Right away, we also had a bunch of contentious political and legal issues. One involved the families of autistic children, in a series of cases they'd brought against the province. A ruling had come down that had haunted the previous government and which we had inherited. It was about the old government's approach to underfunding care of children with autism, and which branch of the state ought to decide the best autistic treatment for Ontario kids: the courts or the government?

The second issue was the salaries of provincial court judges. They had just been awarded a 20 percent pay increase by arbitrators. The question was whether the government was going to appeal the arbitration.

The third issue was what to do with Highway 407, a toll highway. We had promised to tear up the Harris government's agreement, which had sold it off to the private sector in a fire sale for quick, easy cash. But it became clear very quickly that we weren't going to be able to tear up the contract, because it was, legally, watertight. Any attempt to vary the agreement carried with it financial penalties. There was no way, legally, to terminate the agreement, absent something too radical, like legislating it out of existence.

The politically expedient thing to do was to yield to the demands of the autistic children's families, to fight the judges' salary increase, and to fight the 407 sale in the courts—truly a façade for action.

The constitutionally pious thing to do was the reverse: to not let the courts dictate the government's autism treatment policy; to leave the judges' raise alone because the agreed-upon arbitration process had been correctly followed; and to stand down on the 407 sale.

I chose the constitutionally pious approach and it landed me on the carpet in McGuinty's constituency office in Ottawa. The Premier was particularly vexed about the judges' salary increase because he felt it was going to hamper negotiations with teachers and other unions.

I told him the Attorney General is supposed to be independent of the government on such things and able to make an independent decision. He understood that. But he wasn't happy about it.

I also made it clear to him that if we allowed the decision to stand on funding for families of autistic children and didn't appeal it, there would be endless numbers of court injunctions that would, in essence, Americanize our system. The precedent being set by these autism funding cases was radical and had to be tested in appellate courts, I thought. If those decisions were allowed to stand, then in the future if a disaffected group didn't like a government decision they could just take it to the courts and let the judges decide—no matter the cost to the treasury—whether program funding was sufficient.

In the end, I rolled over on the Highway 407 litigation. We fought it in the courts, even though there were no decent grounds. We lost that case a couple of years later.

On the judges' salaries, I allowed the appeal period to pass without doing anything—which forever after earned me the displeasure of the Premier's Office, who viewed it as a power play on my part. But I felt strongly about that one and I was willing to risk losing my job for it. I knew the Premier wasn't going to fire me over that, but I realized it might mean a reassignment in the next shuffle.

On the autism file, I convinced the Premier and the Cabinet that appealing it was the right thing to do. Dr. Marie Bountrogianni, an expert in the field who happened to also be the Minister for Children, had developed an excellent policy supported by most experts and many families of autistic children. It was a policy worth defending. Our government couldn't let the courts micromanage government policy, and that's what these decisions amounted to, I argued. So let's defend our policy, and appeal the decision, even if the plaintiffs were the last people you'd want to be fighting in court: families of autistic children. And that's what we did. My political concession was to offer to pay for the legal costs of the families.

The province's arguments were accepted in the Court of Appeal. The court said it was up to the government to set policy and the McGuinty government was, in fact, already doing more than the court would ask for.

And that was the first few months. It was chaotic. I was loving it.

IN JANUARY 2004, I gave a speech at the opening of the courts that was a barnstorming piece of rhetoric on the independence of the judiciary, and the efforts by conservatives to Americanize the courts through so-called judicial accountability where report cards would be done on judges' findings.

Those speeches were vetted. But it was an operating practice in my office to file the comments from the Premier's Office in the shredder. I took enormous pride in it. But it made Julia Hanigsberg very tense and required her to spend a lot of time being screamed at by the Premier's Office.

That summer, I began my government foray into criminal justice policy. In Opposition, I'd been uncharacteristically active on the file, for a Liberal MPP. As I later told federal Liberal Leader Stéphane Dion, for too long Liberals had been stuck in the summer of love. (True, but it was an obnoxious turn of phrase that ended up in a *Globe and Mail* cartoon, portraying Dion as a hippie advocating flower power over gun power.) In any event, I thought that we'd become irrelevant on crime, and McGuinty said as much back in 1999 when he asked me to be the Justice Critic.

But now we were in government, and I wanted to do something about the organized crime operations that had moved from Quebec into Ontario. Thus was born my Organized Justice campaign— "the best response to organized crime is organized justice." I did an interview with journalist Richard Mackie that ended up on the front page of *The Globe and Mail*.

In it, I made no reference to the Hells Angels. But at the time the story ran, two members of the Hells Angels were being prosecuted on extortion charges. So the Hells Angels lawyer subpoenaed me and brought a motion for abuse of process, alleging that my comments had destroyed their chance of a fair trial.

In September 2004, I ended up riding in a squad car to the court, where I awaited the judge's verdict as to whether I was going to be subpoenaed and cross-examined by Hells Angels lawyer Steven Skurka. There had been some concern about my safety, but it was only speculative, not based on any information. Regardless, that week the OPP drove me around. In fact, my family had been up at the cottage at Stony Lake and there was an OPP boat positioned about 100 feet offshore, off and on, all weekend long.

As it turned out, Madam Justice Michelle Fuerst dismissed the motion. But I knew that if it had been granted and the trial was thrown out as a result of what I'd said in that *Globe* interview, I would have had to resign.

As a result of that incident, I realized the stakes whenever I spoke out on crime—that I could be putting prosecutions at risk, and putting my career at risk. Cabinet ministers are warned about this, but the political near-death experience has to be lived. However, I also saw just where the boundary lay. I saw the line that could not be crossed, and that the closer one inched, the greater the risks. I was willing to take those risks, and thereafter I did so with confidence as to exactly where not to step in the minefield of politics and crime.

After that, our next big controversy was over Sharia law. A Muslim cleric had set up a Sharia law institute and said that, under the 1990 Arbitration Act, family-law matters could be determined based upon Sharia law. He was right. That's how the act worked. Anybody could set up an arbitration system based on whatever law they chose, so long as those who went to it consented.

At first the coverage was minimal. Then the *Toronto Star* ran an editorial criticizing the government for quietly allowing Sharia law to operate in Ontario. We complained and the *Star*'s ombudsman wrote a piece saying that the editorial was inaccurate, that we had never done anything of the sort. I'm not sure many read the latter, but they definitely read the original editorial. The inaccuracy stuck: the government was somehow to blame for allowing Sharia law to govern in Ontario.

It kept bubbling up in the media, so in June 2004 I asked former NDP Attorney General Marion Boyd, who had a background in women's issues and was a member of the Legislature when the act was passed, to investigate and make recommendations on family law and arbitration in Ontario, including religious-based arbitrations.

Boyd's review of the issue quieted further media investigations into the matter and the furor died away for the time being. This technique, of building a bridge over a contentious issue, is used constantly by governments, recognizing that the issue of the day might not be so in the future, whether the government fixes it or not. (Whether Sharia law was actually something to be "fixed" was to be considered by the *Boyd Report*.)

But another problem was developing, as the world turned, and it had nothing to do with Sharia law or organized crime or the early contentious court cases we'd faced to date. In fact, you'd never think that dog attacks would be the concern of the Attorney General of a Commonwealth province, but dog attacks indeed became my business in the autumn of 2004.

FIVE

Comfortably Scrummed

I have a lot for which to thank the Honourable Roy McMurtry: his personal support, his invaluable counsel, his remarkable public service as Ontario Attorney General, Canada's High Commissioner to London, and chief justice of Ontario. But not everything associated with McMurtry was regal. He was an activist like few other politicians in Canada. If there was a problem, Attorney General McMurtry would find a solution, and often legislate on it.

During his time in government, the Ontario Legislature passed more than 50 law reform statutes introduced by McMurtry, including the first major family-law reform legislation in Canada, the creation of a bilingual court system, and a network of legal aid clinics. On the more mundane side, he created legislation regarding daylight savings time, which meant that when President George W. Bush changed daylight savings time for the United States in 2004, everyone scrambled around to find out which minister would be responsible for responding in Canada. It turned out to be a provincial matter, and in Ontario that meant Roy McMurtry must have legislated on the issue at some point in his decade as Attorney General.

So it shouldn't be surprising that I have Roy McMurtry to thank for my constitutional jurisdiction over pit bulls. Minister of Justice McMurtry responded to a set of public recommendations regarding irresponsible animal owners. Constitutionally, if dog bites man, it's an issue for the Attorney General. If man bites dog, then it's the Solicitor General who steps up. Or this was the formula used by my Solicitor General counterpart, and good friend, Monte Kwinter.

Between September and mid-October 2003, there was a rash of reported pit bull attacks. The first time I got a call on the issue, I was coming back from a speech in London on October 14, 2004. Our office had received a call from Richard Brennan of the *Toronto Star*, a famously pugnacious reporter who was known, for good reason, as "The Badger." He would soon become president of the Parliamentary Press Gallery in Ottawa. For now, he was asking if I was going to ban pit bulls. Here was an example of a reporter putting an idea into the head of a politician. Or at least it was the first time that the idea of a pit bull ban had been raised, to my knowledge.

I turned to Linda Shin, riding in the back seat of the Ministry car with me. Linda was a Bay Street lawyer, from my former firm McCarthy Tetrault, who had come to work in my office through Michael Barrack, a long-time supporter and a senior partner at that firm. Linda was brilliant, innovative, indefatigable, and hilarious. Prior to joining my office, she hadn't had any first-hand political experience. However, she was a natural at seeing political angles invisible to others. The pit bull ban was a good example.

Shin knew that such a ban would be explosive, but also knew it could work. Crone, my communications director, loved the idea, but made it clear that the media coverage of any dog issue would be intense. Linda and I strategized out the issue. Pit bull attacks had caught the attention of editors and producers, so every reported pit bull attack would get media attention in the coming weeks, maybe months. Based on my experience (having fielded calls on pit bull attacks as a local MPP), there would inevitably be more attacks, and the demands for action would increase. So, we might as well decide now what to do.

I'd never been personally attacked by a pit bull, or any other dog, for that matter. However, over the years in my MPP constituency office I'd met several dog owners whose pets had been attacked by pit bulls. I met more than a few people who'd been victims of pit bull attacks. One constituent spent an hour educating me on the history of pit bulls: the Molossians, the Mastiffs; the Greeks, Romans, Brits, Tibetans, and Germans; the cross-breeds. A common theme ran throughout their history: they were the fiercest of fighters, and eventually bred to fight—in wars during antiquity, in dog fights for centuries. Regardless, they were again and again attacking other dogs and people. There is an intractable debate about whether to blame the dog-breeders or the dog-owners, but the bottom line was that pit bull attacks had become a public safety issue.

The idea of banning pit bulls was initially appealing to me. It appealed to my instincts—that pit bulls were inherently dangerous—and to my ego. The audacity of banning a dog breed was right up my alley. But on matters like this, I mostly followed my political instincts: the "gut," as my mentors would say. (Although, my mentor McMurtry was also fond of the cricket strategy: "When in doubt, step out!")

But I knew that before I could tell Brennan anything I was going to have to clear it with the Premier's Office. Dog politics had landed many a politician in trouble. I was fine with the trouble that would come with a pit bull ban, but there was no point trying if the Premier's Office was going to kibosh it out of hand.

At the time, you could pick and choose who you called in the Premier's Office. So I called Bob Lopinski. His populist instincts were superb and he had the best political nose in that shop at the time. He said something to the effect of, "Well, as long as you just say you'll look at it, it gives you some wiggle room."

I knew there was no wiggle room. As soon as I said that we were going to look at it, there would be no turning back. But, technically, I had clearance from the top. So I called Brennan back at about 6 p.m. and said, "Yes, we're going to look at banning pit bulls."

It was huge news. It was on the front page of the *Star*. It became national news. It went international; I ended up on CNN. The decision actually changed my political life. For years afterwards, up to 2009, the average person knew me as the guy who banned pit bulls.

Initially, there was no response from the Premier. But the Liberal caucus immediately began getting emails from angry dog owners, not just pit bull owners. A campaign was launched by the local humane societies, who foresaw the thin edge of the wedge of canine genocide.

Some members of caucus were fully supportive, laughing off the naysayers. Others started getting antsy. They raised it at caucus meetings. They came up to me in the House, telling me they were taking heat.

I recall Brad Duguid, now a cabinet minister in the McGuinty government, approaching me; he was one of many backbenchers getting plenty of phone calls on both sides. He stretched out his hands, and said with a smile: "You're gonna need to stiffen your spine for this one." Duguid was right.

So I tried to stiffen the spines of my colleagues, as I had to for myself. I said, "Trust me. The empty wagon's making the most noise here. This is the right thing to do. The silent majority is definitely with us on this one."

From my perspective, I thought it was important that we did it because Liberal governments typically nibble around the edges of these kinds of things with regulations that are more rhetorical than real—things like training for people who own pit bulls, or new penalties for irresponsible dog owners. That kind of thing.

The truth was, we actually had the legislative tools to deal with this issue. Pit bulls were inherently dangerous dogs, I believed. Let's actually try to eliminate the problem, not appease a host of voices.

The issue came to dominate the media coverage of the government. It didn't matter what we did. Three syllables—*Pit! Bulls! Banned!*—were the story. I was getting a lot of ink, and loving it.

The bill to ban the dogs required Cabinet approval. The formidable Toronto lawyer Clayton Ruby had already beat his chest that he was going to challenge the bill in the courts, on behalf of pit bull breeders and owners. So we drafted something that was as tight as possible.

It hit the Cabinet table and immediately a rural cabinet minister laid into it. A dozen other people raised their hands, some supportive, some not. I had made phone calls, so I thought I had the numbers. But I knew there were some people who were very skittish about it.

McGuinty cut them off, which he rarely does—he usually lets cabinet members air their opinions. He shut down the debate. He said he didn't want to spend any time on it. He didn't want our government to be defined by this issue, but he thought it was good politics and that we were going to do it.

I picked my jaw up off the table, and then passed him a note saying thanks. He just nodded at me when he got the note. I hadn't known his support was coming with such finality.

I later learned that the Premier's wife, Terri McGuinty, was all for the ban, and that McGuinty himself had introduced a bill when he was in opposition, also addressing pit bulls. My bill had the most important support one could get in the McGuinty government, the Premier himself, and that was that.

Later on, a famous pollster reported that the pit bull ban was the most popular public event in Canada since Newfoundland Premier Brian Tobin's rhetorical war with foreign fishing trawlers and his defence of the lowly turbot.

Come January 2005, the pit bull ban had worked its way into the government speaking notes as one of our accomplishments. And today you don't read about pit bull attacks in Ontario anymore.

Malcolm Gladwell, who grew up in Elmira, Ontario, before becoming famous as a *New Yorker* staff writer and then as an author and speaker, took me up on this in an article in the magazine that was later updated and enlarged for a chapter in his book *What the Dog Saw*. In a nutshell, he argued that generalizing about pit bull behaviour is a dangerous business, because it leads to bad public policies like racial profiling. The most obvious example occurs when, based on the overrepresentation of African Americans in U.S. prisons, African Americans are targeted by police for crimes by virtue of their appearance alone. I obviously agree with Gladwell on the evils of racial profiling, but a pit bull ban is different.

Firstly, racial profiling is unconstitutional and wrong because of its impact on *homo sapiens*. Canine profiling impacts *homo sapiens* only as commercial dog breeders and offended owners. Secondly, I think Gladwell is guilty of making a category error, although he accuses me of the same. Category errors, according to Friedrich August Hayek, arise when someone slaps categories onto a group based on some abstract, if not random, description but then treats the categorization as an undeniable truth. For example, whether Pluto is a planet depends on how one defines planet.

I think we can get lost in all this circularity when assuming that dogs and people are in the same category. The same argument justifying the U.S. prohibition of keeping wolves as pets applies to pit bulls. Yes, the categorization of wolf and pit bull is an abstraction. But there's no denying that *something* approximating the abstraction of a wolf, and a pit bull, roams the earth. That we cannot always rely on the abstraction's description doesn't mean we deny the very existence of these dangerous animals. Rather, we categorize as best we can, however imperfectly, and regulate the dangers accordingly. This conclusion and my legislative action deeply offended some people, for whom their pit bulls are hardly "property." They are truly loved ones.

What I hadn't realized at the time was how pit bull owners were demonized in their own communities during this public debate. The consequence was unintended, but I feel responsible for the ill treatment of pit bull owners and apologize when I can to people directly. One kind elderly lady sent me a hand-written note expressing sympathy for my 28 seconds experience but gently chided me for ending her practice of using pit bulls for dog therapy. She, and many others, claim their pit bulls are not dangerous. I have little doubt that domestic wolf-owners would say the same thing.

Those who oppose the pit bull ban include a few people who have (sorry) dogged me ever since. Some have threatened me with violence, publicly compared me to Hitler on Facebook and websites, and otherwise vilified me on every issue regardless of whether it's connected to the pit bull ban. I stand by the law. My bombastic campaign for the bill was over the top, no doubt, although I was careful never to engage in personal attacks on dog owners. The same can't be said of dog owners' words about me. Alas, sticks and stones—nay, pit bulls and wolves—may break my bones, but their owners' slander will never hurt me.

Notwithstanding McGuinty's unexpected intervention in the cabinet debate, more often than not I found myself very fortunate to receive my colleagues' support for the justice initiatives I spear-headed. George Smitherman, Health Minister and eventually Deputy Premier, and Kathleen Wynne, the Education Minister, were important allies, as was my good friend David Caplan, Minister of Infrastructure and later Health, and Rick Bartolucci, the Emperor of Northern Ontario, to name only a few.

Chris Bentley would succeed me as Attorney General in 2007, and he was a veteran criminal lawyer before entering politics in 2003. But he always brought his opinions directly to me, and never undermined me at the Cabinet table. Sandra Pupatello, Minister of Social Services and later Economic Development, was also a good friend and could be called upon for support in a pinch. Greg Sorbara was the most powerful cabinet minister outside the Premier, and during his tenure at Finance, he supported many justice initiatives, including significant legal aid budget increases. The same would be true of his successor, Dwight Duncan.

Then in 2005 came Toronto's "Summer of the Gun," with its explosion of gun-related homicides. By mid-September, 40 gun homicides had occurred, and the year's final tally was 52. One killing took place at the funeral for another's death-by-firearm. The 52nd happened on Boxing Day, near the Eaton Centre in downtown Toronto, when a bystander, 15-year-old Jane Creba, was shot while shoe shopping. The crime garnered international media coverage.

It's worth stopping to consider these statistics. Firstly, as far as gun homicide stats go, Toronto's numbers in 2005 were much higher than in previous years, and since then those numbers have plummeted. Secondly, even in 2005, Toronto's gun homicide rate was a fraction of that found in big cities in the United States. Chicago is about the same size as Toronto, and sees about ten times the number of gun homicides every year. In other words, Toronto used to see about 40 gun homicides a year; Chicago, about 400.

But these numbers belie the tragedy within those stats. In 2009, there was but one cyclist involved in a motor vehicle fatality in the Greater Toronto Area. One. That would be Darcy Sheppard. And yet the tragedy of that enormous loss is trivialized statistically. I've always felt the same is true for crime statistics.

Even one homicide is obviously a tragedy, just as one cycling fatality has impacted so many since the dark night of those

28 seconds, and ended the life of a man. To celebrate the decline of crime statistics is not the triumph of smart public policy over statistical trajectories. It ought to be the celebration of lives saved. More often than not, the media reports on lowering crime statistics as a "gotcha" political salvo aimed at tough-on-crime politicians and as a critique of justice budget expenditures.

There is, without question, a political or media trajectory that exists for crime sprees. Once the tipping point is met, every additional crime, whether it be a break-in, a carjacking, a rape, or a gun homicide, receives urgent media attention: namely, the lead story on a newscast, or above the fold on the front page of the newspaper. Every single one. Therefore, at some point the numbers reached a critical mass such that in 2005 we had the Summer of the Gun.

But each of these crimes are terrible stories and chapters and volumes of sorrow. Consider this. On January 21, friends Justin Hodge, 20, and Damian Muirhead, 22, were shot to death at Apt. 313, 180 Niagara Street, Toronto. On February 11, Szilvia Veres, 35, was shot to death in the underground parking garage at 15 Brookbanks Drive. Her 47-year-old husband was injured. Her former boyfriend, John Kovacs, 52, was charged with first-degree murder and attempted murder, but later committed suicide. On February 12, Orlando Grundy, 22, was shot to death with "multiple undetermined firearms" in Apt. 1308 at 2777 Kipling Avenue in Rexdale. Two other males, ages 24 and 25, were wounded. On February 15, Selvakumar Sellaiah, 26, was shot to death in the 17th-floor stairwell of 275 Bleecker Street.

Those are five of the more than 50 gun homicides of 2005. The year ended with a crescendo of gun homicides that left Toronto dumbfounded and angry. On December 1, part-time used-car salesman Sepehr (Danny) Fatulahzadeh-Rabti, 25, was shot to death by two men after a fight at his family's car lot at 4877 Steeles

Avenue West. On December 23, Cordell Charles Skinner, 25, was gunned down on the grounds of 5 Turf Grassway. On December 26, Jane Creba, 15, was shot and killed while Boxing Day shopping with her mother and sister on Yonge Street near Elm. Six others were injured.

Because I had been the tough-on-crime guy for the Liberals, I became the government spokesperson on that issue, one that was almost impossible to manage publicly and personally. I found it excruciating, less because of the media fury than because each death felt like a punch to the heart. There was a lot of self-medication by bourbon going on that year, to be sure.

During that fall and winter, one Question Period bled into another. The issue had boiled up to the Premier's legislative desk, and he fielded many of the questions himself. Sometimes he would send them my way, and some days he was unable to attend Question Period. On those days, especially, I'd receive a justified grilling by Opposition members about the reports of deaths and more deaths by firearm.

One day I was taking a breather in the West Wing, as it's called: the area between the legislative chamber and the door leading to the hallway outside the Legislature, where media cameras awaited. The wing is always full of MPPs during Question Period. Many are on the phone dealing with a local issue in their riding. Many staffers for the MPPs are also there, particularly for the cabinet ministers expected to be "scrummed" by media after Question Period. If you've not experienced a media scrum, just imagine being outside on a very rainy day, without an umbrella, trying to keep your composure, but instead of raindrops it's TV camera lights blinding you, microphones jutting into your face, and about 25 people simultaneously shouting questions and false mockery to provoke a reaction.

As I stood there beside the coffee station, one of the legislative security officials sidled up to me. These individuals were always extremely polite and did their job well. Conversations were inevitably brief, and I'd never in my years at Queen's Park had a political conversation with any of them. It was all business, with the occasional chat about the weather or the time of day.

"You must have the weight of the world on your shoulders, sir," she said nervously, like she'd perhaps crossed a line.

I smiled up at her (they were always taller than me), grateful for her genuine and generous effort to comfort me. She looked stressed out herself, as if my angst were contagious. Truth be told, we were, all of us in Toronto, anxious about the gun crimes, the homicides. It was bewildering, scary, confusing, wrong.

"Thanks," I said with a big smile. "I'm okay now. Better get back...." And I headed back into Question Period, feeling not alone.

Minutes after Question Period ended, it was showtime in the scrums. I loved being in media scrums, because it allowed me to feel in control of a universe out of control. Scrums were an exaggerated, externalized manifestation of my internal misgivings and self-doubt. I was inevitably harder on myself, alone, than the media were hard on me, live and in person. I rarely felt as if the journalists were truly judgmental, even if they said things like "People think you're lying!" or "Obviously you have to resign!" or "The NDP say you're the worst Attorney General in the history of Canada!!" or "COME ON!! TELL THE TRUTH!!" or "What do you say to the mother of the boy who was shot yesterday ...?"

Moreover, I was always comforted by the fact that I never had to actually *answer* their questions. There was no score kept of whether I did so. They got to ask the questions however they wished. And I got to answer however I wished. Like a tennis rally.

If I repeated myself a few times, it was code for "This is all I'm going to say when you ask that question." Often an Attorney General's rejoinder to any question is that "The matter is before the courts and therefore I cannot comment." It was rare that I resorted to that one, but eventually it was easy to offer enough information that the journalist abandoned the line of questioning. The beauty of a scrum was its self-propelling tornado of questions, and the internal jousting among the journalists themselves, physically, violently, verbally. If I ever felt stuck, I could just wait all of one second, maximum, for the next question to arrive.

In contrast, my own self-doubt and feelings of self-pity were far more judgmental and caustic. A media scrum was a vacation from one's inner scrum, itself a truly suffocating exercise. With some experience, an external scrum could be easily defused by an unflappable demeanour. My media guy, Greg Crone, used to often say, to prepare me for a scrum: "Okay, we're gonna channel Gregory Peck now," and I'd always twist my mind into remembering anything about Gregory Peck, but I got the point. For me, impersonating Gregory Peck was always easier than internalizing the Dalai Lama.

The word "scrum" is a rugby term. When rugby players commence play, it's with arms locked and all crowded around each other—which a media scrum resembles, of course. Both are a sport, a game, no matter how serious: a World Cup match or the wartime scrum of a prime minister. (Ontario Premier Dalton McGuinty, meanwhile, changed the rules of the game in 2009 when he announced, after years of being scrummed, that he'd address the media only if they gave him a few feet of space. The outraged media obliged, of course—at the end of the day, the goat needed feeding.)

Like rugby, there are clearly defined goals and rituals for media scrums. Reporters try to get their product so they can file a story and go home. They do that by getting some content that is newsworthy. The more outrageous the reaction to the questions and badgering and physical smothering, the better the product, from the media's perspective. There would be no need for the physical tsunami of a scrum if we politicians just spit out what reporters are looking for, but we don't, so they try to squeeze it out of us.

Sometimes I looked too comfortable in a scrum, such that I would start answering before they could start asking—handing over their needed content with a bow on top, in one take. In other words, I'd give them their sound bite, including all the elements necessary for filing the story. It was mutual manipulation, really, when it got to that stage of providing "one take," but that usually arose only for less contentious issues. Not so for the Summer of the Gun.

After the 2005 Boxing Day shooting of Jane Creba, I found myself on the telephone with the Premier, which was a rarity. He called me on the 27th to brainstorm a bit on what we had to do as a government. McGuinty never overreacted to events, in my experience. So if he was worried about something, it was serious. The overall competency of the government was on the line here—in a rare moment when unanticipated, urgent events could topple an otherwise successful administration.

It was on this telephone call that we discussed the so-called "Guns and Gangs Centre."

What's a Guns and Gangs Centre? At some point in December, prior to Boxing Day but amid the rising homicide toll, I flopped into the chair across from Linda Shin in her office on the top floor of the McMurtry-Scott Building, where we worked.

"So what the hell are we going to do?" I said with a sigh.

Plenty of micro solutions were being kicked around but I wanted to hear—perhaps not for the first time—the macro solution. Linda said: "It's the Guns and Gangs Centre. That's it."

The concept of such a centre had originated with efforts, before my time, by Deputy Attorney General Murray Segal and his Chief Prosecutor John McMahon, to better coordinate police and prosecutorial efforts. A lot more could be done, they thought, if the traditional obstacles to collaboration were removed.

Keep in mind how it normally works: a municipal police force enforces the provincially prosecuted *Criminal Code* provisions, plus the federally prosecuted drug crime provisions. The provincial police stand in for the municipal police in the smaller towns that basically outsource a local police force through the provincial police. The RCMP have still separate jurisdiction themselves. Each of these police and prosecution divisions is then further divided by time and space. Each city with its own police force (or provincial police), each province with its separate prosecutors, and so on. Sound confusing? It's confusing for the justice system and wonderful for organized crime. Sometimes a single operation involving organized crime can involve over a dozen different jurisdictions in Canada. This is not organized justice. Therefore, the Guns and Gangs Centre's innovation was putting them all together, physically and otherwise, into one space, to focus on large-scale investigations and prosecutions.

My Crime Policy Chief Linda Shin, together with Deputy A.-G. Murray Segal, took that concept and put meat on the bones. About $100 million worth of meat, in the form of more prosecutors, more police, and a state-of-the-art *CSI*-esque building that housed all the officials who traditionally were, literally, miles and miles apart. Toronto Police Services, the Ontario Provincial Police, the RCMP, and Interpol were put on the same floor as provincial and federal prosecutors, and all their databases were combined into one.

This unprecedented coordination amounted to the "Organized Justice" that I later trumpeted in speeches. It allowed a hundred people to be arrested in a couple hours and prosecuted simultaneously, which meant that entire gangs could be excised from a neighbourhood by the time most of its residents were having breakfast.

Overnight, communities could be transformed. By 2011, gun crime in Toronto was down to 26 out of 45 homicides, the lowest in 25 years, despite the continued population growth in Toronto. In 1995, it was 52 out of 80 homicides.

(But wait a minute! Now that I've been on the other end of being arrested, am I not bothered by the idea of arresting a hundred people at a time? You'll have to wait for a later Chapter for that answer.)

BY THE FALL OF 2005, the Sharia law issue was boiling over. A 1991 provincial law on arbitration had inadvertently given statutory authority to Ontario family disputes being governed by Sharia law, if the parties consented. This development angered many people, and they wanted their government to fix it—yesterday. There were protests on the Queen's Park lawn. Protesters were burning the Premier in effigy. Sandra Pupatello was the minister responsible for women's issues; she and I were tasked with settling the issue, which boiled down to whether gender equality trumped religious freedom. That I failed to recognize the obvious answer was "yes" might be attributable to my frustration with those who failed to see how racist the issue had become. This was an example of me personally imagining that I could will a result different from its destined conclusions. Obviously, the politically expedient thing to do was to nod approvingly at those who would vilify Sharia law. But this too required looking the other way. For shoulder-to-shoulder with women's groups protesting Sharia law were bigots who yelled "go home" to Muslims who protested the anti-Sharia protesters. To this day, I believe that this issue would never have seen the light of day but for post–9/11 Islamophobia.

This is obviously not to lump together the gender equality champions with the bigots. Some women made it clear to me that they were uncomfortable with their allies in the fight to rid Ontario family law of Sharia law arbitration. The compromise solution that Pupatello and I had put together had the support of some women's groups but not all. All that was left was for Cabinet to approve the package.

But on the weekend preceding that cabinet meeting, Margaret Atwood was one of the signatories to an open letter to the Premier that ran in *The Globe and Mail* demanding that he defend women's rights against the possible imposition of Sharia law. It was not the first or last time that Margaret Atwood had got the attention of a political leader. I find Atwood to be discriminating and usually devastating in her public political missives. (Not always successful, mind you; her support of the Stéphane Dion Liberals against Conservative cuts to the arts didn't stop a Conservative minority re-election in 2008.) But the very fact of her weighing in on an issue means it's serious to Canadians. Really serious.

On September 11, 2005, I was at a Sunday Liberal Association event, munching on a hot dog while chewing on the impact of Atwood's letter. Somebody stuck a BlackBerry in front of me showing me a Canadian Press news story. The Premier had announced a ban on Sharia law in Ontario.

I had no idea he was going to do it. I also knew that we couldn't do it. There was no constitutional way to ban Sharia law in Ontario. So I told the Premier's Office what I could and couldn't do, as the cabinet minister who would be introducing legislation on Sharia-based arbitrations. A meeting was convened with McGuinty and his staff from the Premier's Office. "Tell me why I can't do this, because that's what I said I'd do," Dalton demanded. "You've got to make this happen." It was as heated as he ever gets. Civil by anybody else's measure, but heated for him.

We found a way to allow the Premier to stick with his announcement and yet not introduce blatantly unconstitutional legislation. We also got lucky because the Catholic Bishops of Ontario, through their lawyer, worked with our office to endorse the new legislation. The bishops, of course, were worried that the bill might do something to affect Catholic annulments. They just wanted the government to get out of the business of regulating anything to do with the church and marriage and divorce.

Ontario's second-ever Catholic premier, Dalton McGuinty, loved the idea that the bishops were supporting our bill. I thanked God for the bishops. The bill passed without any fanfare.

IN THE SUMMER OF 2005, Karla Homolka, the former wife of Paul Bernardo and the woman who was convicted with him in the horrible kidnap, rape, and murder of two teenage schoolgirls, was due to be released from prison in Montreal after serving her 12-year sentence. Nobody reported it at the time, but my deputy minister, Murray Segal, had led the team that prosecuted Homolka. He was the prosecutor who made the "deal with the devil," as it was known in the media. The deal was necessary because investigators didn't know at the time of the existence of videotapes chronicling the abuse. The prosecution needed Homolka's testimony, they thought, to convict Bernardo. So a plea bargain was struck.

Notwithstanding the public outrage at the plea bargain, a public inquiry held to scrutinize the plea bargain thought otherwise. Segal and his colleagues' conduct was found by Justice Patrick Galligan to be "professional and responsible." The deal itself? "Unassailable" under the *Criminal Code of Canada*, the judge concluded: "the Crown had no alternative but to ... [negotiate with the accomplice] in this case" as "the 'lesser of two evils' to deal with an accomplice rather than to be left in a situation where a violent and dangerous offender cannot be prosecuted."

When Homolka's release was approaching, Segal, the man who made the deal as a prosecutor and who was now the Deputy Attorney General, knew what to do. We created a set of proposed restrictions on her freedom, for the purposes of protecting people from the potential dangers that she posed.

A number of issues arose for public debate. Hadn't she done her time in prison? If so, how could we pile on more restrictions? Was she really still dangerous? Were we (the Crown), motivated by a bad deal—a "deal with the devil"—trying to, in essence, re-write history? Indeed, Karla Homolka had served her sentence in its entirety. The National Parole Board had ruled that she remained a risk to commit another violent crime, and therefore had to complete her sentence without possibility of parole (or early supervised release). Why a risk? In prison, she had developed a relationship with a convicted murderer—exactly the behaviour that had led to the carnage and sex crimes with Bernardo.

Our efforts in court regarding Homolka's release were not to amend her sentence, but to deal with the here and now. It was intensely practical. She was going to be at large. If she were a risk, as we believed her to be, was there nothing the justice system could do? In fact, there was something to be done. The restrictions we sought in Quebec Provincial Court, pursuant to a "recognizance order" (a peace bond, but that sounded too soft to me), were not an extension of a sentence completed. Rather, these restrictions were preventative, and required evidence that she posed a danger to society. Under the *Criminal Code*, a prosecutor could get such an order. Most orders of this nature are based on consent, as the person posing the risk agrees to not engage in the risky behaviour, more often than not in a domestic context (until they get drunk or high or angry, and then violate the order at their peril).

We provided evidence of the risk Homolka posed to society. Her criminal conduct resulting in the rape and murder of two teenage girls, and the rape-death of Homolka's sister (it was never established in court that the sister was murdered by Homolka, albeit she likely would have been so convicted had it gone to trial). That was pretty damn dangerous. The National Parole Board findings supported the argument that she remained a risk.

In a dramatic flourish, we sent our best Crown attorney, James Ramsay, who was fluently bilingual, to appear at the hearing. Ramsay was the Crown attorney for the very region where Homolka had committed the horrendous crimes. She had been incarcerated in Quebec for her safety, which meant that she was released onto Quebec streets. The Quebec Attorney General agreed to let an Ontario Crown attorney, Ramsay, argue the case.

A two-day hearing was held before Judge Jean R. Beaulieu in June 2005. He ruled that Homolka, upon her release on July 4, 2005, would still pose a risk to the public. As a result, using section 810.2 of the *Criminal Code*, certain restrictions were placed on Homolka as a condition of her release: she was to tell police her home address, her work address, and with whom she was living; and she was to notify police if any name change was attempted or if she planned to leave home for more than 48 hours. Homolka was forbidden from contacting Paul Bernardo, or any other violent criminals, or the families of her victims, Leslie Mahaffy and Kristen French. Homolka was forbidden from being with people under the age of 16 and from consuming drugs other than prescription medicine. She was required to continue therapy and counselling, and required to provide police with a DNA sample. It was the most restrictive set of conditions imaginable under Canadian law.

Essentially, we got everything we asked for and more. The media reaction was very positive. One *Toronto Star* reporter wrote the following description of me: "When Karla Homolka shuffled into a Quebec courtroom in leg irons this week ... [s]he never saw the rosy, puckish countenance of the man who pulled the strings. That was Michael Bryant, Attorney General of Ontario and the victor in the battle to rein her in when she's released from prison next month. Bryant is Karla Homolka's worst enemy, and maybe her best friend. She may not like it, but he sees himself as the buffer between her and mob justice."

A Quebec Superior Court later overturned the initial ruling, but we were seen politically to be playing hardball with her, instead of defending the deal with the devil.

But that kind of positive media wasn't just bad for my rapidly inflating ego—it was bad for relations with the Premier's Office. At one point, I was basically hauled in after something that my communications head Greg Crone leaked to the *Star* had, in effect, overshadowed an announcement by the Premier. I apologized immediately and then told Crone to be more careful with any leaks, to stop leaving our fingerprints behind. It felt like a power play to me, *un grand jeu*.

THEN CAME THE Christmas tree debacle of 2006, furthering the estrangement between myself and the Premier, at least in the media. The presiding judge at the Jarvis Street courthouse had ordered the court staff to take down the Christmas tree. This decision hit the news. My response was an attempt to defuse the issue through humour: "We don't see the need to bring a *habeas corpus* application to free the tree just yet. Amnesty International has not called to date." I went on to joke that a Christmas tree "protocol" would be the subject of my next discussion with the chief justice of Ontario. I'd hoped to demonstrate the absurdity of the issue being in the media.

That day McGuinty contradicted me, publicly urging the judge to put the Christmas tree back. So I got kneecapped, and that was the media story. This action was unusual for the Premier. He was certainly entitled to have the last word on government policy, but he didn't like contradicting ministers because it made the government look incompetent. Maybe he wanted to put me in my place. Or maybe he just had strong views about Christmas trees. Either way, I joked my way through the scrum. That's how I got out of it. I made fun of myself. But it was so theatrical that John McGrath from CBC Radio ran the whole scrum on air.

When the cameras and microphones were turned off, some reporters expressed astonishment with the fir fight. Such was the puerility of Queen's Park politics. Only through this fatuous lens was there a rift between McGuinty and myself. But that was the impression left to this day.

FROM THE COMIC to the tragic: During the winter of 2006 and into 2007, it became apparent to me that the Ontario Human Rights Commission had failed to live up to its lofty mandate. If you brought a human-rights complaint in Ontario, it typically took up to seven years to get it resolved. I was determined to fix that.

So we created a new system where complainants bypassed the commission and went straight to a human rights tribunal and got a result within a year. The new system works well now, by all accounts.

The political problem with all this was that we were shrinking the role of the Human Rights Commission. And the biggest objector was David Lepofsky, one of my Crown attorneys, a blind man who is in the media regularly for his tireless fight for rights on behalf of those with disabilities. He was castigating me for the changes to the Human Rights Commission.

Most agreed the new system was very good policy, but very bad politics. The Premier's Office was determined to kill my bill amending the system, if only because we were getting too close to a provincial election to be in a fight against people with disabilities. However, I became convinced that his office was not reflecting the Premier's wishes. I held the perhaps naïve hope that McGuinty would choose good policy over messy politics.

At that point, it was all flying just below the media radar. So I leaked some background to Ian Urquhart, the Queen's Park columnist at the *Toronto Star*, who wrote a column that, in effect, dared the Premier to do the right thing.

He did. At the cabinet meeting on the human rights bill, we had a big long debate. And, once again, the Premier backed his Attorney General.

McGuinty drew upon his experience as an MPP. When people came in to see him in his constituency office with a human rights complaint, he would wearily tell them to go to the Human Rights Commission, knowing that nothing would happen. He hated that. He thought it was stupid and that we should have a human rights system that actually worked.

When it counted, Dalton McGuinty had my back. In fact, he supported me on almost every justice initiative I brought forward: on the Guns and Gangs task force, on pit bulls, on paralegal regulation, on electoral changes, on the Law Commission being revived, on human rights reform. I was grateful for his support, but never so grateful that I was willing to let my ego take a back seat to my talent for garnering headlines.

I was starting to think that this run I was having as Attorney General couldn't continue. It was too good. The bar was happy with me. The judges were happy with me. The police and prosecutors were happy with me. Stakeholders were relatively happy. I just knew it couldn't last. So I thought, "Maybe I should do something different anyway after the election. Maybe I'll go and do energy, or infrastructure, or health, or something like that."

Then, near the end of the 2007 campaign, when my riding association was flush with cash, somebody suggested that I send some money to help other candidates in a few key ridings. I called up Greg Sorbara and asked what he thought of the idea. He welcomed the extra help. He was doing it himself. So that's what

I did. I sent money to a handful of candidates. They all won. It seemed like a good investment.

This was taken by the Premier's Office, however, as akin to Paul Martin's machinations as he sought Jean Chrétien's job. They thought I'd stepped over a line, that I was overtly campaigning for the leadership. Really, I was just naïve. I thought, "Well, Sorbara's doing it so it's probably fine." In hindsight, it was a mistake.

David Caplan called me up. He said, "I'm worried about you, buddy. I'm hearing things ... bad things ... like maybe you're going to get punted from Cabinet or demoted. I'm hearing that they've gone nuts over you spreading money around." I shrugged off his worries, convinced of my invincibility.

Then, the week before McGuinty made his final decisions on his new Cabinet, former Prime Minister Jean Chrétien's memoirs were published—with media reports of his "regret" that he hadn't quickly fired Paul Martin and his "self-serving goons" for undermining his leadership. This rather paranoid attack on Martin, I'm convinced, might have had an impact on McGuinty, who had an opportunity to send a message to any pretenders to his throne.

As history records, we won a second majority government in October 2007. But when the cabinet call came a little while later, it turned out not to be quite the magical moment it had been four years earlier.

THE PREMIER TOLD ME he was appointing me Minister of Aboriginal Affairs and Government House Leader. I was surprised. But I saw immediately what he was doing. The combination made it clear. He was trying, with the House Leader's job, to keep me close to home at Queen's Park. When I wasn't, I'd be up at the far northern communities that most Ontarians didn't know existed.

He was burying me. He went on to say, "I need you to be

more thoughtful" and less quippy. But I'm not sure he expected my reaction.

I said, "Oh, this is great! This is the portfolio that demands your leadership, Premier. I can do this. After all, I've got my two graduate degrees in aboriginal affairs."

There was a pause. "I didn't know that," he said.

Immediately, I started spinning madly in the media that this was *great news* for me. People were trying to get me to complain, but I didn't. I refused to acknowledge the obvious: it was an intended demotion by the Premier.

It was great!! The best thing that ever happened to me!! And I got kudos from columnists in *The Globe and Mail* and the *Star* for not pouting. But we all knew the score. Greg Sorbara came up to me and hugged me and said a crummy thing had been done to me and to hang in there.

The day I was sworn in, John McGrath from CBC Radio asked me when I was going to Caledonia, the site of a standoff between police, residents, and one of the largest and most powerful First Nations in Canada: Six Nations. My predecessor in the ministry hadn't gone to Caledonia (against his private protests to the contrary), nor had the Premier. And that was the subject of some criticism.

At first I ignored the question. I hadn't cleared anything with the Premier yet. But then I looked at McGrath with a familiar twinkle in my eye, and he repeated the question: "When are you going to Caledonia?"

"Tomorrow!"

So I got hauled once more into the Premier's Office. The conversation was pretty heated and went on for a long time. I can't speak for Dalton McGuinty, who was no doubt frustrated that I was headline-grabbing yet again. But I can speak for myself as to what was happening between the Premier and me.

From where I sat, our relationship had unravelled into a power play. I refused to be controlled and he, perhaps, felt that his own authority was being undermined. While I did have a keen sense of just how far I could go, in defiance of any attempt to rein me in, in hindsight I see that I must have looked totally out of control. The truth was that I was deeply stung by the perceived demotion. My ego did not respond well. Out of defensiveness and fear of failure, I became further unrestrained.

Meanwhile, I noticed that the size of the cabinet binders was shrinking. While the binders we used for cabinet meetings used to be about the size of a breadbox, now they were less binders than thin folders. The government's electoral agenda would take a few months to be rolled out. It would be a full year before some of our key plans could be implemented. That created a vacuum that I was happy to fill with new initiatives in aboriginal affairs.

A week after becoming Minister of Aboriginal Affairs, I attended a gathering of First Nations chiefs, where I took aside Tom Bressette, Chief of Kettle and Stony Point First Nation. It was the home of Ipperwash Park, where Dudley George had been shot dead by a police officer. Bressette brought Dudley's brother, Sam George, along to our impromptu huddle.

During the Second World War, the federal government expropriated land adjoining Ipperwash Park to build a military base. Aboriginal families, including Dudley George's family, were moved to Kettle Point reserve and told their land would be returned after the war.

In 1995, Dudley George and others occupied the park to protest Ottawa's failure to return the expropriated land and to protect sacred burial grounds. George, 38, died when OPP members fired on the protesters.

I told Chief Bressette and Sam George that I had a proposal for them to consider. I couldn't help with their federal claim, but the province did own a piece of the park. If I just handed the park over, local non-aboriginal residents would have been outraged. So I offered to give the First Nation the title to the land, but that the park would be jointly managed by the local community and the First Nation. We shook hands on it, and the deal was done.

Then in February 2008, two things happened that led me to believe that my time in the political arena was soon up. Up in the far, far north of Ontario, a First Nation called Kitchenuhmaykoosib Inninuwug, or "KI," had begun to receive national attention. Chief and council were defying court orders, and were willing to be jailed, in protest to an attempt by a junior mining company to explore and mine disputed lands. I went up there three or four times to try to find a resolution.

At the same time, a dispute over casino gaming between the government and Ontario's First Nations was finally going to trial after years of talk. So I tried to negotiate a solution. It took a week, literally day and night negotiations. We booted all the lawyers out of the room, except for me. So it was just me on one side of the table and five chiefs on the other.

Day and night we negotiated in a windowless room on the conference floor of the Delta Chelsea. Except for one day, when I travelled to KI in a last-ditch effort to forestall incarceration of Chief Donny Morris and KI councillors. I returned after a gruelling day to recommence negotiations with the chiefs—at 10 p.m. It earned their respect. A couple days later, we shook hands. We had a deal.

The agreement saw all of Ontario's First Nations share in all of Ontario's gaming revenues. The agreement, worth an estimated $3 billion over 25 years, will provide the long-term, stable funding needed by First Nations to invest in improvements to quality of life in their communities.

That was the first time I thought, "OK, I think I'm ready to leave politics." I thought I'd done something concrete that would serve a community for years. I also felt exhausted. And I was tired of fighting the Premier's Office. For the first time, I opened up the want ads section.

About halfway through my political career, in 2005, I gave an interview where I speculated about how long I'd stay in politics. I said then, "I'm here for a good time, not necessarily a long time. I don't want to be a career politician. I am here only as long as it makes sense." Quite suddenly, in the spring of 2008, it no longer made sense.

I came to believe that it wasn't right for someone in Cabinet to be job-hunting. So after spending the summer discussing the matter exhaustively with Susan, I decided I was going to leave.

When I told the Premier in September, he was at first confused by my explanation. I was nervous and therefore verbose but inarticulate in explaining what I was doing. Or perhaps my reasons for leaving were not compelling.

"I don't understand," he said. "*Why* are you leaving?"

I paused for a moment. Looking back now, I wonder if the thought crossed my mind that, in fact, there was no good reason for me to leave, only bad ones. Was I leaving because of ego, pride, or fear? I don't think so, but nor could I pinpoint my motivation, other than a strong intuition that it was time to go. Or, as I'd said in that interview years earlier: "I am here only as long as it makes sense." In short, it no longer made sense *to me* that I remain in office. And ten years of public service was enough, I thought, to refute the argument that I owed it to the people to remain an MPP regardless of my own sensibilities.

Moreover, I'd always believed that the second an MPP lost his or her mojo, it was time to go and give someone else that opportunity. (Which is exactly what happened: Dr. Erik Hoskins, former head of War Child, a non-profit organization assisting child victims of war, was elected Liberal MPP of St. Paul's in a by-election after I resigned.)

To McGuinty's question, then, I blurted out: "I just know in my gut that it's time to go, Dalton. It's just time."

Suddenly, the Premier became laudatory, cheerful, and, for him, effusive. I couldn't help but think he was thrilled to learn of my decision to leave, but perhaps that's unfair to him, and more than a little self-flattering. Perhaps he was just happy for me.

At the time, I didn't have a job to go to but didn't think I'd have much trouble landing one. But before I could finish drafting my farewell speech to the media that same afternoon, I got a phone call from Peter Wilkinson, the Premier's chief of staff and enforcer in the government.

"You can't leave now," he said. The Conservative Leader John Tory was without a seat in the Legislature. He'd lost his seat in the general election, having lost his bid to unseat Education Minister Kathleen Wynne in Toronto. Now he was hunting high and low for by-election in a winnable seat.

"If you leave, John Tory will run in St. Paul's and we don't want to give him an opportunity—"

"So I'll hang onto my seat 'until further notice,'" I replied. Wilkinson rejected that and every other argument I had for stepping down from Cabinet.

"We have our foot on his throat," Wilkinson said, "and we can't take it off at this time."

I didn't see why having John Tory as Conservative Leader was such a threat to McGuinty, given his overwhelming victory in the polls in 2007. However, as ever I underestimated the political prowess of McGuinty and his team. In hindsight, a John Tory–led Conservative Party might very well have succeeded in the 2011 election.

Wilkinson asked me to stay until the spring of 2009, because he figured by then they'd be rid of Tory. (They were right.) It was less than a year, which was not unreasonable.

He then said that the Premier wanted to offer me the Economic Development portfolio, to ensure that I didn't get stuck in a portfolio prone to elongated standoffs. I didn't want to bolt from Aboriginal Affairs next spring if tensions had arisen between a First Nation and a local community or police, which happened sometimes. Little did we know that the economy was about to take an interesting turn.

So I agreed to stay. And on September 18, 2008, I was sworn in to what would be my last cabinet post. Susan, Sadie, and Louie came to the small swearing-in ceremony. Afterwards, a photo was taken at the press conference that had me literally flexing my biceps, with McGuinty caught in the background looking perplexed. Thus began a crescendo of ego flexing that would end abruptly—in 28 seconds.

The weekend after I was appointed Economic Czar, Lehman Brothers collapsed, the global financial crisis blew up, and the automotive crisis hit the largest manufacturer of vehicles in North America: Ontario.

Politically, the portfolio was stressful but invigorating. I went to Congress with my federal counterpart and friend Tony Clement to lobby Congress and the administration to assist Chrysler and General Motors. I found myself at the largest boardroom table I'd ever seen, and ever will see, at Chrysler headquarters in Michigan, across from Chrysler CEO Bob Nardelli (he of golden parachute fame for his $200-million-plus take from Home Depot).

Nardelli was incredibly charming, joshing with each of us like we were old friends. Then as we sat down, he blurted out, "We're going to go under if you don't give us a loan." I was flanked by the Finance Minister, Dwight Duncan, and the International Trade Minister, Sandra Pupatello, both of whom represented the auto-manufacturing capital of Canada, Windsor.

"How much you looking for?" I said, before I could stop myself.

"Oh, I dunno," waving his hand around, "$100 million to start?" Nardelli then looked over at one of his executives, who went poker-faced and silent.

I marvelled at the chutzpah, the arrogance, of this flippant request for Ontario tax dollars, pulled out of his butt. But the number didn't matter so much, I would see: Nardelli was looking to generate some momentum for a government bailout. Start with Ontario, then shame other jurisdictions to follow: the State of Michigan, the Government of Canada, and finally the big kahunah of cash, the U.S. Treasury.

Nardelli would eventually have to resign as CEO, as would his counterpart at General Motors. In fact, all the global executives at Chrysler and GM turned out to be remarkably glib about their request for "free cash," or government-backed loans.

But loans were clearly not the way to go. Early on in the auto crisis, I called a financier in New York City at the behest of my classmate Joe Freedman, now at Brookfield Asset Management. Freedman thought that Steven Rattner, a private equity executive, would have some insight. I called Rattner at his offices at Quadrangle, in NYC.

"I don't know anything about the auto industry," he said, "but I know about restructurings and that's probably what these companies need." Of course, Rattner went on to do just that as Obama's Car Czar some months later.

During this time, I had the privilege of getting to know some remarkable union leaders: Buzz Hargrove and then Ken Lewenza of the Canadian Auto Workers; Leo Gerard, the Canadian head of the United Steelworkers; and Doug Jolliffe, president of the Ontario Secondary School Teachers' Federation. Labour politics is remarkable, to me, for its unabashed member-based populism. Labour leaders cannot survive without convincing their members that they are fighting for them no matter what, even during labour negotiations, when this process is highly professional and pragmatic. It's tough politics, and Lewenza, in particular, showed tremendous heart in all our conversations. I admire him a lot.

Then came my exit. Early in 2009, I was meeting with delegates from the City of Toronto to discuss their new economic plan. Under the mayor's leadership, they were setting up Invest Toronto and Build Toronto, two new agencies intended to revitalize the city. Councillor Kyle Rae mentioned offhandedly that they were looking for a new CEO for Invest Toronto.

So, after the meeting was over, I pulled Kyle into the adjacent office. I said, "What do you think of that job? Would you take it?" He told me he was getting out of politics altogether. But he mentioned me to Mayor David Miller. The mayor called me. We had breakfast.

During that breakfast, he made it clear that he couldn't just appoint me to the position. We didn't know each other well enough for him to know that I wasn't expecting the process to be anything other than transparent and unbiased. On the contrary, I wanted to get a fair shot at the job. That's all one could ask. He said that I'd have to apply for the job like anyone else, and go through the interview process like anyone else. So I did. And I got the job.

In the week before I left my political post, I gave another variation on a "Reverse Reaganism" speech I'd been giving at various places. I learned that the Canadian Club of Toronto wasn't like various places. The speech caused a splash, mostly because I said it was the job of government in the new economy to identify what enterprises to back. The Premier immediately undercut it, giving one of those "what-the-minister-was-really-trying-to-say" scrums, which is the equivalent of a public spanking.

Anyway, that sort of thing would soon be behind me. On June 3, 2009, ten years to the day after my first election, I said farewell in my last speech to the Legislature. For most of us who have the honour of occupying one of those Legislature seats, we are probably never as seized by the magnitude of that honour and responsibility than on the day that we arrive and on the day that we leave.

"To all of you who share this chamber, on all sides of the House: I have learned much," I said. "I have listened much. I have spoken much—much too much sometimes; sometimes a little too loud and brazen for some Upper Canadians. The best we can do here, I suppose, is to be ourselves and hope for the best. That's what I did, and I have no regrets."

I had so many people to thank. And the thanks one is able to say in so short a time—to my wife, my children, my parents, my constituents, my staff and colleagues—just never seem enough.

"My final words are to my family," I said. "To my mom, a multiple sclerosis conqueror extraordinaire, who taught me I could do anything that I wanted to do; to my dad, who taught me exactly how to do it; and to Susan, for putting up with all this, for supporting me in all this, for sharing me with a lot of people and a lot of priorities. Thanks for letting me live this dream."

After ten years at Queen's Park as the member for St. Paul's, I resigned. I was off to Invest Toronto. I was on top of the world. And, less than three months later, what happened during 28 seconds would knock me off that pedestal but good.

SIX

Last Call

Of all the memorable dates in my ten-year thrill ride through Ontario politics, other than my kids' births, the one that matters most is March 7, 2006.

That day had nothing to do with landmark legislation, or creative policy initiatives, or precedent-setting court cases, or media extravaganzas designed to enhance my profile and reputation. Rather, it was—as turning points often are—my bottoming out, my occasion of personal bewilderment and abject defeat.

It was the day I stopped drinking. And it arrived, this day of reckoning, in its own time and not a moment too soon.

Drinking problems are hardly a rarity in politics. Once upon a time they were almost commonplace, the injudicious antics of inebriated politicians unreported by press galleries whose inhabitants were usually just as habitually besotted.

After all, the business is almost tailor-made for such indulgence and excess: the pressure, the travel, the socializing, the boredom, the loneliness, the euphoria of the very public successes and the humiliation of the very public defeats. The lifestyle practically screams for something to level out the highs and lows. And no few politicians have answered the bottle's seductive call: Sir John A. Macdonald, Sir Winston Churchill, Ulysses Grant, Boris Yeltsin, Edward Kennedy.

Former Texas Governor Ann W. Richards died in her seventies, sober for more than a quarter century, during which time she served as Governor of Texas and became an international celebrity after her speech at the 1988 Democratic National Convention. Her reign as governor was cut short by one George W. Bush (also in recovery) in 1994. Richards had begun drinking heavily after first being elected in her local county. Sober and in recovery, she was elected as state Treasurer, and then Governor in 1990. She was always open about her alcoholism recovery: "I like to tell people that alcoholism is one of my strengths," she said.

Other famous recovering alcoholics: Sir Anthony Hopkins, Sir Elton John, Raymond Carver, Stephen King, Robin Williams, Stevie Ray Vaughan, Betty Ford, Eric Clapton, Joe Walsh, Johnny Cash. The list of those who died from alcoholism or addiction is much longer. John Barrymore, George Best, Richard Burton, David Byron, Truman Capote, Raymond Chandler, Peter Cook, F. Scott Fitzgerald, Errol Flynn, Alexander Godunov, Ernest Hemingway, William Holden, Billie Holiday, Jack Kerouac, Veronica Lake, Joseph McCarthy, Jim Morrison, Chet Baker, Franklin Pierce, Edgar Allan Poe, Jackson Pollock, Hank Williams, W. C. Fields, Kurt Cobain, Amy Winehouse.

The list of politicians and artists who've done battle with alcohol is long enough, and star-studded, but that's no surprise. Alcoholism is everywhere and politicians cannot escape it by virtue of their station. Almost one in ten men, and one in 25 women, are alcoholics. That's true for Canada, the United States, and the United Kingdom.

The cost of alcoholism is profound. Most are surprised to learn that alcohol is more costly to our society than tobacco. (Yet governments around the world are increasingly supporting efforts to denormalize smoking, through advertising prohibitions, health warnings, class actions, and massive taxation; not so with alcohol consumption.) Moreover, the devastating effects of alcoholism on families are impossible to quantify.

Neuroscience is still in the process of explaining the cause of alcoholism. As the late (alcoholic/addict) David Foster Wallace summed it up in *Infinite Jest*, "addiction is either a disease or a mental illness or a spiritual condition (as in 'poor of spirit') or an O.C.D.-like disorder or an affective or character disorder...."* For most of those afflicted, the great (and alcoholic) American writer William Faulkner may have put it best: "God damn! Why do I do it!?" The answer for most alcoholics, right down through the generations of human experience with grapes, hops, and distillation, is that they don't have a clue.

It remains the case that recovery from alcoholism and addiction is rare. Most who need help never seek it. So many of those who do seek help do not end their days clean and sober. It is a fatal affliction for those who suffer rather than recover. And it serves up an utterly undignified end.

That's why March 7 is the most important day on my calendar each year. And March 7, 2006, just weeks shy of my 40th birthday, was maybe the most important day of my life.

The first time I got drunk I was about 9 years old. I was babysitting my little brother with my best friend, Doug Stark. We opened the doors of my parents' liquor cabinet. The first clue to my drinking lineage was right before my eyes. The cabinet was enormous. It held dozens of bottles; almost all were nearly empty. We sipped on a few liqueurs and some rye. Then I tried a beer. It was Labatt's Blue in a brown stubby bottle.

Infinite Jest, at p. 1079. For more on Wallace, see David Lipsky, *Although of Course You End Up Becoming Yourself: A Road Trip with David Foster Wallace* (Broadway, 2010).

Then we went down to my room, lined my door with a wet towel, opened my window, and smoked one of my grandfather's Colts. It was a wonderful experience. And it grew increasingly more wonderful in my teens and early twenties.

The second half of my drinking career would get progressively worse. That's the way of alcoholism. It always gets worse. The pathology is as predictable as it is pathetic. It's good, and then it gets very bad. There is recurring drunkenness that, just like William Faulkner, even the drinker can't explain. People get hurt. Damage gets done.

The first time I felt addicted—like I truly needed as opposed to wanted alcohol—was the summer of 1986. I was 20 years old. All summer, I'd come home to my parents' basement, after working the night shift as a janitor at BC Transit. I'd bought a beer fridge and filled it. While listening to music or watching TV, I'd have a few, which was probably rounded up to five or six, then go to bed. It was a beloved ritual.

One night, I opened the fridge, and it was empty. My stomach clenched, my heart pounded. I broke out into a cold sweat. I tore apart my garbage-dump of a bedroom searching for a beer. Finally, I found a warm Rainier Pilsner in an empty pizza box. I drank it immediately. I vowed to never allow myself to run out of booze again.

So began my obsession. When I wasn't drinking, I was fretting over my supply.

As this twisted logic came to settle into my twisted brain, as the disease began its work on me, there was a sliver of recognition that my reaction to an empty beer fridge was abnormal. This lingered for a nanosecond, then flew away. For about 20 years.

At the University of British Columbia, the distance between the pub and the hospital is approximately 400 metres, which was a good thing for me. As a student I occasionally wound up in the emergency ward, intoxicated to a dangerous degree.

I awoke in the hospital one day in 1989, shivering in a post-operative fog, having just had my appendix removed. Waiting for me was a surgeon and an anaesthetist. They'd been waiting for a while, and if you know anything about hospitals, you know that doctors and anaesthetists don't wait around for much.

Barely conscious, I listened to them silently. I was shocked by what they said, even if I wasn't surprised.

"You have a drinking problem," a female surgeon in her forties said without emotion. "Your tolerance for anaesthetics is at a level consistent with alcoholism or drug addiction."

The anaesthetist chimed in: "I would give you a very large dose, and then your body demanded more. If I hadn't kept pumping you full of [the anaesthetic], you would have regained consciousness and the pain would have been unbearable."

"You need to do something about this. You're too young to be—"

"Look, I gave you enough anaesthetics to kill a horse," he said, a couple times, and then they left.

I couldn't wait to tell my drinking buddies. It seemed riotously funny to me. But on some level, I must have been worried by their warnings, so I raised it with my family doctor at the time. Unfortunately, he dismissed their diagnosis out of hand.

The summer before I left for law school, I began to notice that my roster of friends was depleting. I chalked it up to people moving away, getting on with their lives, but the truth was a little harsher. My UBC friends had had enough of my drunkenness.

One night I was awakened by a flashlight in my face. I was clueless as to where I was. I could smell ambulance attendant on the man's hand as he pulled up my eyelids. I remember hearing: "He's alive. Yep, he's alive." This got relayed to someone via a radio. I heard it again. Or maybe it was an echo in my brain.

I'd passed out, on my back, in a bush on West 41st Avenue,

near Larch Street, having been ejected from the BC Transit bus for reasons I can only imagine.

Five hours earlier I'd taken off my chicken costume and thrown it at Barney Bentall and the Legendary Hearts, on stage at War Memorial Gym. Halloween. I was now wearing shorts and a UBC Boxing Club t-shirt, stained with something foul. Someone driving by had telephoned 911, reporting a dead body in a bush.

"Either you tell me your address and show me you have the cab fare, or you're spending the night in a drunk tank," they said. "You could have died here, you know. Aspirated on your vomit, lying on your back like that."

I was unable to speak a coherent sentence, but I found some ID in my sock, with my address on it. I was delivered to the Sigma Chi house and passed out in the hallway, never making it to my room.

I was aware that I drank just a little more than almost anyone else in the fraternity. But I was heading off to Osgoode Hall Law School soon. Then everything would be better, I thought.

At Osgoode, I began drinking alone with a frequency that marked a rite of passage on the pathology of alcoholism. There was nothing social about my alcohol intake now. In fact, it was antisocial. It just seemed necessary for my survival.

I'd brought a small black-and-white television to Toronto from my fraternity house, and rented movies from the corner store that would be conducive to black-and-white viewing. I remember watching a bunch of Woody Allen movies, and *The Godfather* many times. And drinking beer. Lots of beer.

One night, I called my only friend at law school at the time, Joe from Timmins. He was a teetotaller, he said, because there was a history of alcoholism in his family. Joe was generous and hilarious, and would become a great friend for life.

"HELLO!" Joe had a very big voice. Think Jabba the Hutt.

Whatever I said was so slurred that he couldn't understand, but he wasn't laughing. After many efforts, I told him I was worried that I "drank too much." Joe called me the next morning to talk about it, and would inquire after my drinking, on and off, until I sobered up 20 years later.

At the time, all my classmates were reading cases and writing case summaries. I had begun to research the locations of Alcoholics Anonymous meetings. The problem was, I was still debating in my mind whether I really *was* an alcoholic, or whether I wasn't just overreacting to a bit of bad luck.

The meeting I attended was somewhere in Toronto. I don't remember where. I was terrified of being spotted, which is absurd considering I had no friends in Toronto of which to speak. I recall nothing of that first meeting other than that the makeup of the crowd was not what I had expected. It was a mix of successful-looking people and those who appeared to be down-and-out. That's all I remember. It was a long time before I'd return.

Near the end of my drinking career, I was ruining everything. I was missing the experience of the babies growing up, and I would have missed everything after that had I not stopped.

I was ruining Susan's life. She'd never complained about my drinking until the last year, and so, really, she saved my life. Not for the last time. And she somehow knew just what to say. Rather than preaching to me, or demanding changes, she just told me what it was doing to her.

She was embarrassed for herself and for me, when I was intoxicated among friends at social gatherings. She felt alone, she said, even when we were together, because I simply wasn't there anymore. In that, she nailed the essential ailment of the alcoholic—estrangement from the human race. I was never present, always emotionally elsewhere. Unavailable. Inaccessible. Drinking, drunk, or recovering from being so.

Susan felt pity for me, as I tried to sleep off hangovers, missing weekend mornings with the kids. Or as I lingered over cocktail creations rather than tucking them in at night. Or as I slurred my words during their bedtime story.

For the final year of my drinking, I'd wake up every morning with a hangover that felt like I imagined chemotherapy would feel. I would lean against the shower wall, a creaking sound echoing in the bathroom, as I breathed, and often I'd just lie down, always alone, in the shower.

I was completely out of sync with Susan. She'd usually be gone for work when I was in the shower. In the last few months, I was getting in to work at 9 a.m. or so. For the Attorney General of Ontario, this was the equivalent of taking a sabbatical.

On the job, I was squeezing ideas out of my head like they were the dregs of an empty toothpaste tube. When I was first appointed Attorney General, I'd have several crazy ideas a day, and a few per week would be worth pursuing. By the end of my drinking, I hadn't had a new idea in months.

During my morning shower meltdown, I'd ponder what I'd said to myself the morning before: *I really need to do something about my drinking.* But by sundown, I'd be looking at my best friend: a martini, Manhattan, gin and tonic, rum and ginger beer with bitters, Scotch and soda, bourbon and soda, white wine, red wine, champagne, vodka, and finally just bourbon or gin or vodka or rum. Whatever it was, I had only one requirement: that there be lots of it.

Near the end, Susan was making it clear that she was not satisfied with what her life and marriage had become. Again, her gift to me was not judging me at all. She just told me the consequences of my actions, which I never doubted to be true.

I knew there was a limit to how long I could look at Susan every morning with a saggy hungover gaze as she described to me the evening before, as if it were a play she'd watched but I'd missed. Each day, I'd vaguely promise to do something about it.

"I'm going to go see my doctor."

"When?"

"Today."

"You said that last week."

"Okay, true, but ..."

Weeks would pass. I would wake up to hear her weeping.

"I'm going to go see my doctor."

As I said it, I heard echoes of promises past.

"Shit."

"Will you call him right now for me?"

To keep the peace, I finally did. To my dismay, I got an appointment that very day.

My G.P. asked how much I was drinking.

"Daily."

"How much?"

"I don't know."

"A bottle of wine a night? Or the equivalent?"

"Yes. No. Sometimes more. Usually more. But my tolerance is dropping. I'm getting drunk quicker."

"How are you functioning as an ... Attorney General?"

"I don't know. I just am. I've got lots of help. I mean, Churchill saved the free world as a drunk; I can do my job. I've avoided being drunk at work or in public. I usually just drink at home, or at a friend's. But always eventually at home, alone."

"What do you want?"

"A therapist that specializes in this stuff."

He referred me to the late Dr. Max Himmel, a psychiatrist. I would not call to make an appointment, however. Nor would I tell Susan about the referral. Mercifully, she didn't ask that night, and

I fabricated a story about getting the thumb's up from my family doctor, and more tests forthcoming.

In November 2005, I received another warning, this time from a great friend. Les Scheininger had been my political godfather since the beginning of my Ontario political career. He'd run for MPP himself, and was a past president of the Canadian Jewish Congress. Les always had a stable of politicos whom he mentored. I was lucky to be one of them.

"I have something I want to say.... It's not easy for me to do this."

I figured either he had cancer or he was going to tell me that I was drinking too much.

"People are noticing," Les said, "that you're ... They're noticing that you're in your cups a lot. In public. Like last weekend ..."

I quickly defused the matter.

"That night was an exception," I said. "But I appreciate ..."

It took a lot of guts for Les to tell me what he did. I was full of excuses.

"I'm just saying that people are talking about it," he said again.

I was filled with shame alternating with denial. *Really?* No. *Who?* Never mind. I didn't really want to know.

In the coming days I would resent his diagnosis, but later on I would come to see it as a life-saving gesture on his part. I ordered no wine at our lunch, but had an extra mickey of Scotch that night, seized by the juggernaut of self-loathing and pity, with a shot of self-righteousness for good measure.

Then, on New Year's Eve 2005, I had one of the worst binges of my life. I awoke on the basement floor, face to carpet, fully dressed, with a distinct, very distinct, sense of amnesia. I did not know where I was, even as I looked around the basement of my own house.

After five minutes staring at the ceiling, I got that much. But I couldn't remember anything else. I didn't know the date. I didn't know anything other than that I was in the basement. And that it had to be bad.

Coming up the stairs, the pungent scent of alcohol preceded me. In the kitchen, I found a newspaper that gave me the date. New Year's Day, 2006. Susan filled in the rest of the blanks. We'd been at the final night of Le Select Bistro's tenure on Queen Street West. Most of the people in the back room, which we'd taken over, were her colleagues in the music and legal industry. I'd had to be carried out to a cab by the restaurant's owner, Jean-Jacques—and we weren't leaving voluntarily.

That afternoon (I'd slept past noon), no ultimatums were made. No promises were made. But she wanted my commitment to never do it again. I provided it. But I had no idea if it was a promise I could keep.

On January 4, 2006, I walked into the office of Dr. Max Himmel. I'd called to make an appointment and was offered something in February. Then, a cancellation and a call back. It was the first of the lucky breaks, or little miracles, that guided me on my way.

His office was at Bay and Bloor, an intersection that would later figure large in my life. The first time I went, in my overheated self-centredness I feared the paparazzi would be lying in wait in the lobby. They weren't.

"Why are you here?" Dr. Himmel asked, after we'd sat down across from each other.

"I want to moderate my drinking."

"Well then," he said. "We will work on you moderating your drinking."

Dr. Himmel, who I did not realize was dying of cancer at the time, knew perfectly well that abstinence would be my only real hope. He eventually referred me to a fellowship of recovering alcoholics whose program is based on abstinence. Had Dr. Himmel told me on that first visit that I needed to abstain from drinking permanently and start attending meetings regularly, the first visit to his office would also have been my last.

"What's moderate, for you? How many drinks a week?"

"A week?!" Pause. "Two or three a night would be moderate, no?" It never occurred to me that social drinkers seldom had cause to keep count of their drinks.

"Which: Two? Or three? A night."

"Two," I said.

"Two it is."

"Okay."

"That's it for today," he said.

I was a little stunned. Maybe he had another appointment. I was hoping to talk about myself a lot and was disappointed.

Then, he raised his finger: "Except for one thing," and his eyes brightened and he smiled.

"I need you to go downstairs. Take the elevator. And then when you leave the building, turn left onto Bloor Street. You'll be heading east, okay?"

"Okay."

"Go to Grand & Toy—you know it?"

"I know it."

"Good. Now," he took a sip of water, "buy a notebook. Okay?"

"A notebook. Okay. How big?"

He winced. "Doesn't matter. You're going to keep a journal."

"A journal?"

"Yes, a journal. You're going to write in your journal every night. You're going to write about your two drinks a night. Every night."

"I'm going to keep a journal of my moderation efforts?"

"Yes. But don't lie to the journal. You can lie to your kids, lie to your mother, lie to your wife, even lie to me. But don't lie to the journal. Write everything down that you think. It's very important."

"Okay," I said. "When do I start?"

"Ah, yes. When do you want to start?"

Susan and I were due to go to an all-inclusive resort in Jamaica in five days. It seemed contrary to the Geneva Conventions to be a moderate drinker at a Jamaican all-inclusive resort—for a moderate drinker, that meant all drinks included in a lump-sum price; for an alcoholic, it meant all you can drink.

I told Dr. Himmel about Jamaica. He asked if I thought I could moderate my drinking at the resort. I began sweating. He was forcing me to feel the disease with these questions.

"Michael," he said, "I'm not a big drinker, but I will have an occasional drink. I'm a moderate drinker, you might say."

He allowed that to sink in. To this day, I think he was fudging it. He probably was not imbibing alcohol at all at the time, so nauseous did chemotherapy no doubt make him. But he was making a point.

"I, moderate-drinking Max, could go to that resort, and drink moderately. Can you?"

My immediate thought was: I'm different. Nay—I'm special. I need it, Max, way more than you. You don't understand.

"Oh, but I do understand," he said.

"How did you do that?"

"What?"

"Did you just read my mind?"

"Did you just speak your mind?"

I'm not sure what happened. But I said that, yes, I would start January 9 with Project Moderation.

I reported this great news to Susan and she was quietly supportive. Not excited. Promising forecasts were nothing new to her. Many had turned into the dreariest of days.

"What about between now and our trip? Can you abstain from drinking for five days? Just to prove to yourself that you can?"

I knew that the correct answer to this skill-testing question was yes, so I said yes without thinking. I was going to dry out, I thought. And keep a journal.

Headaches, hand tremors, inability to sleep, extreme agitation at the cocktail hour, obsession with other people drinking alcohol and with alcohol generally were some of the symptoms revealed in my newfound habit of keeping a journal. That journal saved my life, even if it is one of the sadder contributions ever made to English literature.

As often happens with alcoholics, I was able to abstain for a few days, after which we convince ourselves that we can abstain whenever we want to, at which point we drink again. Until the next round of excursions "on the wagon."

Being sober for a few days, besides having some painful detoxification effects, alerted me to new feelings and thinking. I hadn't gone sober for four days since 1999.

As the plane began its descent into Kingston Airport, I was weeping. I thought about skipping the moderation effort altogether and abstaining. But that thought lasted only until the slightest incident—luggage delayed by half an hour—and I was toasting our arrival in Jamaica with a sip of Red Stripe.

Here's what I wrote in my journal that night: "After many delays and a little stress, we were left to wait in Sandals Resort Lounge until the shuttle arrived. Free beer. Susan had one; I poured a sip to "toast"/taste with her. More for thirst and relief than out of a strong desire, but there was no way I was going to pass on it. Had my sip (2 ounces of beer). Wanted more, but just because it was so available.... Arrived at resort 9:20—ugh. Champagne greeted us. I had it. Stressful check-in. SHA and I fought (her fault!). We sat down for dinner, hungry and fighting. We each ordered a drink. I had a double. Then food was crummy so we went to grill for fast food and each had a beer. Again, the occasion demanded one—I'd already decided that beer sip and mini-champagne did not count. So I stuck to my 2 but knew I hadn't: thus 2.5...."

There are a few things of note in those jottings. The blame-game is rampant. I drank because of the "occasion" or its "availability" or "stress." Not because of me. I fought with Susan but it wasn't my fault. I lied to myself and others about how much I had in fact had to drink.

This would be the pattern throughout the coming months. I lied to the journal in parts, and told the truth in others. I was explicit about my mental gymnastics of justification, like this entry on January 11:

"How do I justify 2–4 [drinks], when I'd committed to only 2 drinks? Holiday, I say. Still very much in control, but for 2–4." Oh sure: totally in control there.

Or January 16: "1 Beer today. Not hungover, but tired and cranky so very bad. Pissed off at that huge cocktail last night (a triple bourbon before dinner, 6 drinks in total). Very little desire for a drink but had two beers with SHA at airport [returning home from Jamaica to Toronto]. Then stopped."

Good God, the denial. The denial that I harboured back then, oblivious to the rank absurdity of this thinking. Who has "very little desire" for something only to consume 16 ounces of it!? Breaks my heart every time I read it.

But some entries make me laugh. Jan 12: "5 drinks (sort of—1 cocktail, 1 champagne, 1 beer, 1 more cocktail (double), ½ beer, ½ wine ... 4½?" Or Feb 2: "Skipped Wed night because drunk."

Many days were blank. Some days were explicit about a binge. January 20: "Missed last night. Fell off wagon but not too hard. Hungover today. Fine tonight. Moderate? Almost. Not counting ... That first drink has become too important."

Starting that night, I stopped counting. Or, as I put it that night: "moderate but not counting." Two and a half months passed.

The worst of my life. I didn't moderate. I didn't drink two drinks a night, unless you count two mason jars of bourbon as two drinks. I lied a lot to everyone but the journal and Max Himmel, to whom I lied only a little.

The true genius of the alcoholic is for self-delusion and rationalization. One night, I would say I wanted more booze because it was so freely available. Another night, it's for the taste of the wine. Another night, it's to satisfy a ritual behaviour.

Even when I admitted the truth of how much I drank, there were always the excuses of some event, circumstance, or other person. Bad sommeliers. Boring company. Not enough non-alcoholic beverages available.

At a certain point, I began referring to Susan as "The Cop," demonizing her in my journal.

"Not moderate last night. The Cop's absence clearly a factor. Buzz factor at work and the freedom to crawl inside the bottle. Discipline impossible when intoxicated. Booze like a friend to spend time with and I like getting on the phone. Partying alone" (Jan 31, 2006).

There were occasional, and melodramatic, cries for help, mixed with self-pity. "WHY? Point is that boozing at night, even in moderation, is too much of my life. Planning, thinking, booze-obsessed" (Feb 2).

"Friday night: the excuse du jour. I thought about [moderation] then (get this!) decided that I shouldn't obsess—so just drink!! What an idiot.... I'm devolving. I'm NOT disciplined. I'm a royal piece of shit ... PA-thetic" (Feb 3).

As February turned to March, the writing itself, the penmanship, began to deteriorate. It painted a picture of decline that I can now see just from flipping the pages with my thumb; an animation of that last chapter of boozing.

My hands were shaking, increasingly, starting when I woke

up and easing up once I started drinking in the evening. During Question Period that winter, I reached for a glass of water while answering a question, and I could barely get the water in my mouth, while the cameras were rolling. I stopped drinking water at my legislative desk after that.

Throughout the journal, I mention needing to spend more time reading to my children, playing games, showing them "how much I love them" (Feb 5). Regret and Shame became my other children, each receiving far too much attention.

My entries grew more succinct. "Tues., Wed., Thurs. Tired. Drunk. Hungover."

Apparently, I wasn't able to date an entry past February 13. The entries grew more random: "Sat/Sun ~ Drunk/Hungover/Drunk.

Wednesday.

"Better, but still in that drinking rut, which begets cranky days. One or two too many tonight....

Thursday.

"Same as yesterday."

Friday.

"Worse than yesterday. Fuck."

Saturday.

"Better?"

Sunday.

"Very moderate, but could have had one less. I need to stop at dinner (or cheese).... I'm hoping to wake up tomorrow feeling ok."

Then, on the last night, March 7, I attended an awards ceremony for Ontario Crown attorneys, at which I had a couple glasses of wine. Photos taken, speech delivered, many laughs, maybe all fake. Then to the Air Canada Centre to watch the Leafs play the Canadiens. I was turning 40 on April 13, but this night, March 7th, was a pre-birthday celebration hosted by a former colleague from McCarthy Tetrault, Michael Barrack, and attended by half a dozen of my most generous donors and closest advisers. They pitched in for a Leafs jersey with my name on the back, #40, and AG stitched onto the front where the "C" for Captain would be. It was a cool and generous gift, from a group of good friends. I barely acknowledged their existence. My only friend was being served to me in liquid form.

I proceeded to get New Year's Eve shit-faced again, right in front of Susan. At some point in the final period, I left without saying goodbye or anything to anyone. I got lost somewhere downtown, the alcoholic Attorney General on his last night out. I don't know how I got home.

I woke up, remembered nothing, sat up in bed, and remembered enough.

"What are you going to do?" Susan asked. Her face was red and tear-streaked.

"I don't know. *But I know that I'm not going to drink anything tonight.*" The words tumbled out of my mouth, and I heard them as if not my own. It was the first sensible thing I'd said in a very long time.

Thus began the revolution, the rebirth, the surrender. I just gave up, gave up trying to figure it out, gave up on my old life, ready for a new one. My head shook very slowly, as the words echoed back to me: "I'm not going to drink anything tonight."

And I didn't. Not that night. Or the next. Or the next. Or, by the grace of God and one day at a time, in any of the days that have followed. Not since March 7, 2006, until the time of this writing, in 2012, and of course I pray to continue this streak, one day at a time, until I croak.

I was a reader, and thought that I could read my way through this. So I bought up every memoir by a drunk or addict that was in print, and even found some that were out of print.

It was an important first step: reaching out for the experience, strength, and hope of others who had recovered from their addiction.

Here's how it worked, for me. I would read something that Cheevers or Burroughs or Sykes or Knapp or Hamill said about their affliction, and I'd connect with these authors. That's just like me, I'd think. And you're telling me that you're an alcoholic? I must be one too.

A few nights into sobriety, I wrote about a dream I had: "On a plane, dozing off, suddenly a glass of red wine in my hand. I looked at it, thought about it. And poured it out. I was CONSCIOUS of its power. Poured out it was powerless. I am now conscious of the power of alcohol over me."

Then a couple weeks later: "Finishing bio on Bill Wilson, founder of AA. I feel a little re-born; must enjoy this but not overdo it."

Then I experienced a huge drop in energy, heightened anxiety, and the need to sleep a lot. Many ups and downs, but throughout a sense that nothing was as bad as when I was drinking. I kept opening up the journal to remind myself of how pathetic life had been as a drinker.

At some point, within the first month of drying out, I admitted to myself that I was an alcoholic: "Loving Knapp memoir [Caroline Knapp's *Drinking: A Love Story*]: she confirms for me that I'm an alcoholic (rough word). Felt a tug at a bottle of wine in the fridge but then called it EVIL out loud. Had another cigar."

A couple of months later, my journal recorded a tough night following a roughing-up by the Opposition in the Legislature: "Very down. Normally booze would have flowed; tough not to but not really tempted. Just hard to deal with that feeling without escaping from it.... But then it's over; it ends; I move on. Building the muscle."

There are a number of firsts in this re-birth. The first time in a cocktail lounge or bar or restaurant or party, at a wedding or the cottage or a staff party or a birthday, all sober. They were dreaded, but never lived up to the fears I'd generated in my head. After some initial self-consciousness, it was fine.

For many days after I'd admitted alcoholism to myself, I still couldn't admit it to others. I constantly dreamed at night about drinking booze and awoke relieved that it was just a nightmare. Indeed.

Eight months into sobriety, I started to go to the meetings Dr. Himmel mentioned. I heard stories. I related. I felt understood. I felt hope. But still I kept to myself, did not share what was going on inside me.

I was, if not sober in the best sense of the word, certainly abstaining and alcohol-free. I kept that journal until December 14, 2006. My last entry was: "I feel better sober. Much, much better. Happy to be sober."

Come the night that everything changed, I hadn't had a drink for more than three years. And a good thing it was.

SEVEN

Twenty-Eight Seconds

As Susan and I licked honey from our fingers in a Greek bakery on the Danforth, at about 9:30 on the evening of August 31, 2009, we could never have anticipated the storm of primal fury that was blowing our way.

Not terribly far away, the man we would presently come to know as Darcy Allan Sheppard, part of Toronto's hardy, scruffy, aggressive sub-culture of bicycle couriers, was having the latest in a lifetime of turbulent days.

For most of his troubled 33 years, Darcy Sheppard had fought addiction to alcohol and crack cocaine. On this day, his string of eight sober days had come—once again—to a dispiriting end. He appeared on the city's radar a little after 7 p.m., as Susan and I were parking the car at the restaurant where we would have our shawarma dinner. It was then he showed up at the apartment of his girlfriend on George Street, in a notorious zone of men's hostels and crack dealers in one of Toronto's grittier quarters.

For a time, Sheppard and his girlfriend had lived together. But, after a dispute, she had asked him to move out. Now, he was back at her door, drunk on arrival. She wanted him to sleep it off. For a time, he reportedly did. Then he awoke and apparently decided to leave. There must have been a disagreement in the apartment about the wisdom of this.

Around this time, Susan and I would have been exchanging anniversary presents, and walking on the sand, along the lake shore at the Beaches. The moon was three-quarters full. On the other side of town, someone was howling at that moon.

At 9:12 p.m., the Toronto Police Service received a call from another resident of the building, complaining of noise coming from the apartment of Sheppard's girlfriend: screams, crying, the sound of things being thrown. The caller told police that Sheppard was observed outside the building a few minutes later, assaulting a homeless man.

Police arrived at 9:21 p.m., as Susan and I were finishing our baklava on the Danforth. They noted that Sheppard was belligerent and had been drinking. Sheppard's girlfriend would later tell reporters that she, along with other friends who showed up, asked police to allow Sheppard to return to the apartment, but the officers refused to permit it.

Instead, police warned him not to return to the address. They cleared the call within 10 to 15 minutes, about the time Susan and I were paying our bill at Akropolis and heading toward our car to drive home.

Sheppard "was asked to leave," a police spokesman would later tell the news media. "The officers left. And that was it."

Except, it wasn't.

Darcy Allan Sheppard—extremely intoxicated, fresh from an argument with his recently estranged girlfriend, from beating up a homeless man, and from his latest encounter with police—was allowed to ride off on his bike.

As Susan and I approached Yonge Street, it was Darcy Sheppard who had snarled traffic by throwing pylons and garbage across the intersection. Then, in something of an athletic marvel—despite an alcohol level more than twice the legal limit—he did figure eights curb to curb, along Bloor Street, as drivers like myself hung back, refusing to take his dare to pass him. Until he finally forced a vehicle over to the side of the road, and I drove on by.

It was Darcy Sheppard who, moments later, drove within inches of my driver's side door, as our Saab was stopped a little farther west on Bloor Street at an intersection near Avenue Road.

It was Darcy Sheppard who then pulled directly in front of our car and spun his bike around to confront us, sneering at me. *"Now what're ya gonna do?"*

By 9:48 p.m., on the night of my 12th wedding anniversary, the 28 seconds that changed my life forever, and that abruptly ended Darcy Sheppard's, were about to begin.

IT'S ABOUT THREE KILOMETRES—and many tax brackets—from that apartment on George Street to 102 Bloor Street West in Yorkville, which houses a store called L'Occitane En Provence. That shop, specializing in vanity products, is what Yorkville is all about. L'Occitane started in the south of France and is now listed on the stock market in Hong Kong. The company aspires to be, in its own words, "the worldwide reference for Mediterranean well-being, with unique body, face, and home products." The shop smells wonderful, the scent of money not least among its allures.

The store also has two security cameras, one facing southeast on Bloor, the other facing to the west. Some of what happened that night was captured by those cameras. Some of the video is fairly clear. Some isn't.

What it did show, what a later investigation would show, and what I recall, is this:

Before the 28 seconds began, I had been unsettled by Sheppard's antics and had lost sight of him. I was anxiously trying to spot him in the passenger-side rearview mirror, assuming that if he showed it would be near to the curb. Susan took the direction of my glance for attention and chatted away about work.

As Sheppard passed on my left and cut in front of us, the traffic light had just turned green and I was starting to move the Saab forward. As he passed, he slowed, coming very close to my side door. I sensed him swipe his hand at me. I ducked instinctively to my right, hitting the brakes and turning the wheels to the right. It was then I stalled the car, presumably taking my foot off the gas and clutch while putting on the brakes. When I looked up, he was straddling the bike, facing us, taunting me. *"Now what're ya gonna do?"*

The 28 seconds began.

His front wheel was within a couple feet of the Saab's front bumper. I knew he was too close for me to drive around him. In a millisecond, my eyes darted up to my rearview mirror, then back to this man. I saw that there were cars behind me, so I couldn't back up. I couldn't move forward. Trapped. He was big, drunk, and raging. I feared for Susan and myself. I wondered if he had a weapon on him.

The thought of confronting him was never an option—it was our anniversary, for God's sake. *Susan was with me.* Neither did staying put make any sense. *Susan was with me.* Either to fight or sit tight might put her at risk.

I needed to get away. I'd no idea how. But I knew I couldn't escape the situation until I started the damn car. I tried to keep an eye on him and at the same time I tried to start the engine. It turned over, but kept stalling out. Frustration and panic were both rising fast.

As the car started and stalled, it bounced and lurched forward a little bit. This growling man saw this, the car lurching, and he seemed to get more and more agitated. He seemed to be howling at me.

I gave up on the eye contact with Sheppard. I looked down at the pedals and the stick shift and the ignition to see why the Saab wouldn't start. As my eyes darted back up, I saw that it finally was moving forward—for all of a second. I hit the brakes. Another second. Now, Darcy Sheppard was draped over the hood of the car.

During my frenzied attempts to start the car, as it stalled and stalled, the Saab lurched three times. The first, with the wheels angled to the right, moved the car away from Sheppard. With the second, there was still no contact with him or his bicycle. The third caused Sheppard to land on the hood. But it was at low speed, brief in duration and, because he was already so close to the car, left no discernible injury.

But now he was furious. His bike was caught under the front bumper. He screamed at people on the sidewalk, "You're a witness! You're a witness!"

By now, Susan was also yelling something. I don't know what. And by now, I no longer cared what was behind me. I didn't care if I had to ram the car behind me and push it back to Bay Street. I needed to get us out of there.

I was now especially terrified of taking my eyes off him. But in order to back up, I had to. I looked behind me, turned my back on the beast. It looked clear enough. I put the Saab in reverse. As I was looking back, Sheppard hurled his backpack, containing a heavy bike lock, at us. It went sailing over my head.

I put the car in first gear and tried to drive around him. Outraged, he raced toward the front of our car. I remember Susan screaming, "Oh, my God!" over and over.

Chasing after us, he leapt at the Saab, as if in slow motion. Sheppard landed hip first, to break his fall, the way you see stunt-men-as-cops do the hood slide on crime shows. It made a crunching noise. I felt the impact of a man over 200 pounds landing on my car. He then grabbed the windshield wiper and bent it back toward him. He began pulling himself toward me, hand over hand, as if the wiper were a rope. The strength of the man was extraordinary. He seemed almost super-human.

His upper torso was now on the hood's edge, driver's side, with the car still moving forward. He swung around, put his right arm inside the door, his left armpit around the side mirror. He held up his legs, a feat of some strength, no doubt assisted by the adrenalin that, I later learned, Darcy so often sought.

The car suddenly swerved sharply to the left, almost 45 degrees. I have no recollection how that happened. He must have grabbed the wheel. In wrestling for control of the car, we crossed to the south side of the street, heading westbound into the eastbound lane.

As it registered in my mind that my escape attempt had failed, I tried again. So I slammed on the brakes. But the Saab has anti-lock brakes. The stop wasn't sudden enough to dislodge him. Nevertheless, there was a fair bit of torque. I could see him bending forward and hanging on, the side mirror cracking under the pressure. I remember thinking how strong he seemed to withstand that torque.

Then, he said to me, with a crooked grin: *"You're not getting away that easy."*

Less than 20 seconds had passed since he had said, "Now what're ya gonna do?"

Next, I tried to push Sheppard off the car door. It felt like trying to push over a telephone pole. He pushed back. I pushed again. He pushed back. Then he started climbing in the car. Susan grew louder and more frantic. "No! No! No! No! Stop! Stop! Stop! Stop!"

This was the only physical contact between us. The car remained stopped while this shoving was going on.

I had stopped the car and couldn't get him off. It seemed that when the car was stopped, he got closer to being on top of us; when the car was moving, he wasn't.

I started moving forward again.

It felt to me like the Twilight Zone, where familiar streets are oddly abandoned. I registered no cars, no people. We just seemed to be heading into a tunnel. And it was getting smaller and smaller and smaller.

The car never left first gear. It was very noisy, because the Saab was still in first gear and the car was revving so high, almost red-lining.

At one point, it seemed like Sheppard was skiing beside the car, making the kinds of whooping noises you'd make if you were intentionally road-skiing for sport. A witness would later say his bicycle shoes were setting off sparks on the pavement. I remember thinking: he's done this before.

I couldn't take my two hands off the wheel even if I'd wanted to. I was struggling with Darcy Sheppard for control of the vehicle.

Then he was gone.

All of a sudden, he just wasn't there. I didn't see him fall. I heard a sound, maybe a groan.

From the moment of him jumping on the car to the point where I stopped the car with him on it, we had travelled about 100 metres.

At first I felt relief, but for less than one breath. Now what was I going to do? Should I stop right now? I shouldn't leave the scene of an accident. But I wanted to get away from this guy. Is he coming? I was not going to stop the car and let him come at us again after finally getting away. There was no one to help. I wanted to get somewhere safe.

I looked up and saw Avenue Road in front of me. I saw the Hyatt hotel. It's where our marriage counsellor had an office that could be entered through the hotel lobby. I routinely tore up in front of the Hyatt, getting overpriced valet parking because I was running late for our sessions in the marital intensive-care unit.

So I turned right on Avenue Road and drove into the hotel's circular driveway and found, I thought, sanctuary.

I stopped the car and pulled up the emergency brake—for what would be the final time. I couldn't find my cell phone. Susan offered hers. Neither of us today recall what was happening on her side of the car, other than that she was there, frozen, and terrified.

I dialled 911. I began to describe what happened. I wanted police to get there quickly—to protect Susan and me. I said we'd been attacked by a man on a bicycle on Bloor Street. A transcript was made of this, of course.

"He was literally picking fights with people on the corner of Yonge and Bloor, and putting obstacles in the way and trying to stop cars from going," I told the operator. "We all avoided him, drove past him, and then he came back. I'm in a convertible so he came back and he started—I mean, I thought he took a swing at me, but whatever, he missed. And then he pulled in front of me and stopped. I slammed on the brakes and I tried to get away, and then he—the next thing I know, he's, like, literally trying to climb into my car."

When asked where Sheppard was, I said: "Somewhere on Bloor, I assume." She said an ambulance was on the scene. It was the first time it occurred to me that Darcy Sheppard had been injured.

I told the operator I'd just "wanted to pull into a place where ..." She seemed to understand. "Where you felt a little safer." "Yeah," I said.

I suggested to Susan that she take a taxi home to relieve Sarah and care for the kids. I figured that I'd be only a few minutes behind her, depending on how long it took to give a statement to the police about the attack. That's where my head was at: we were attacked, he was the attacker, and now he was to be arrested and charged.

"I'll be home soon," I said to her.

At 10:01 p.m., the police arrived as Susan climbed into a cab.

My rescuers, I thought. But as soon as the constable driving got out of the car, I knew something was wrong, though I couldn't say what. He was a huge guy. I walked up to him, to get close to him in case Sheppard arrived.

The constable promptly manhandled me around to a spot in front of his squad car. He started pushing and poking me. He said I was in a lot of trouble. He kept asking how much I'd had to drink. In five different ways, he asked me if I'd imbibed. I told him I didn't drink alcohol, period. "Yeah, okay," he scoffed.

"What's going on?" I said. I couldn't understand why I was being questioned. I'd called the police for protection. It never occurred to me that I'd done anything wrong.

Susan was off to the side. She'd stepped out of the cab when she witnessed the police pushing me around. I assumed she was being questioned by the other officer. But she wasn't. She was just watching, thinking, and trying to call for help—on a BlackBerry that suddenly kept resetting on her, over and over.

"You're in a lot of trouble," he said again.

It wasn't registering. Why was I in trouble? I felt like we just had to get the have-you-been-drinking part over with, then reason would prevail and he would give me an update. I was imagining that Darcy Sheppard was in handcuffs right now.

"You better hope he makes it back there," the officer said. "You're in a lot of trouble. It's touch and go...."

The constable was talking on the radio to his superior officer. The hotel valet handed me and the constable a bottle of water. I took it; he refused. There were more people milling about the driveway. Cars were pulling in and people getting out, and some were getting into cabs. I couldn't see where Susan was standing. I was worried about her.

Suddenly, I was being handcuffed. I was flabbergasted. I remember seeing the constable pulling the cuffs out, and my overpowering feeling of disbelief. Were these for me? Handcuffs? Really? REALLY! What will Susan think, seeing me being cuffed? I imagined she'd want to throw up.

The kids were being babysat by our beloved Sarah; she started work at our place pretty early, so she didn't like late-night babysitting. I knew that it was after 10 by now. Someone needs to contact Sarah, I thought. Susan should call her mom for support, I thought. I was suddenly ashamed of being in cuffs, and angry. They put my head down and sat me in the back of the squad car. Less than ten minutes had passed since the police had arrived at the Hyatt.

"The cuffs are over the top," I said to the constables, who were sitting in the front seat, whispering to each other, though I clearly could hear every word. "I'm not going anywhere. I could have sat in here without the cuffs."

"It's standard procedure," said one of the officers.

For what? I thought. *Standard procedure for what? What the hell was happening?*

There was more whispering and radio talk. Seconds became minutes became 20 minutes. Then we'd been there, waiting, for almost an hour. I didn't speak a word after my outburst about the cuffs. At some point in that hour, the constable who'd been aggressive with me opened the door beside me, and finished his conversation on the radio:

"Yeah, I'll do that now," he said.

Do what now?

I knew I was being detained pending investigation. I had a burning desire to talk with the constables but nothing came out. Something told me to shut up.

"You're under arrest ... Dangerous driving ... Criminal negligence ... Right to retain a lawyer ..."

"I'm aware," I mumbled, but I don't think he heard me. Susan appeared inches from the side window on my left. "Are you okay?" she mouthed through the closed window. Then to the constable: "Can I talk to him?"

Silence. They ignored her. "Hey! I just want to talk to my husband?!" More silence. "Just roll down the window." They kept ignoring her. "Fine!"

"MICHAEL!!" she yelled through the front window to me in the back of the cruiser. "WHO SHOULD I CALL?"

I was happy to see her. She didn't seem panicked. She seemed heroic.

"A lawyer," I answered, less than helpfully.

"WHO!? WHO SHOULD I CALL?"

Blank. Between those 28 seconds, being cuffed and put in the squad car, and then read my rights, I was unable to process much. The former Attorney General of Ontario, who'd spent most of his adult life rubbing shoulders with hundreds of Canada's leading barristers, couldn't name a single lawyer at the moment he most needed one.

Then, I thought of someone who could help. I thought of Nikki Holland. Nikki had been my chief of staff for a time when I was in Cabinet. She was the first person I hired in the autumn of 1999 as a rookie MPP. Nikki was 23 back then, in '99. I had hired her again at Invest Toronto, a decade later. She was extreme in all her qualities: eager, loyal, smart, and diligent. Nikki is part older sister, part mother, part younger cousin, and all best friend.

So Susan called Nikki. As it happened, Nikki was driving home from a Liberal campaign meeting, less than a mile away, a meeting to support Dr. Eric Hoskins in his bid to win the by-election in St. Paul's—the riding I had recently vacated. In the car with her was Emily Bullock, Hoskins's campaign manager and my former political staffer extraordinaire for many years.

Nikki saw the call display, so she answered the phone. She

heard the words "Michael" in the same sentence as "arrested" and "the Hyatt." Three minutes later, she was there.

When I looked through the front window of the squad car to see Nikki materialize, I did a double-take. She and Susan would be a formidable force together. Watching them was my first experience with the freedom of helplessness. Others would help. I'd no choice but to let go.

Big-city news media live by the police scanners and reports of the latest calamity to befall some citizen or other. Already, they had heard the report of what happened on Bloor Street and a crowd of reporters and cameras were gathering at the Hyatt.

"Get me out of here," the constable driving our squad car said over the radio to his superior officer. "There's media *everywhere.*"

Indeed, the media trucks would follow the car, filming me in the backseat. The "perp-shot," they call it. I was in a blue Club Monaco t-shirt, jeans of some sort, and Converse sneakers, sitting on my handcuffed wrists.

The constable's words about getting out of there were somehow a welcome relief. I was enduring the experience of an arrest and squad-car detention, and I wanted to move on to whatever was next.

The problem with *next,* I would learn, is that most of it took place in my head, in a cell, in a police station. I was about to enter my dark night of the soul, a crucible reserved for all of us, often delivered without notice. But for me, the action was over. The rest of my story would be played out by others.

Still, my life story at least would continue. Darcy Sheppard's would not. It turned out that on the sidewalk near 131 Bloor Street West, there is a fire hydrant. The side cap of the hydrant points toward the north. It's about a foot from the curb. As we drove past it, still fighting for the steering wheel, the side cap caught Darcy Sheppard's left side, causing him to fall from the car. He struck the right side of his head on the curb or raised patch of asphalt, fatally damaging his brain stem.

He was dead by the time the squad car, with me handcuffed in the backseat, headed south out of the Hyatt, toward the Toronto Police Service Traffic Division. He was declared DOA at the hospital. I would not learn that for several more hours.

EIGHT

The Cell

For five long minutes, we were stuck outside the door in the sally port at the police station at 9 Hanna Avenue. Two constables and me, the alleged perp, with cuffs on tighter than ever, my wrists swelling a little from having sat on my cuffed hands in the squad car with media trucks running alongside. They'd buzzed twice at the door. Now a third time. The constables were visibly embarrassed about being locked out of their own division headquarters. Here they were with their prize turkey with no one to let them in.

I knew that giving a statement was the last thing I should be doing, given that almost all arresting officers are more interested in building their case than in investigating it. In my case, within minutes of arriving at the scene, eyeing Darcy Sheppard dead or dying on the curb, the police had decided I'd committed a crime.

I pondered saying something humorous to lighten the mood. It's almost reflexive with me. I was one of those people who couldn't stand awkward moments, so I always tried to rescue everyone—or, really, to rescue my own uncomfortable self by showing how clever and funny I could be.

But a little wire had grown between a corner of my mind and my mouth, it seemed. The wire had wrapped itself around my tongue, and looped twice around my jaw. That corner of my mind pulled the wire taut as my reflex to speak pushed against my mouth's door. The more I pushed, the tighter the wire got. I would not speak a word to these people, as it turned out, ever, other than asking for a toilet.

It was divine intervention or a lifetime in the law that strangled me at that moment. I needed to speak with my counsel first. I needed to think through whether to give a statement. I needed to remember that the right to remain silent was well worn, well established for very good reasons. The right to not self-incriminate was a powerful right to be exercised, not to be trifled with. People under arrest or otherwise facing police questioning need to consider that before they speak to the police. Be sure that you know what you're doing when you waive that right, dispel its power, and ignore its history and its lessons. When in doubt, say nothing.

Finally, the door opened. There were bright fluorescent lights and hallways, video cameras everywhere. The officers took inventory of the items on my person: keys, wallet, cigar cutter (eyed with suspicion), receipt scraps from my anniversary dinner and dessert. I signed a form.

A large metal door was unlocked and opened. Around midnight, they pointed me into that room and that was that. This was the cell they would hold me in for the next 15 hours.

I was alone in there. Most of the time I remained seated on a grey-painted metal bench, about the size of a chair, jutting out of the cement wall. The bench was a shinier grey, contrasting the bland white-grey paint covering the cement. At times, I leaned on the bench, resting my head on my arms. But that wasn't working too well because I was in a t-shirt and it was cold on my arms, too cold to sleep.

Besides, my mind was in overdrive.

I stared at the wall. The wall paint itself was actually more a lazy cleaner than something to add colour. The excrement and urine and saliva and blood and pus that had visited those walls got scrubbed a bit before another layer of paint went on.

Under that paint lay years of mendacity, self-mutilation, beatings, wails, delusional rants, tantrums, weeping, untreated injuries, echoes of babbling drunken tongues, sickness, pain, death, senselessness. That cell was quiet but I could barely hear above it all. Interior madness, painted over, coat upon coat, layer upon layer. A chip away from breaking out, filling your nostrils with something acrid, sore, stung, rasped, scraped, ripped, rotted.

And my mind raced faster still.

"Where should I start," I thought to myself. "I'm in charge.... No, I'm not."

First began the *what-ifs*.

What if the internet payment for baklava on the Danforth hadn't cleared the first time and the proprietor had run the transaction through again? We'd have been delayed a minute or two maybe. Then I never would have seen him. He would have terrorized someone else.

What if we'd decided to get Susan that book? Then, I would have turned left on Bay Street, and never encountered Sheppard parking his bike in front of me at Bloor and Belair.

Or what if I'd just turned north on Bay Street to go home, winding up Bay and over to Davenport, then right on Avenue Road? It would have taken me well north of Sheppard's path.

The what-ifs were making me sick. I stopped. I felt panic brewing inside.

Now, to stop the terrifying sound in my head, I started going within myself, in a fashion I'd not experienced before, trying to hide from my thoughts.

I grew up beside the Pacific Ocean, and knew that beneath the blowing whitecaps and the churning waves, down under there, things are quieter, calm, moving very slowly, darker, but not scary. It's the flip side of the wild Pacific, as if the inside were balancing the outside. On the surface, my head bobbed among the whitecaps, amid a gale. So I went within, down below, deeper, deeper, where it was quiet and slow.

Once I was safe from my own thoughts, I knew that this little cave within a cave that I'd found would become useful. It wasn't a comfortable place, by any stretch. But sometimes, when my thoughts became overwhelming, I'd go back there. My sanctuary. It was the place where one's dignity cannot be touched, the soul protected.

Hearing that we're powerless over people, places, and things (like booze) is not uncommon. Grasping this concept intellectually is one thing. Experiencing powerlessness is another. The experience in that cell was not unlike the sweet surrender I'd experienced more than three years previous, when I'd surrendered to my powerlessness over alcohol. Because I had to, because I was worn out, because I couldn't keep going anymore. Not because I wanted to. I had to.

The same was true after the 28 seconds. Many times, when chaos fogged up my vision, I'd have no choice but to surrender, to crawl into this cave within a cave, powerless. It became home, that place of surrender.

After I don't know how long, I began to be able to think again. I considered whether I'd be charged with something more serious. I knew Darcy Sheppard was hurt. The police said he was in very bad shape. But I still didn't fully believe them.

What's the charge? If he dies, it's criminal negligence causing death. What's the legal test? Oh, I knew the legal test. After all, I'd helped write it.

It was 1993 and I was clerking at the Supreme Court of Canada for Madam Justice Beverley McLachlin. I'd been asked to write the first draft for *Hundal, Creighton,* and *Finlay*—a trilogy of cases that established the legal test for criminal negligence. I borrowed heavily from the jurisprudence of the retired judge from my home province of B.C., Bill McIntyre.

A few years after the trilogy was released, I would publish a scholarly article on the resurrection of his previously discarded jurisprudence. It only underscored my familiarity with these charges that I was no longer writing or studying, but living them.

The constitutional issue was whether someone could be convicted of a serious crime without being consciously aware that they were engaging in dangerous behaviour. On one side of the debate were the subjectivists, who argued that the accused had to think dangerously. On the other were the objectivists, who argued that it didn't matter what the accused was thinking if his thinking was so idiotic that a reasonable person would have found it to be dangerous. In that case, the *mens rea*—or criminal mind—part of the test was met.

Basically, I advocated that McLachlin take a hard line. An objective test would suffice for a conviction, and the majority agreed with Justice McLachlin. Now, sitting in a cell in the early hours of September 1, 2009, I found that I'd written a test that would threaten my future. It was quite a reckoning.

Still, as I went through the test in my head, I believed that my conduct had not come close to being criminal. The reasonable person, I thought, would have done what I did. They would have tried to escape from the attack. I would be okay, legally.

I didn't feel okay. I still didn't know the condition of Darcy Sheppard. And there were other questions. Would my wife be furious at me? What would the kids think of me? How would the media respond? Would I be employable hereafter? Was this the end of any future return to politics?

In case I needed reminding of how drastically my prospects had changed, I could hear the arresting officer somewhere down the hall, talking on the phone. They'd accidentally left the door open a crack for about ten minutes, so I'd heard the constable clearly. He seemed to be reading my Wikipedia page to his wife or girlfriend.

"This guy's the Chief Legal Officer of Ontario," I heard him say. "This is huge!" He sounded very excited about the night's collar.

Next I began contemplating my next vocation. A teacher, probably, at a small community college. No university would dare appoint me. I gave up all my lofty aspirations there and then. It wasn't as awful as I'd expected. I would just have to change my dreams. I'd have to change my life's map. This inner conversation happened while I was sitting on that bench, sitting up straight at that moment, facing the opposite wall, the one with nothing on it.

But when you're in a room for 15 hours with nothing to do but stare and think, some dangerous thoughts come unbidden also. When I was released from custody, would I have my first drink in more than three years? It would be a Manhattan, I knew: Maker's Mark bourbon, some agostino bitters, and the red vermouth, I think it was. One cherry. Or maybe a very dry gin martini. Or blended Scotch and soda, on the rocks.

I stood up, arms crossed in front of me, looking low on the wall. I decided in that moment that drinking would be worse than this. Having a drink, being drunk again, being hungover again, being beholden to alcohol again, being something other than myself, being medicated and fake—that was worse than anything that could happen to me sober.

So I sat back down, just overcome with fatigue. Crossing my arms for warmth, I leaned back against the wall, fists balled up into my armpits, crossing my legs to stay stable.

A couple or many hours passed. I was clueless as to the time.

The metal door was opened.

"Someone is here to see you.... A 'Cynthia Fromstein.'"

"Yes, I'll see her."

Cynthia is a criminal lawyer who had joined my Liberal constituency association a few years earlier, one of many overqualified members of the riding executive. When she got the call,

Cynthia climbed out of bed and came to the police station, just after midnight. She'd spent all hours of that morning speaking with police, consulting with her colleagues on the defence bar, and occasionally being allowed to squeeze into a tiny cement telephone booth with me, so that we could speak privately.

We huddled together in that phone booth built for one. Cement, like the cell. Same paint as the inside of the cell, too. And a phone; a black phone or a pay phone, I can't remember (quaint, now that I think of it; one day I'll have to explain to my kids about "pay phones"). A stool was jammed in the corner of the cement booth, but nobody felt like sitting, so it served only to diminish our space.

"How are you?"

"I'm okay."

"Good. Good." She looked upset for me, but something about being in a police station made her feel comfortable, simply at work.

"I can't thank you enough for coming here tonight—"

"Don't be silly. I'm so glad I can do something. This is crazy. Michael, you're going to be released soon."

In fact, I wouldn't be released for another ten hours.

"They're still looking at manslaughter, but I can't believe they'd do that," she said.

Manslaughter?

"Michael," she said, her face blushing red now, "Michael, he died.... He's dead...."

When the words came out I just buckled, slid to the floor, face in hands, pushing my palms upward into my eye sockets. She told me they were going to charge me with criminal negligence causing death and dangerous driving causing death. Maybe manslaughter.

After a while, Cynthia left.

Sometime before 5 a.m., when I must have looked asleep on the surveillance camera, the door creaked open. A detective came into the room and introduced himself. He was overweight, with a moustache, balding. He didn't really need to introduce himself as a detective. This man was a cop and looked like one probably at birth.

"We have a lot of evidence. Witness statements, and *a lot* of video. *A lot.* Now, we need some context to put it all together."

It sounded so attractive. I was tempted to help him. It's a natural human inclination. I wanted to provide context because I knew I was innocent and wanted to avoid being charged with an offence.

Now, finally, was the moment I'd been waiting for, in many ways. It was time for me to act, make a decision. Since the 28 seconds, nobody had asked me to actually do or say anything, until now.

He repeated his request for some "context," and then made a mistake. He said: "we're looking at charging you with dangerous driving causing death. Or maybe vehicular homicide. That's what we're looking at right now."

This was not news to me. But just the way he said those words, the charges, I knew they were operating in a parallel universe where there are no innocents. It was now clear to me that the police at this division were not debating to charge or not to charge. Rather, they were debating how serious a charge they could lay. My "context" was not "context"; he wanted a statement to incriminate me. Something that could be contradicted by a witness, or some video. They didn't think I might be innocent. They thought I was a killer. They wanted me to help them ruin me.

"This *context*," I said, finally. "Are you asking me to make a statement?"

"Yes," he said immediately.

There was a pause. I knew the answer was no but wanted some more time. I asked to speak with my lawyer. It happened within about 20 minutes.

"These guys are trying to build a case against you," Fromstein repeated. "We shouldn't help them. They're not your friends."

I came back into the room, where the detective was waiting. I was tired but very alert, very careful. I thought about how to say this, how to say I wasn't going to make a statement. Do I explain why? Am I bitter, nasty, or accommodating, apologetic? The video camera purred silently above me.

"Declined," I said quietly, as I sat down on the metal pallet. The detective nodded, unsurprised, and walked outside the room without a word, locking the door behind him.

CYNTHIA HAD ALREADY TOLD Nikki and Susan about the death. They had returned to our house in Nikki's car to arrange for a "heavyweight" defence lawyer. They began making calls, getting advice. They phoned my friend Michael Eizenga, a class-action lawyer and former president of the Liberal Party of Canada, who said, "Get Marie Henein."

I'd met her once, at a dinner with Eizenga. The way we'd all been seated at that celebratory dinner, which now seemed centuries ago, I hadn't had much of a chance to chat with Marie. But by 8 a.m., Susan had retained her as my interim lawyer.

Sometime in the morning, a detective asked if I wanted anything to eat. Then: "Can I get you anything before you get released?"

"Yes," I said. "Am I right to assume that media are waiting for me?"

"Oh boy, yes," he said. "Never seen so many out there."

I figured there would be some kind of a perp walk, or certainly photographs taken, maybe a statement demanded, and I was in a t-shirt and jeans, both much the worse for wear by the last 12 hours.

"Okay, I don't want my kids seeing me on TV in a t-shirt and jeans. They'll know something is off. Whenever they see me on TV or in the newspaper, I'm in a suit. So can you ask my lawyer to find me a suit to wear, from my house? They'll bring it here."

So the officer told Cynthia Fromstein that I wanted a suit. Cynthia told Susan, who asked Nikki for help. They chose the most boring suit and tie they could find. They asked two of my best friends to pick it up and then pick me up.

Stephen Granovsky was a law-school buddy and a mensch extraordinaire. I'd been emcee at his wedding. He put my suit and shoes in a paper bag and headed to the station with another best friend, Andrew Evangelista, also a law-school buddy now with his own civil litigation law firm.

Back at the station, all morning there had been a debate about whether to release me on conditions from the police station, or to Old City Hall for a bail hearing before the Ontario Court of Justice. There was a strong likelihood that bail court would be presided over by a judge or JP that I'd appointed, but the debate was over whether I ought to be treated differently—which is to say more harshly—than any other accused with no criminal record who presented no flight risk.

Police consulted with the independent prosecutor, B.C. lawyer Richard Peck, who had by then been appointed by the Ontario Crown Attorney's Office. Cynthia Fromstein addressed Peck's question about whether being released by the police, rather than going before a court, constituted special treatment. They spoke by telephone.

"I've been practising criminal law in Toronto for a long time, Mr. Peck, and anyone but Michael Bryant would have been released from custody 12 hours ago…. The police laid charges way, way before it was necessary. They're still collecting evidence, for goodness sake. What was the rush? Because you guys ARE giving him special treatment, all right. Especially UNFAIR treatment. And as for his release: gimme a break!! You can't tell me that this guy is a flight risk. If you take him to City Hall it will be a circus, and it's only because you're going overboard here. Way, way overboard. Release my client, Mr. Peck. Now, please."*

Her argument won the day.

At about 2 p.m. on September 1, the heavy metal door was opened and I was escorted down a hallway to another room, which looked like an office that had become a large storage closet. I sat in that room for a few minutes. I didn't know what was to happen next.

There was a knock on the door. I didn't answer at first, thinking that it wasn't for me to answer it. I felt like a prisoner, not like I was in an office/storage room, which I was. Finally I answered the door. And there were the last two people I expected to see: Stephen Granovsky and Andrew Evangelista. Steve pushed a paper bag into my arms and told me to get changed.

Those two best friends of mine had waited for some time at the station with the suit they'd been given by Susan and Nikki. At some point an officer took the suit away from them, presumably to give it to me. The bag got lost somewhere. So after a treasure hunt in the Traffic Division, another friend was called to retrieve suit #2. Lorne Sossin, now the Dean at Osgoode Hall Law School, and another classmate (and co-clerk), violated several speed limits in an effort to deliver suit #2. Then, apparently, suit #1 got located and was returned to Steve and Andy.

Much was made of me in that suit after I was released. The fashion critics would have been amused to know how shambolic the whole wardrobe matter had been. I even had to borrow a belt from Andy and dress socks from Steve. And, for the record, I didn't shave. I wanted to look respectable, not groomed.

---

*Cynthia Fromstein's recollection of the conversation was repeated to me soon thereafter. She referred to her notes; however, there is no transcript of the conversation.

All I cared about was that the kids would think I was at work and what my daughter Sadie would say to me that week. "Daddy's in the newspaper!!" she bubbled, just as she always did. Every newspaper box lined outside the kids' public school had me in that blessed suit, photographed from various angles, all week.

When I was given the suit, Andrew also handed me his BlackBerry.

"Okay, Mike, Susan is asking you to read this."

On his BlackBerry was a message, a "statement," that Andy suggested I read. Andrew has his own firm, a civil litigation operation on the top floor of the austere Toronto Dominion Bank Tower. Besides being a terrific lawyer, Andrew was one of my earliest supporters, politically very smart, and cautious as the wise counsel he was. His advice is important to me.

"I'm recommending that you read it to the media. Then nothing. Don't answer any questions. Just read it and walk away."

Andy told me how it had been produced. Susan and Marie Henein and Jaime Watt, from the consulting firm Navigator, had worked on the statement. When I heard Watt's name I was pleasantly surprised. Watt had worked as a senior strategist and communications guru for Conservative Premier Mike Harris and was Jim Flaherty's consigliere. After his time in provincial government, he had transitioned into a successful private-sector career. I'd first met Jaime at a dinner party held by Neil and Marie Finkelstein. Neil is one of Canada's leading barristers and Marie was also a lawyer and a renowned artist. They'd been political supporters of mine and hosted many a dinner party, often mixing and matching people who might not otherwise get to mingle together. Conservative Jaime Watt and Liberal Michael Bryant, for example.

Susan and I met Watt and his partner Paul Ferguson at a dinner party and an instant friendship was born. We had them over for dinner and we'd been hosted by them at various functions.

After I was arrested, Susan called Jaime for advice. He cleared his day and gave Susan all of his time. Jaime and his colleagues at Navigator would give me countless hours of help, at a time when I was literally incapable of thinking or reading, let alone deciding about communications matters. Watt refused to charge me a cent for the work they did for me, on and off, for months.

Navigator's efforts on my behalf were both pilloried and celebrated in the media. Some thought I was yet again obsessed with my reputation; they found it deeply cynical. The reality was otherwise, but that's no matter: people will think what they will think. A few days after the accident, there was still a huge appetite for more media on the Bryant–Sheppard story, but no new facts. So media editors and producers turned to shaky journalism and much commentary on process, rather than substance. In other words, they reported not on *what* was happening (nothing), but on *how* it might have happened. In other words, they set their sights on Navigator.

On September 1, Watt got Navigator's media-scan machine kicked into gear for crisis management. He suggested a statement be made and drafted one. At first, Marie Henein said forget it, no statement. Susan went back and forth between the two and they came up with wording they could both live with.

This was the statement that Andy brought to show me on his BlackBerry. He asked if I was up to it. I noticed that there was no reference to the man who had died or to his family. I said I wanted that added, and scribbled down something about the "deceased." I wasn't confident that the police had accurately identified the man who'd died the night before.

Andy assured me that the police were positive that the deceased's name was Darcy Allan Sheppard. I'd never heard or seen that name before. Marie reviewed the amended statement and she okayed the wording.

"The media are outside the station," Andy said. "There are a lot, Mike. But I think you can handle this. You can do this, buddy. Make this statement and then you're done. You can go home. If you don't say anything, they're gonna stalk you all over town. They're on your front lawn now—"

I gasped a little at that thought. Not in surprise, but to hear it made me realize my worst fears for my family.

"Okay, I'll read it," I said.

I asked Andy to help me scribble it down from the BlackBerry onto a piece of paper—literally, the back of an envelope. I stood just inside two sets of glass doors, looking out at the media throng. It was huge. Granovsky and Evangelista took me by my elbows and guided me toward a microphone on a podium. I stood facing the wrong way, with my back to the cameras.

Then I felt some hands on my shoulders. I was gently turned around, to face the cameras, by Global TV's Catherine McDonald, a friend and a veteran crime reporting specialist. Neither of us could have ever imagined this scene. Too unbelievable.

"Okay, Mr. Bryant. Whenever you're ready."

When I began to speak, it just happened. My voice was cracking and I was having trouble getting the words out.

"May I ask for your understanding in not making a statement today on last night's tragic events. At an appropriate moment I will, of course, speak to you. I would, however, like to extend my deepest condolences to the family of Mr. Sheppard. To all those who have offered support to my family in the past 12 hours, thank you." I barely got out those two words.

"May I ask that the media continue to respect my family's need for distance and privacy ... for the next few days. Thank you."

I started walking away, and was steered back toward the front door of the station by Granovsky. Andrew walked up to the podium as if he were to make a statement. The photographers followed me but the rest homed in on Andy, who waited until I was safely inside the station, at which point he said not a word and walked back into the station.

Next I was in the passenger seat of Granovsky's giant SUV, driving along unfamiliar streets. I don't recall saying anything for a long time.

"Can you slow down a bit?" I said. "I'm having a little trouble with this."

"Sorry. Sorry, buddy. Of course."

I stared through the car window. The day was gorgeous, apparently. The weather reports said it would be sunny and warm without exception in Toronto. We drove past the Sobeys in Liberty Village, a new café kitty-corner from it, the familiar gentrified stores on Queen Street West, people sitting on patios, then the hockey card store on Bathurst.

Everything looked different, like I was wearing pain glasses hooked up to my stomach. It was all in monochrome to my eyes. The colour had been bled out of everything and I felt like throwing up.

I looked curiously at lovers strolling, workers on a smoke break, parents walking with babies, people shopping. It was as if everybody's lives were continuing on like they had been 24 hours ago. But I was no longer part of that world—the sunny, normal, pedestrian world of ordinary life. I was no longer of that world. *Will it always be like this? Was I going to spend the rest of my life being this way?*

Granovsky was now driving up to Avenue Road. We were a few minutes away from my house. I was in the passenger seat, my jaw clenched, sweating a little. I should call Susan, I thought, and began dialling in a guilty panic. I should have called her minutes ago!

I couldn't dial the number. Stephen did so for me. Susan answered. We wept and spoke some words to each other that would temporarily mark a blessed spike, an apex maybe, in the arc of our marriage.

Then she snapped into her role as four-star general. "Okay, we're ready for you. Pull up to the side door. There's media camped out front—"

Stephen had overheard my conversation with Susan. When excited, she tended to amplify her already loud voice for telephone conversations. It was as if Stephen had been conferenced into the call.

"How is she?" he asked.

"Strong. Heroic."

"She's been amazing," Stephen said. "Unbelievably strong. Orchestrating everything: your lawyer, media help, getting her own lawyer, getting us to the station with the suit. Getting people in and out of the house with media everywhere. A rock."

Fifteen hours earlier, as I was cuffed in the back of a squad car, heading south to the Traffic Division on Hanna Road, Susan was following—Nikki at the wheel, Susan on the phone. She was calling lawyers—one asleep in Greece; another, Cynthia Fromstein, asleep in Toronto—her mom, her Uncle Harvey, who'd spotted me on television, and Sarah, with the kids, now for the night.

At the station, she was assured that I would be released soon enough. Eventually, the police figured out that taking a statement from Susan would be good police work. Like any lawyer, she knew the risks. Like any spouse, she wanted to help me. But how?

Female police officers started showing up in the waiting room, trying to offer Susan comfort. Later, they would call her, pretending to be a shoulder to cry on, offering to meet. To "just hang out," one said.

I pity the fool who underestimates Susan Abramovitch. But this was complicated for her. This was not just about police manipulation, it was about her husband's liberty. She was doubting her own instincts, and she was in shock—also enduring post-traumatic stress disorder, of course.

Nevertheless, she made the right choice, and the only real choice in that situation: she provided no statement to the police. In those situations, any statement would be used only to incriminate, and not at all to exculpate. I've no doubt that the police would say otherwise. Regardless, the experience of being hunted by the police, to be used as a pawn in their investigation, only compounded her rage about the rush to judgment that led to my arrest. That rage has left her, to this day, contemptuous and fearful about policing in Canada.

At some point around 3 a.m., she was told by Cynthia, my lawyer, that the man on the bike was dead. Susan heaved a bit to herself, and had to sit down. She later told me that she knew right then that our lives had changed forever.

When it was clear that there was no releasing me anytime soon, she went home to sleep, then awoke Nikki at 5 a.m. Soon enough she was on the phone with Marie Henein, retaining her on my behalf, then retaining Doug Hunt as her own counsel. This was all before most people had gotten out of bed that morning.

As Granovsky and I approached my house in his SUV, I spotted the media gauntlet. Incredibly, they didn't spot us, despite driving slowly and carefully through them, all chatting away, standing aside for this SUV driving up Michael Bryant's laneway. Once in the door, I ducked into the basement, away from any windows. Susan ran downstairs where I was waiting with my arms open wide.

I squeezed her and spun her around.

"Daddy's home! Yay!"

"Daddy!!!!"

Sadie and Louie said it like I'd just got home from work. Another day at the office.

"Daddy! Daddy! Are you going stay? Are you going to stay?"

That was always their question. Was I home to see them during dinner then heading out somewhere, or was I staying home to play with them, help them brush their teeth, tuck them in, perhaps read them a story.

"Too hard," said Louie as I squeezed him. Sadie slipped under my other arm. We kissed cheeks staccato-style. Louie wiped the kiss off his cheek, something he did in his sleep if we kissed him at night before turning in ourselves.

I turned back to embrace Susan again. She was crying, happy.

We had been married 12 years and a day.

NINE

Stretcher Bearers

To be suddenly on the wrong side of the law—especially if you were once a well-known politician, especially if you'd been Chief Law Officer in the jurisdiction, especially if you were still widely thought to be politically ambitious—is to discover how abruptly and totally the world can turn on its axis. In important ways, in trivial ways, and in every way in between.

From the moment I stepped out of that police station on Hanna Avenue into the disorienting sunshine of September 1, 2009, nothing in my life was as it had been just 15 hours before. It was as if I'd stumbled through Lewis Carroll's looking-glass, or entered the Wachowskis' Matrix. Everything that was familiar, everything I'd once taken for granted, had changed.

The most immediate was my relationship with the news media. For better or worse, I had always been one of those politicians regarded as never having met a microphone or TV camera he didn't adore. I courted and cultivated relationships with reporters. I tried to figure out their needs and fill them. When it suited me, I leaked to reporters, unless it involved my Chief Legal Officer duties, wherein I was uncharacteristically circumspect. Otherwise, I spoke freely and at length with reporters. I loved leading newscasts, loved making headlines, loved the whole gratifying rush of being at the centre of any scrum—the cockpit of politics, where reputations and careers can nosedive fast.

Now here I was, the just-released accused, no longer a media-hound but the hunted, saying nothing, taking no questions, pleading to be left in peace and privacy. My arrival home shortly afterwards, with the news media all over our driveway, would illustrate again my new world order. A day earlier, that sort of reception might have been my idea of paradise. Not anymore.

It would be a little while before I'd realize how little those reporters really needed any more to chew on, and how much they'd already gorged on the story.

The best chronicle of the media performance in the early hours of this story would be published in the spring of 2010 by the *Ryerson Review of Journalism* (RRJ). Within hours of the accident, wrote RRJ reporter Matthew Halliday, *The Globe and Mail* and the *Toronto Star* had run brief online stories describing a hit-and-run on Bloor Street. Neither story named me as the driver, but rumours were apparently already making the rounds.

Just after 5 a.m., the RRJ said, 680News reported that I was the driver in police custody, after having been involved in a confrontation with a cyclist while returning from a night on the town.

"As night turned to day in Toronto's newsrooms, phones rang, in-boxes pinged, a journalistic reveille rallying the incoming army of editors and writers," Halliday wrote.

He quoted *National Post* reporter Matthew Coutts saying: "It got pretty exciting pretty fast.... Right off the bat it was all hands on deck. A lot of people get into journalism for that rush."

The feeling was apparently widespread in a profession whose best days are usually other people's worst.

"I shouldn't call it a great day," Kelly Grant, then Toronto editor of *The Globe and Mail,* told Halliday. "But when a story breaks that everyone wants to read and I have this stable of incredibly talented reporters I can throw at it, that's not a bad day. That's a great day."

If this story involved the worst moment of my life, the *Ryerson Review of Journalism* suggested that it hardly became journalism's finest hour, even if it provided a peek into the sort of thing that most energizes newsrooms.

As Halliday wrote, unsubstantiated rumours went viral through Toronto newsrooms. "Bryant had been cavorting with a mistress." "Bryant had been drunk." Almost instantly, this was Toronto's own *Bonfire of the Vanities*. This was Michael Bryant's personal Chappaquiddick.

"The dream was," *Toronto Star* city editor Graham Parley told Halliday, "Let's find the ritzy restaurant in Yorkville where Bryant ate and count how many bottles of expensive wine were on the table.... It would have been sensational to find him drinking with some mystery woman before jetting off in his luxury convertible. You know, 'What a story! Mmm, yeah!' In a crude way, you could say we went looking for dirt and didn't find anything."

In short order, the *Bonfire of the Vanities* narrative, the drunken-Lothario-on-a-spree that had the potential to be such a circulation and ratings booster, began to unravel. No luxury convertible. No ritzy restaurant. No expensive wine. No mystery woman.

"It would've been a better story for us if he had been drinking," Parley told the respected Ryerson magazine. "No question we were going out there with a bit of 'Gotcha' in mind, and the facts were the opposite of 'Gotcha.'"

On many levels, though, they still got me. Eyewitnesses were quoted, with accounts of events that were practically hallucinatory. They had my Saab travelling at 100 kilometres an hour or more, when it would eventually be proven that it never left first gear or got above 34 km/h; they had the driver trying to bounce the assailant on mailboxes, when it would be proven the car never so much as touched a curb. (Yet more evidence to prove the fallibility of human memory and eyewitness accounts.) The goat I'd once sought to feed was feasting—with gusto—on me. The gods can never be accused of lacking a sense of humour.

Even worse, some media had my home address in a database and others read it on the *Toronto Star* website. The *Star* had published my address, even provided a map showing where the house was—which was, in fact, about 100 yards from my children's public school. There were photographs of my kids, ages 5 and 7, on the website, with their names under each photo. Susan would ask someone to get the photos taken down, but it didn't happen until the new year, about five months later (though I am grateful to the *Star* reporter who fixed it).

The mainstream media had nothing, however, on the world of blogs. There, I would find out only later, I was routinely called a murderer and denounced as the "Butcher of Bloor Street."

Still, if I found myself the target of anger, hate, and vitriol by some, the events that followed my return home on that first day of September 2009 also opened my eyes to qualities of unconditional love and friendship, of consolation and support from people and places I'd never anticipated.

When I first went upstairs to our bedroom that first day home, and lay down on the bed to rest, I saw a pile of books beside Susan's night table. On top was a memoir by Abigail Carter, a woman who had lost her husband in the 9/11 attacks on the World Trade Center in New York. Her book was called *The Alchemy of Loss: A Young Widow's Transformation*. I opened the book to the first page. It began with an epigraph from the Persian poet Rumi's "Zero Circle":

> *Be helpless, dumbfounded,*
> *Unable to say yes or no.*
> *Then a stretcher will come from grace*
> *To gather us up.*

I read it about 20 times. I took great comfort from it. I knew that I'd already received stretchers from grace, to gather me up. Intuitively, I also accepted the prescription to "be helpless, dumbfounded / Unable to say yes or no." This required a measure of surrender. A surrender of the will—quite a different approach to the world than I was used to.

I'd always felt immune from surrender, out of pride, and willed everything myself, I thought, since I was old enough to remember. What happened to me, from the time my troubles began that summer of 2009, has been the regular appearance in my life of those "stretchers from grace," to gather me up in my lowest moments.

Friends had already come to my rescue, within minutes of the accident, before we knew how tragic it had been. Susan was both stretcher bearer and in need of a stretcher herself. Nikki Holland spent the evening and the next day helping Susan rescue me. Together they'd contacted lawyers, and the suit-bearers and jailhouse liberators Andrew and Stephen—one sockless, the other beltless—who showed up at a moment's notice in the middle of the day to literally give me the clothes off their back.

Meanwhile, I needed all the help I could get. Unemployed and staying mostly at home, I was physically and psychologically incapable of doing much more than eating, sleeping, jogging, and writing thank-you notes, at my most energetic, for months after the accident.

As I later learned from my psychiatrist, I had PTSD: post-traumatic stress disorder. The definitive explanation of PTSD describes it as "exposure to an extremely stressful traumatic event that involves personal experience with actual or threatened death or serious injury; a response of fear, helplessness or horror; repeated re-experiencing of the event; persistent symptoms of increased arousal [i.e., stress]; and clinically significant impairment of important areas of functioning (e.g., social or occupational)." In a word, I was shell-shocked.

Spiritually, I'd experienced something that liberated me from the bonds of reputation management. Legally, I could say *nothing* on or off the record that would compromise my defence. Police, prosecutors, and the defence are not supposed to comment on matters before the court, to avoid the appearance (or reality) of influencing the judge or potential jurors through the media. As I knew from my days as Attorney General, violation of this rule could lead to contempt of court, or the dismissal of a case for abuse of process. Even if this principle is flouted in the U.S., it tends to be narrowly observed in Canada and other Commonwealth countries, most of the time, and certainly I could not violate the so-called *sub judice* rule as a former Attorney General.

As the sun rose on September 1st, Susan had called the managing partner at her firm, Peter Lukasiewicz, to alert him to the emergency, and explain that she wasn't sure when she'd be in the office. Peter was at his desk and was soon going through his Rolodex. He told Susan that, with her permission, he'd assemble a short list of the best criminal lawyers, and the best forensic professionals. He knew that my defence team (which didn't yet exist) needed to be assembled immediately and start collecting evidence before the crime scene was completely useless.

Experts had to comb the streets for skid-marks, evidence of where the car had travelled, and any evidence on the fire hydrant or mailbox. They had to dust the car for fingerprints before the evidence became "contaminated" by the fingerprints of others. (But it was too late. There were about a dozen different fingerprints on the vehicle, rendering the evidence useless; the police had failed to contain the scene.)

IMMEDIATELY AFTER DELIVERING me home, Stephen, a modern Orthodox Jew who thought food was an answer to every problem, asked if I was hungry. And it wasn't just Stephen who made sure I wouldn't go starving. The day I was released from the cell, the food started to arrive and kept on coming. Care packages from good friends and simple acquaintances. There was enough food for a week: casseroles and lasagna, smoked meat and bagels and verenikas and deliveries from stores.

Then there was the unforgettable conversation I had with Toronto Mayor David Miller. As mayor, Miller was chair of Invest Toronto, the economic development agency he'd created and to which I'd been hired as founding CEO.

His hopes, like mine, had been high on May 25, 2009. "Michael Bryant is exactly the person Invest Toronto needs in this important leadership role at this time of challenge and opportunity," read the press release at the time.

Now, Miller's CEO was charged with killing someone. I was no longer anyone's idea of the ideal global business cheerleader. So I called David Miller on September 1, standing beside an unlit barbeque in my backyard, to offer my resignation.

"I don't think you should resign," he said.

"Thank you, David," I said after a long pause, as I tried to gather myself. I had a huge lump in my throat. He wasn't thinking about Invest Toronto or himself. He was thinking of me.

"No, seriously. You're innocent. Innocent until proven guilty means something to me. It means something period. You should rethink this."

"I've thought about it," I said. "I've gamed out the scenarios. The media will howl for a resignation starting late tomorrow. Let's not allow them to push me into this. I want to get ahead of it."

"No, I won't accept your resignation," he said, "... or at least resign pending the completion of the investigation—"

"Oh, the investigation is complete," I replied. "It lasted a few minutes. They charged me within seven minutes, my lawyer tells me."

"I mean resign pending the conclusion of the prosecution."

"Well, I think that's half-pregnant. Either I'm the CEO or I'm not. If I'm not, I resign. What happens afterwards is—"

"Just sleep on it," he said.

I slept on it and resigned the next morning, September 2.

"I do not believe ... that I can continue in this position on account of the circumstances of the past two days," I wrote in my resignation letter. "Let me be clear: I am innocent of the very serious accusations made against me. It would, however, be unfair to you, the Board and above all to the residents of Toronto to allow this event to distract from the vital efforts of Invest Toronto."

A FEW DAYS AFTER the accident, I went back into the offices of Invest Toronto to collect some personal effects.

I logged onto my (old) computer to check emails that had been sent over the past week. A couple of messages were nasty. "Subject: MURDERER." But more than 20 emails of support had come in, including one from a PC MPP. I printed them up and literally hugged them against my chest.

One had been sent at 7:30 a.m. on September 1. It was the first one that responded to the media reports of my arrest. At the time it was sent, I was in a jail cell. At that moment, the media were reporting that a former Attorney General was arrested for a road-rage death in Yorkville after a night celebrating with an unnamed blonde. So the sender of this message had the worst possible version of the events. When I read it, I shook my head.

"I know you may feel very alone right now. You're not. All your many friends are with you and will stand beside you. Sincerely, Michael Ignatieff."

Ignatieff was the Leader of the Official Opposition in Canada's Parliament at the time. The last thing he needed to be doing was sending words of support, in writing, to an accused felon, well before hearing all the facts. As it stood at that moment, what was known was ugly. But Michael Ignatieff found the time and humanity to send his support anyway.

I'd supported Ignatieff for the federal Liberal leadership. But that perhaps warranted an annual, electronically signed Christmas card. Not a personal, poetic missive of friendship.

That first morning I awoke at home after spending the previous night in jail, Susan's Uncle Harvey and Aunt Maura were at our house, looking after the kids or looking after me, whichever seemed most necessary. They greeted people who showed up at the door. Which happened often.

That week I got a visit from Margo Timmins of the Cowboy Junkies, a great client of Susan's and good friend to us both. Full of wisdom and kindness, she spent hours with me, drinking coffee. Then the doorbell rang.

It was an older man and his son, the proprietors of Dutch Dreams Ice Cream. I'd frequented their delightful establishment on Vaughan Road near St. Clair Avenue, as the MPP for the area, and provided the token celebratory local scroll. Now, they came to comfort me with their greatest gift. The father had tears in his eyes and litres of ice cream under each arm.

The look in their eyes, those Dutch Dreams proprietors, told me something. The 28 seconds had clearly had an impact on people, many people I'd never meet. Strangers would approach me again and again with the same sentiment. "There but for the grace of God, go I." My unexpected life change had rocked some people, I realized, because they seemed to feel, quite viscerally, the lack of control we all have over our lives. The fragility of our pedestrian existences left people feeling powerless. To see that in people's eyes, and hear it in their words, made me feel as if I were not alone.

The next thing I noticed was that people were helping me without me even knowing it. One day Rob Oliphant, then Member of Parliament for a Toronto riding, and a former United Church minister, rang my doorbell. He had a card with his numbers on it, and told me to call him. Then we spoke.

In the days that had followed the 28 seconds, he decided that the best way to help me was to help my former political staff, all of whom were understandably freaked out by what had happened to their former boss. Political staff are like family, except they don't always get remembered like family. Oliphant took the time to sit down and talk with them. This was a comforting thought— that someone was caring for those I was unable to care for at that moment.

Oliphant's actions inspired me. He looked the picture of serenity, and he was doing good deeds. Meanwhile, it's a tenet of alcoholism recovery that in times of high anxiety, it's best to get out of one's head, and to be outward-facing. In particular, it's suggested that we engage in service to others.

In my case, I started to reach out to people who were clearly worried about me. I wanted to assure them that I was doing okay, and that I was all the better for their generosity of spirit. In fact, hundreds of messages had come my way, by email or Facebook or instant messages, or by phone calls, visits, and many, many hand-written notes. I decided to write everyone back.

First step, a stationery store. I wasn't employed, so there was no fancy letterhead for me embossed with Invest Toronto or Government of Ontario or Legislative Assembly of Ontario. Next step, an email address. This sounds odd, but the truth was that my identity was wedded to my old email addresses. I spent days—not hours, but days—figuring out an email address. The same was true for the stationery. That it took so long to complete these simple tasks was evidence that I was in a serious funk. Psychic numbness, depression, shock, PTSD equals serious funk.

Finally, I decided on an email address with no reference to my past vocation, and bought blank, cream-coloured stationery. I began writing thank-you notes to people. Getting them addressed on an envelope often took five times as long as writing them. Getting a stamp for them took still longer. And then getting them to the mailbox became an odyssey. This became compounded by the fact that I didn't keep track of my thank-you notes, which meant that some people might have received several cards, some received none. During the day, I carried a briefcase with files full of kind notes from people, another file with my thank-yous, and another with envelopes. Often I'd leave one or the other at home. This was not the Manhattan Project, but I was pretty useless in those days.

In addition to writing notes and calling people, I visited people—at their workplace or a nearby coffee shop, or at their homes. Making the appointment was one thing. Keeping it was another. I stood people up inadvertently because I failed to put appointments in my calendar. It would have been comic if I hadn't so inconvenienced the very people I'd wanted to reach out to. I was behaving more like Mel Brooks's Young Frankenstein than a Harvard graduate with lots of time on his hands.

September and October remain a fog of time spent in front of a computer, at a coffee shop, in the gym, or in our backyard, writing notes, and ... meeting at Marie Henein's office. I don't recall much.

I wrote very little at first, although I did start keeping notes of my daily life at the advice of a generous friend, Doug Pepper, father to my daughter's best friend and a book editor/publisher. I went to meetings with recovering addicts and alcoholics twice a week, and sometimes more often. All those people who met with me, all those people in those meetings, everyone, did a lot to heal me. I wondered whether I should send a thank-you note to follow up on the thank-you note, a running commentary of my gratitude. Susan and I decided that was a little much.

Meanwhile, there was a debate raging in the media to which I was oblivious. After August 31, I never read newspapers and never watched the news. It was only by accident that I'd come across something. More likely, Susan or Marie or a friend would point something out. Family friend Frank Iacobucci said to me one day: "What Patrick said: that's how we feel." I nodded, not knowing the reference, which I later looked up.

In a media interview, the Dean of Osgoode Hall Law School, a former professor of mine, Patrick Monahan, made a strong case for why, if anything, the justice system was likely to overdo it in my case. The police and prosecutors and the judge were so paranoid of appearing biased in my favour that they'd be biased against me. But when asked whether he was a friend of mine, which might taint his legal opinion, Patrick was blunt: "I'd do anything for Michael Bryant."

And then there were what I came to call "The Drivers." A series of angels, disguised as ordinary drivers, would pull up beside me on the street, every other week, sometimes more frequently.

Some of them I knew—like Brad Duguid and Peter Fonseca, two cabinet ministers from the McGuinty government (who were driving themselves; where was *their* driver?). But most were complete strangers.

One man was in his sixties, a former Conservative activist in his time, he told me. He was driving a beautiful BMW convertible. He thought I'd like to be driven in that for a bit. Just like that: he saw me, recognized me, and offered me a lift to where I was heading.

Another time a beige SUV pulled up beside me, a mom behind the wheel and two occupied child seats in the back.

"Michael Bryant?"

"Yes."

"I heard about what happened to you and know you can't drive so ..."

So she gave this accused felon a lift down Avenue Road with her kids chattering in the back seat. ("Mommy, who's dat man?!")

When I wasn't receiving this treatment from Toronto drivers, I got around town by bike. I purchased one from Duke's Cycle about two weeks after I returned home.

Now, keep in mind that cyclists had filled Bloor Street in memoriam for Darcy Sheppard the day after his death. It made the front pages. And bike shops are obviously a hub for any cycling news. More than a century old, Duke's Cycle was a veritable Speaker's Corner of cyclist hobnobbing. But I was completely out to lunch in those early days, because nothing was sticking in my brain.

I walked in, looking like Michael Bryant, and after a few minutes of perusing the bikes, a man came up to me. I realized that the place had gone very quiet the last few minutes.

"Can I help you?"

I explained what I was looking for and ended up purchasing a fold-up bike that would allow me to cycle and subway easily. The gentleman assisting me suggested that I give it a test drive before buying it and asked for a piece of photo ID. So I handed over my driver's licence.

By this point, every worker and customer in the store had stopped whatever they were doing, and awaited the verdict. The man behind the counter had brown curly hair, a toque on a warm September day, and a beard that was braided, pencil thin, at his chin. The friendly fellow, who was working the cash register, looked down at my licence and announced to everyone in the store:

"Yep, it's Michael Bryant alright!"

Then I was helped down the few stairs of the Richmond St. W.

entrance for my test drive. The pencil-bearded fellow ran the transaction through and explained everything to me regarding tune-ups,
the warranty, and the like, as he'd done with countless others.

Then he shook my hand, held it fast, leaning in to whisper:
"I'm with you, brother."

Other stretcher bearers arrived unbeknownst to me. Witnesses
who came forward had to figure out *how* to come forward in a
manner that allowed them to provide direct evidence to the
defendant, rather than to the police.

One such witness was a successful engineer living in Yorkville.
During the 28 seconds that I struggled for control of my car, he'd
been enjoying a smoke at his window in his condo on the Mink
Mile, above one of the shops on Bloor Street West.

He ended up getting a bird's-eye view of almost everything
that happened. His version was quite helpful to my defence. The
engineer turned out to be an important witness. Besides providing
a professional and credible accounting to both our defence team
and the police, he was willing to swear an affidavit about a chilling
exchange with a police officer on the telephone, within a few days
of the 28 seconds.

The police officer he spoke to said that he, the witness, was
"fucking up" their case and asked him to reconsider his exculpatory
statement.

To me, this sounded like Mark Fuhrman planting a glove
in the O.J. case. Marie didn't seem fazed, assuring me that this
happened more than I'd like to think. Needless to say, that incident
has permanently changed the way I think of police investigations.
Even assuming that particular police officer to be a bad apple, the
point is that such apples exist, and they have enormous, frightening
powers.

Another witness was a successful hair stylist, who had been on
Bloor Street when it all happened. She too recalled a version of

the events that squared with mine. One of the stylist's long-time customers was a bencher at the Law Society of Upper Canada, the regulator of the legal profession. Benchers tend to be the most successful lawyers of their generation, and this one was no exception. Although not a criminal lawyer, she well understood how difficult it could be for a defence team to connect with positive witnesses. So, upon hearing the stylist's story, she dug up Marie Henein's number and made her call my lawyer.

MY LAW-SCHOOL CLASSMATE Richard King was awake around 1 a.m., September 1, when the broadcasts of the Bloor Street *Bonfire of the Vanities* started airing on TV and radio. Rich happened to catch a glimpse of the perp shot of me hours before the media would confirm my identity. He stayed up that entire night, listening to newscasts, and around 5 a.m. started calling my friends. King lined up Evangelista and Granovsky to liberate me from the Traffic Division.

A few weeks later, he'd plant the idea with John West, head of the Toronto office of Ogilvy Renault, home to former UN ambassador Yves Fortier and former Prime Minister Brian Mulroney, that maybe I would be a useful addition to the firm's growing Energy and First Nations Business Law practice. Less than three months later, John West approached me to discuss my becoming a senior adviser at that firm. Ogilvy Renault was more than a century old, and one of the leading Canadian law firms, and would soon merge with the global U.K.-based megafirm Norton Rose.

I may have been a former Attorney General, but I was also an accused felon. Law firms are primarily commercial enterprises—the mega ones, anyway—so they don't need much of a justification for taking a pass on a new lawyer joining their firm, with the inherent risks and overhead. Usually, a couple of indictments are more than enough to do the trick.

Yet John West teamed up with the national managing partner, John Coleman, and the firm's chair, Norm Steinberg, to convince their partners that they should employ me. If innocent until proven guilty is to mean something, they argued, then we have to judge Michael as an innocent and therefore eligible to serve as a senior advisor here. So, in December 2009, I got a job. Having their support, and, just as importantly, a vocation, was instrumental to my life in the wake of what had happened. I would work there for just over two years, and I remain grateful for their courageous decision.

Sometimes the act of kindness seemed minor, but the impact allowed me to feel like the Rumi quote: caught by stretchers. For example, Linda Martell of Fiorio salon had been cutting my hair for over a decade, and the kids' hair since they were born. She knew I was due for a cut, but unlikely able to venture back into Yorkville for an hour of styling. She offered to cut my hair at her apartment, and loaned me some wonderful books that had helped her during a time of great trauma.

But Linda wasn't done. One of her clients kept talking about me, wishing out loud that he could share his own experiences with me. Finally, Linda hooked us up, and we met for lunch.

He was a senior executive at one of the top-ten investment banks on the Toronto Stock Exchange. Over lunch, he shared his very personal experiences, and passed along his top three books that had helped him the most. Two of them I was familiar with, but one I had not read. Oscar Wilde's *De Profundis,* written from a jail cell, became a bible for me. My new friend and I have kept in touch ever since.

SOMETIMES, kindness and support came utterly out of the blue. A chin-up phone call from Brian Mulroney, then a wonderful letter from his son, Ben—neither of whom I'd previously known. A month or so after Darcy's death, I received an email from a stranger. It was an invitation, from E. James Barton, who went by Jay, to have breakfast at the Royal York Hotel. Barton emailed, at first, then somehow got my cell number. I never returned the call but he kept at it, emailing me regularly. He proposed that I attend a breakfast meeting with street people, homeless people, some local celebrities, ex-NHL players, and a broadcaster. I finally responded.

"Thanks for the invite, Jay. I'm no longer the CEO of Invest Toronto. But I can pretend to play the part. You still want me?"

He did, and seemed fully aware of my circumstances. I showed up late for the breakfast, held in a private room off the main dining room of the Epic Restaurant. The Royal York Hotel is exactly like it sounds: dark wood, formal bellboys, thick Eastern rugs, a pipe tobacco shop in its gallery of jewellery and art stores within. Now part of the Fairmont brand, the Royal York is where a wealthy person would stay in Toronto if the Four Seasons was considered too nouveau riche.

Barton was dressed for Bay Street: pinstriped suit, tailored; perfect white shirt with a collar seemingly hard as cement, a Polo tie, French cuffs, shiny buttons. His jawline resembled that of the animated superhero in *The Incredibles*. If he weren't so cultivated, that chiselled chin would have regularly knocked over his water glass. Even his hair was courtesy of central casting for rich people you loved to hate: blond curl in the front of a fresh cut and a hairline that wouldn't move until he was six feet under.

"Okay, let's get this party started," I choked out, into a quiet room full of bacon smells and awkward conversation sounds. Nervous laughter exploded. Yeesh. This would be difficult.

They'd all been seated and were halfway through breakfast. I was half an hour late.

Jay repeated my joke, then nodded to the man beside me: "Michael, this is Jimmy, who was really looking forward to talking politics with you." I looked at Jimmy. And everyone, all 12 men, cast their gaze at Jimmy and me, who were now expected to talk politics. Seconds passed. Nothing but the sound of coffee steaming. Yet soon enough, the different worlds of prosperity and poverty, brought together for breakfast by Jay, were one.

The day after, I got a call from Jay Barton. "Hey, Michael, thanks *so* much for coming to the breakfast. It's really important for the homeless guys and it takes major stones for the successful people to get out of their comfort zone, you know?"

In the months that followed, Jay Barton invited me several times for coffee. I either ignored the invites or made excuses. I became suspicious that his efforts were just guilty white dudes getting their annual absolution by coming to breakfast with poor people at the Royal York. But one day I happened to be in the neighbourhood where his proposed coffee klatch took place, so I sat down with him over an Americano.

Jay was wearing a faded green Polo shirt and long khaki shorts. A bicycle helmet sat on the chair beside him. Hmmm. This didn't fit.

He told me his story. It's private, but I related to it. Suffice to say, there's more to the man than the fancy clothes.

E. James Barton, in fact, makes enough "cake" to stay in a certain "snack bracket," but also enough to allow him to volunteer about half his time to helping people living on the streets. "Front-line work," serving meals and talking with "guys and some gals." Jay had organized the breakfast club to give some impoverished Toronto residents, with mental illness or suffering from substance abuse, an opportunity to interact with another world. And to give the "conventionally successful" an opportunity to interact with another world.

Jay Barton had become, in essence, a street worker. Mediating, breaking up fights, escorting junkies to and from a downtown church; talking, listening, feeding, cleaning.

He had learned, he said, "what it's *all about*, ya know? Maybe all I can give them is some dignity but that's a lot. To find an inebriated person a couch, to lay a blanket on them, so they could sleep it off *with dignity*, right?"

I found that I wanted some of what Jay Barton had. I wanted some peace of mind and purpose. I wanted the kind of happiness that comes not from getting what I want, but from giving something without judgment or expectation.

"I'm the luckiest guy, Michael," he said. "You've no idea."

"Will you take me along sometime?" I asked.

He would. We'd meet at the Starbucks "by the Sanctuary at Yonge and Charles Streets." This was a couple of blocks away from where I first laid eyes on Darcy Sheppard.

Through Jay I learned about Sanctuary Ministries, a Christian charity that is much more than a soup kitchen (if only because the food is fantastic). Sanctuary houses a community, but no beds. It's a community of the homeless, of Rosedale scions alongside squeegee kids, of university students, and of hardened street soldiers. They all are shoulder-to-shoulder in that basement, or upstairs helping those who sometimes can't help themselves. Through drop-ins, street outreach, and one-to-one relationships, they provide food, clothing, and basic health care. Mostly it's a bunch of friends helping each other.

I was not allowed to "volunteer," Greg Paul told me. He's their leader, though not formally. An ordained man of the cloth. Hair buzzed back, slim, fit. He resembled a rock star or a professional cyclist, rather than a minister to people of the streets.

We were in the basement of the Sanctuary, originally a stately mansion before it was overrun by porn video shops, condos, shawarma joints, and parking lots smelling of urine, around the corner from the gay village. The Sanctuary basement smelled of food and wet socks.

"What do I do when I come here?" I asked Greg.

"Just grab a seat. Hang out. If someone asks for a coffee, go ahead and get it for them but you don't get to hide behind the authority of being a volunteer kitchen worker. We have staff for that."

"But what about them?" I pointed at women and men passing out plates. They'd come from another job, wearing official and unofficial uniforms of the employed.

"They're members of the community. Earned the privilege of serving others. You need to become a member of this community first, if you'd like."

Greg was treating me like a celebrity, introducing me to people, and he'd clearly blocked off time for me, at the behest of Jay. Greg showed me around the place. The office. The health-care "centre" (a room), the "library" (a book shelf), Marie's Kitchen (where Donny is the "boss"; I make a Donny and Marie joke), the "chapel" (a gymnasium upstairs), where there would be a book and CD launch, Greg told me.

The next night, the chapel was converted into a bandshell where books and CDs were for sale. The back room had Styrofoam cups full of Cheezies and cans of generic-brand pop and coffee, but that room didn't get opened up until after the festivities began. When it was announced that the food room was open, there was a stampede of dozens—about half the crowd—from the metal chairs facing the stage.

I was too afraid to dance to the band's rock but I wanted to. Everyone was dancing. The dance floor was full. Everyone was happier than any group of people I'd ever seen, outside of my fellowship of recovery. I sat on a chair beside a fellow who was mentally handicapped in some vague fashion. Stuffing his mouth with Cheezies, he was bragging about being able to live on his own. On the other side of him was watchful Jay, who got up periodically to check out empty rooms in the church for sleeping giants. A woman was crying, makeup going all Alice Cooper on her, and Jay took her someplace where dignity was restored. This is what Jay Barton does.

I was welcomed completely, but not yet part of the community. It would take some time. But that night it felt, after an hour or so, that it was time for me to go.

I shook Jay's hand goodbye. He followed me out to where a guy with an Expos hat stood, apparently on duty for general crisis management. We all shook hands again and I walked down the stairs. They stood at the top of the stairs, chatting; my back was to them as I descended.

Then something happened.

The band was playing music loud enough to dance to. Perfect volume, actually. It was very difficult to have a conversation amidst that volume but not impossible. So Jay and his friend shouted at each other, not worried that I could hear them over the din.

But it was as if the music were a breeze, a breeze that blew all sounds down those stairs. So I heard their conversation perfectly. I don't understand the physics of it all, but I overheard them.

"You met Michael?" Jay asked.

"Yeah, good to have another tall guy around here." We were apparently the same height. It took me a few seconds to realize they were talking about me.

Jay's voice: "Yeah, he's *really* hurting—"

"Yeah, for sure.... Read in the newspaper—then heard from Greg ... Yeah, Jay, you did outreach ... outreach—for Michael? ... — for how long?"

"A while. Called him—about a month after the arrest. Yeah, REALLY hurting ... and also ... even after charges dropped ... after the breakfast.... Had to keep calling ... hurting.... Then another coffee, you know HOW IT IS.... Slowly ... Came yesterday ... but he's getting better—"

I was frozen now, at the bottom of the stairs, looking out onto Charles Street, the sidewalks full of people in their twenties mostly, the 8 p.m. crowd. The music seemed far away, Jay's words echoing in my head. I felt like Bruce Willis's character at the end of *The Sixth Sense*.

I'd fallen for the oldest charity trick in the book: thinking that I was offering charity to others, in helping Jay Barton, while the opposite was true. He and all the other people at the Sanctuary were helping me, bringing me back to life, to connection with other human beings, to my own humanity.

TEN

For the Defence: Marie Henein

Marie Henein should have a comic book series done on her. Her Clark Kent nameplate says criminal defence counsel, but she's a superhero to me and everyone she rescues. It's impossible to describe Marie without saying the word tough. Street legal worn, turned out tough. The toughest I've known. My ex-wife Susan is considered tough by many, and Susan was plain old scared of Marie.

"She should be," Marie replied when I told her. Without smiling. But tough is often misunderstood, I think. Former Supreme Court Judge Frank Iacobucci explained this to me. He said, for lawyers, you've got to be smart to be tough. Otherwise, it's just bluster. To be tough requires forging a path against great resistance, full of obstacles, with a clear, difficult target on the horizon. It was John Wayne who said, "If you've got them by the balls, their hearts and minds will follow." That's smart/tough.

Doorbell rang. I could see the silhouette of Marie Henein and a young man, through the translucent curtains covering the front door window. It was around 6 p.m., September 1. When I opened the door of my house, to let in Marie with her associate, I was surprised at how pretty she looked, for someone who was clearly ferocious. Her high heels looked particularly expensive, which said something because lawyers like their shoes. Often it's the only accessory that's their own, once they have the generic black gowns put over their white-collared barrister shirts and black vests.

I recall that she had an overcoat on, and shook out an umbrella. But that makes no sense because it never rained that day. Her height was difficult to discern. Those shoes were high, the leather looked like it had come off an endangered species, and the cut was something that could have been in the Museum of Modern Art.

Marie has different looks, different masks. Of Lebanese descent, she's dark and her hair is short; curvy and lean at the same time. Her brown eyes are big and brooding, hard and unhappy. Jovial is not how I saw her most of the time, during our time together with me as her client. Marie is in the rescue business, after all. Like a veteran paramedic, she's seen it all.

Standing in my doorway, briefcase in hand, Marie shook Susan's hand, said hello sweetly to my inquiring kids, then switched from mom to poker-faced lawyer while I blinked.

Marie had a look about her that I'd not seen before except in a boxing ring, or on Reggie Jackson's face as he went up to hit his third home run in one night during the World Series. The Yankees' manager, Billy Martin, said that the look on Reggie's face was such that he'd have been shocked if Reggie had NOT hit a home run at the plate. Marie had that look and I'd see it over and over again as we worked together.

We went to the top floor of the house. Her associate, Jordan Glick, sat at the desk because he was using the computer. I sat on a chair across from Marie, who was nonplussed to be sitting on an uncomfortable bench. We formed a triangle.

"So what happened?" she asked.

ONE DOESN'T HAVE TO BE a former Attorney General to figure out that the first order of business after being arrested is getting a lawyer. Or at least I should have been able to figure that out. However, the process of retaining someone to represent me through to a trial, of finding someone to save my life in a courtroom, was complicated by my state of mind. Having kept my wits about me during the period of incarceration, which followed on the heels of the 28 seconds itself, my brain basically shut down. Although I needed to make some critical decisions, the store of my mental faculties was closed for business.

Upon reflection, this would be common for most people charged with crimes, which is why the presumption of innocence is so important: the vulnerability of the accused is acute; their capacity could not be lower, and the risk to their freedom could not be higher.

The morning after I'd been released, September 2, I wandered into the kitchen a few minutes after waking to have a telephone waved in my direction. I felt as if still in a trance, and I wondered how I'd gotten from bed to kitchen floor, and I had no idea why I was taking the telephone and putting it to my ear.

"Hello?"

Men's voices began coming out of the telephone receiver. It sounded like adults do in Charlie Brown cartoons. I held the phone out and asked Susan what was going on.

"It's Peter Lukasiewicz and P—," she was whispering loudly. These were her partners, technically her boss was Peter. And they'd been put on hold for about five minutes so the indicted Mr. Magoo could get his butt downstairs to get the urgent advice as to whom he ought to retain as his criminal defence counsel.

Lukasiewicz and P— had consulted with the best minds on the subject, and were offering to me their learned shortlist of defence counsel that I should retain, given the (freakishly unprecedented) circumstances.

"Oh," I said to Susan, then put the phone back to my ear.

"... which is why we'd recommend the following, in no particular order...." And they listed the names of five criminal lawyers who were well known to me, followed by their expert analysis of each.

They were careful not to be unequivocal about anyone. It's true that any one of those five people would have done an excellent job. It was September 2, and I was feeling capable of little more than breathing at that moment, and also maybe of drinking coffee. I have no recollection of how I responded to this telephone call. At some point I hung up.

The next few days were long and slow. Everything moved glacially in my brain, as if underwater, or like the dreams where you're sprinting in quicksand. Each day that passed, I gathered a little more information about whom to retain. (On my behalf, Susan had retained Marie Henein as interim counsel, but all concerned understood that I'd need a little time to make a decision about who would be my lawyer beyond the interim stage.)

Other lawyers I would call for their counsel on counsel included criminal lawyers Peter Dotsikas, David Porter (a former colleague from McCarthy's), and Alison Wheeler, a brilliant criminal lawyer with whom I'd clerked at the Supreme Court of Canada. She was a contemporary, but always a little on the scarier side of scary-smart. She'd also been mentored by Eddie Greenspan, Canada's most famous living criminal lawyer, and Alison had worked with Marie Henein, who was on everyone's shortlist.

Alison gave me good advice early on in my search: "Here's what everyone accused of a crime should consider when choosing their lawyer. You need to get on with your life. You're innocent, Michael, and you need to recover, get a job, be a husband, be a dad, live your life. You can't be co–defence counsel on this case. You need to let go of the case. That means finding someone you trust to do more on your behalf than you could possibly do yourself."

There was a consensus about Marie Henein, although not everyone put her at the top of their list. Some men found her aggression to be too aggressive. I'd experienced this benign sexism before. Aggressive men are tough, they'd say; aggressive women are "shrill."

That initial decision of whom to retain took longer than it should have, but my brain wasn't picking up much speed. I could digest a little information each day, but not much more. Near the end of that first week, David Porter was instrumental in talking me through all the factors at play in my case. He pulled over to the side of the road and gave me close to an hour on the phone, and had clearly put his mind to it in advance.

While I was making the decision, Marie continued to act as interim counsel. It could have been uncomfortable but she made it otherwise. When it came to making decisions about the case, or presenting the analysis, she was extremely direct. When it came to whom I should retain, she was gracious and patient.

In our first conversation, she said, as interim counsel: "I don't need the file, Michael. You won't hurt my feelings if you retain someone else. Just make a decision about who's best for your case."

"SO WHAT HAPPENED?" We're on the top floor of my house. A few hours previous, I'd been in a cell at Toronto Police Service's Traffic Division. Jordan Glick is at his laptop, sitting at my wife's home-office desk. Marie is seated across from me.

I spoke for about an hour, and I've no recollection of any of it.

After we'd finished talking we went down the stairs. Following some preliminary talk about meeting the next day, Marie and Jordan left and went back to the office. In the car, she was quiet. Thinking loudly.

"What do you think?" he asked.

"Not sure yet."

Something didn't seem right to her. She'd heard the media reports, which had already found me guilty of the road-rage killing of a cyclist. Marie would hear her client out, of course, but she was used to clients having a warped sense of what had happened. They often were terrible witnesses of their own actions. Ideally, they are never called to the stand to testify. The mind plays tricks on people, constantly, especially amidst the chaos of an incident that ends in death.

Road rage, road rage, road rage. News of my release on conditions was leading the radio newscasts on their drive back to Marie's office. The call-in shows were discussing road rage, some with a psychologist as the special guest, all speculating on what had happened during the 28 seconds—though no one knew yet that's all it took.

When Marie was first telephoned by Susan, early on September 1, she hadn't leapt to any conclusions about my actions. Keep in mind, the seasoned defence counsel does not start every case convinced of their client's innocence. It's not the point. The point is that defence counsel must represent their client, to the best of their ability, in defending the charges. Regardless of Marie's personal judgment, she would represent me as best she could.

So if, in fact, the evidence had confirmed road rage, Marie's job would have been to dismantle that evidence: exclude it, discredit it, contradict it, drown it, destroy it with advocacy and evidence to the contrary. Motions to throw out damning evidence, cross examinations to impeach witness testimony, defence experts throwing doubt on the prosecution's case. That was totally up her alley.

But this case quickly appeared to her to have nothing to do with a road rage incident.

Firstly, the people claiming to be witnesses, who were interviewed by the media, weren't describing the driver (me) yelling or shaking his fist or honking his horn. Secondly, while Marie didn't know me personally, even the damning media reports admitted no history of my having anger issues. Lastly, her office was getting phone calls and emails from people, many directed to her through Andy Evangelista. People were calling about Darcy Sheppard. A picture was forming in Marie's mind about the man who'd died. In her mind, that man was sounding less and less like a road-rage victim, and more and more like a road rager himself.

THE NEXT MORNING, September 2, the day after I was released, I took a taxi to Marie Henein's office. I was about two hours late for the appointment. No idea why.

I stood outside her building, looking at the address on the door, and looking down at the note I'd fished out of my pocket. It was one and the same. I recall the day as raining, pouring, but when I double-checked the weather for September 2, 2009, it was sunny and 20°C.

As I stood there on the sidewalk, I overheard two people having a conversation.

"No, I thought that he was with his wife—"

"Yes, his wife. That's what I said. But the courier didn't hit the wife. Where'd you hear that?"

I followed them. They were talking about me, and my case, unaware that I was in earshot.

"What's going to happen, you think? ... When will it go to trial?"

"Who knows? Feel sorry for the ..."

I stopped. Not sure who was the object of his sympathy. As I walked the half block back to Marie's building, someone spotted me from across the street. The person pointed straight at me, elbowing their friend, all in slow motion, it seemed:

"There'sssssss ... Michaelllllll ... Bryyyyyaant ..."

I scurried into the building and up the stairs to Marie's office.

Walking up the stairs, I couldn't find the offices at first. Then I poked my head into the reception area, where I was waved in.

"Hi. I'm Michael Bryant, here for Marie Henein."

A professional-looking receptionist blinked. In front of her was a *Toronto Star*, the entire front page of which was completely devoted to "Bryant's Deadly Duel," as the headline read. Half the front page was the face standing before the receptionist. She blinked again.

She firmly took my coat.

"Take a seat. Coffee?"

I accepted and sat down in the waiting room. I'd never done that before, waited for a lawyer. I'd never been a client before. I stared at the table covered with magazines, but the words made little sense to me.

Marie's office is in downtown Toronto, broadly speaking, as nondescript as one would expect of a defence counsel's office. Criminal defence practices are lean operations. Most are sole practitioners. Most clients can't or won't pay their full bill. For almost all, and for most of their career, the earnings pale in comparison to high-priced corporate lawyers (boardroom) or civil litigators (courtroom). Moreover, people allegedly involved in crimes are not infrequently the targets of other crimes. A criminal law practice may not be at a secret location, but neither is it Rockefeller Center.

To the right of the reception area was a large boardroom. The doors were usually closed. To the left was a hallway. At one end was a coffee room, washrooms, and some storage rooms. At the other end of the hallway was a larger bullpen of secretary work stations, a photocopier, and huge filing cabinets. Along the wall were offices: Marie's, her associates', and a few offices rented by sole practitioners with their own practices separate from Marie's.

The lawyers who worked on my file, as Marie's "associates" or juniors, were all young, serious, smart, and anemic from the workload. Margaret Bojanowska, Matthew Gourlay, Jordan Glick, Danielle Robitaille. Margaret was the second-in-command.

As I waited with my coffee, staring at the hardwood floors, the sound of expensive heels on hardwood echoed off the walls, building louder and louder, until Marie appeared in the reception area, slightly hunched, unsmiling, eyes peering forward, as if she were looking over reading glasses that weren't there. A stylish, expensive suit was on display, and again the shoes of a countess. Countess Henein, at your service.

"You've got coffee. You found the office. You're late but that's okay because you're all dumb from what happened. Would you prefer to talk in the boardroom or my office?"

"Ummm."

"Follow me."

We went to her office. There were two white chairs, but only one didn't have books on it. A gargantuan Apple computer sat atop her desk, along with a few file folders, and some notes. She smiled and then relaxed, asking me, quite carefully, how I was doing.

The next few days, that first week, I was in her office a few times but not much could be done until I decided whom I was going to retain. When I finally made the decision to retain Marie, I called to let her know.

"Good," she said, no more or less excited to represent me than any other client. "Can you come into the office tomorrow? I want to go through what we've got so far."

As it turned out, what she'd collected "so far" was nothing less than a bucket of bombshells.

ON THE MORNING OF September 2, less than 24 hours after Marie had been retained on an interim basis, she arrived at the office to an overflowing voicemail box. It wasn't yet in the media that she was interim counsel, nor did we want that to become public. If I'd ended up retaining someone else, it would have been bad form to have identified her in any way as an also-ran.

Meanwhile, my buddy Andy Evangelista had been fielding calls non-stop since he'd landed himself on the front page of every newspaper in Canada. Andrew was there beside me when I'd been released. The media identified him, incorrectly, as one of my lawyers. So he received an avalanche of calls and emails, some helpful, some not, in regard to the case. It meant that he spent a good deal of time sifting through emails from crackpots and stretcher bearers alike.

Andy quickly began working with Marie.

"I'm getting all these calls from people, and a tonne of emails, all saying that they've been attacked by this Darcy Sheppard guy," Andy told Marie.

Both Andy and Marie, experienced lawyers in their own fields, were rightly skeptical about such callers. Some people might be sharing their delusional fantasies, others their tales of woe that involved a cyclist, but not necessarily the cyclist Darcy Sheppard. Police are very familiar with this phenomenon, wherein callers offer up information that turns out to be useless to their investigation.

However, Marie took nothing for granted, and always checked her own assumptions. She told Andy that they had to take all of these people seriously. Marie and her colleagues in the firm would weed through it all, even if it was a fruitless exercise. Needle in a haystack, Marie thought at the time.

The volume of calls and emails, however, was unlike anything Marie had experienced. Andrew would pass along messages to Marie, and where necessary refer them to Marie directly. She'd sit at her desk with her associates across from her, taking notes, reviewing the transcript of the voicemail or the email. Or they'd go over notes of a conversation she'd taken or those taken by another lawyer. On the desk was her massive Apple iMac, a pile of transcripts, and a notebook. Much coffee was consumed.

Again and again, people were telling stories about a cyclist who'd attacked them in their car, in a fashion remarkably like that described in the media as what had occurred during the 28 seconds. This didn't shock Marie so much—copycat stories, she thought.

One of those callers had the initials B.S., which led to a few guffaws.

This guy had reported that in August he was driving down Bloor Street—less than a month before my 28 seconds, on the very road where it had happened—and saw a cyclist ahead of him weaving in and out of different lanes. Then, at the light, the driver had been blocked by the cyclist while waiting in the passing lane. There was an empty right lane, plus also maybe an empty bike lane at that part of Bloor Street, but this cyclist was using the left lane, without any intention of turning left. So the driver tapped on his horn, to let the cyclist know there was a car behind him. No response. Fine, the driver thought, and drove past the cyclist on the left side as there was no traffic.

The driver continued down the road, stopping at a red light, not giving the cyclist a second thought. Suddenly Mr. B.S.'s window was smacked by the cyclist, and—

"Hold it," Marie said. "Did he say that the cyclist had been weaving in and out of different lanes?"

Pages were flipped backwards.

"Yes," Margaret responded. "He said he could see the cyclist up ahead, weaving in and out of different lanes, near Bloor and Lansdowne."

Marie stared at her associates. Their eyebrows went up, as if to say: "So what?"

"Bryant said that Sheppard was weaving in and out of the lanes, from the top of the street to the bottom, dodging traffic heading in both directions. That's what Bryant told us, several times," Marie said. "But there's no reference in the media reports of Darcy Sheppard weaving in and out of traffic in front of Michael."

Jordan started a search on his laptop to double-check. Nothing in the mainstream media, or the blogs, or anywhere referring to this remarkable feat that I'd seen, of Sheppard weaving in and out of traffic.

"Maybe a coincidence," Marie said. "Keep going."

"Okay," Margaret continued reading from the voicemail transcript. "The caller said that the cyclist came up to his car on the left-hand side and slapped his window. The cyclist was—"

"Wait," Marie said. "Michael said that Darcy Sheppard took a swing at him, approaching from the driver's side. Michael's convertible top was down and window was down. Sounds like this guy's slap to the driver's side window."

"Nothing," Jordan said, having already looked it up in the media search.

Nothing about Sheppard taking a swing at me was in the media, but I'd mentioned it in my 911 call, and also to Marie and her team.

"Keep going," Marie said, her voice betraying nothing.

"Cyclist was angry, inches from the window ... Spitting ... Losing his mind."

Marie leaned forward for the first time that day, her hands on the desk: "Did the caller say that the cyclist was 'losing his mind'?"

"Right from the transcript. He said that he was, quote, 'losing his mind.'"

They all looked at each other. If I'd said that same thing once, I'd said it a dozen times to them: Darcy Sheppard seemed "psychotic" during the 28 seconds, like he'd lost his mind.

But it got even more familiar. Mr. B.S. drove away from the cyclist—who, the driver insisted, looked like the man identified in the newspaper as Darcy Sheppard. Blocks down the road, the cyclist came up on his left and struck his left-side rearview mirror, dislodging it from its housing. Swerving to the right down

Brunswick Avenue, the driver called 911 and told the dispatcher that a cyclist had knocked the mirror off his car. During the call, he watched as Sheppard straddled his bike, just as I'd seen him straddle his bike during the 28 seconds.

As the 911 call confirmed, just as the driver was explaining his location to the dispatcher, the cyclist raced toward the vehicle and threw a brick through the driver's side rear passenger window. The dispatcher could hear the sound of impact. The driver would retell all this to police officers, who obviously took extensive notes, and he kept the bill as proof of body-shop repair that was needed.

Marie has a voice that doesn't seem loud, but is always very, very clear. She doesn't raise it, because she doesn't have to.

"Get the repair bill, get the 911 records, and get me this guy's address. We're going to his house. Right now."

It was Marie's practice to never send private detectives or clerks or stenographers to conduct an interview with a witness. She always did it herself, or had a trusted junior do the interview, but only after having seen Marie do it about a hundred times. They recorded it, and secured a signature from the person swearing to its accuracy, as soon as possible. And it was always done immediately, as soon as they learned of it. Otherwise, memories fade, or people move, or lawyers plumb forget to do it in a timely manner.

When Marie was able to interview this witness, Mr. B.S., she asked him if he recognized the photo of Darcy Sheppard that had been in the media, a copy of which Marie had with her.

There was no hesitation. He'd been attacked by Darcy Sheppard.

THE VOLUME OF CALLS and emails was staggering to Marie. After the first night, she hired someone to remain in the office, through the night, to take messages and get as much information as they could, from dusk 'til dawn.

Marie also completely revamped her law firm's computer security. Wi-Fi was out. Everything was hard-wired, and a big investment was made in new security to avoid any possibility of the files being hacked. A pseudonym was used for my file. If anyone did hack into the system, which would seem impossible with a firewall around all her files and no Wi-Fi, they'd never find a file with the name Michael Bryant.

Of the many emails and calls that Andy received those first few days, one stood out as both too good to be true and too important to ignore. So much so that he made sure that I was copied on his email to Marie, with photographs attached to the email. Supposedly someone had taken photos of Darcy Sheppard attacking a car much like I'd been attacked.

Whatever, I thought. Marie will take care of it. I didn't even open up the attachments to see them. But Marie did, and what she saw blew her mind.

David Wires was a lawyer—a civil litigation specialist, not a photographer. However, Wires had no choice but to become chronicler of the activities of a number of bike couriers outside his offices near Adelaide and York Streets, in downtown Toronto, where he and his clients had faced abuse from the courier cabal. Wires was a disgruntled tenant in his commercial building. He took plenty of photos because there was plenty of unruly conduct to photograph—for the landlord, and potentially for a civil action, or even for the police, one day.

When David Wires saw the media photographs of Darcy Sheppard, he recognized him right away. He'd seen Sheppard many times, and often Darcy was drunk and belligerent. He'd photographed Darcy in just such a state, several times, from his office.

So Wires jumped on his computer and started scrolling through the photographs until he came upon the one that he remembered. There were a number of vivid digital shots of Sheppard attacking a BMW. Attaching the photos to an email, he sent a message to Andrew Evangelista, who forwarded them to Marie and me.

Marie opened the files on her Mac and printed them out on a colour printer. She blinked a few times, recalling my description of the 28 seconds. This seemed a photographic display of my description of Sheppard on my car, albeit it was a BMW in the photo, not my convertible.

IT DID, HOWEVER, have a New York State licence plate that was clearly visible. Marie made a phone call to get the plate traced, and asked her assistant to get the photos enlarged.

When I next saw Marie she opened up a binder with 8×10 photos showing a man launching himself into a car.

I gasped. Marie watched my reaction. I looked at her, my forehead creased. No words were spoken.

Then she turned the page to an enlarged photo of the man, from a different angle. He was clearly visible. Then another such photo.

"If that's Darcy Sheppard," Marie said, pointing at the photo of him attacking the driver of the BMW, "then—"

"That's Darcy Sheppard," I said.

"Okay, but I'd rather someone else confirm that person as Darcy Sheppard."

"The photographer?"

"No, the driver."

My face twisted up. Before I could ask how on earth she'd find that information, she pointed at the licence plate. Pretty clear, all right.

The man driving the BMW became perhaps the most important witness establishing Darcy Sheppard's capacity for aggression with motor vehicles, and the threat that Sheppard posed to a driver. In this case, the driver was a senior executive in the United States with a black belt in karate; he would eventually testify that his encounter with Sheppard was life-threatening. I've never been able to thank either man for the courage to speak out, and for the remarkable foresight of Wires's photography. Many people came forward, but none were more important than these men.

"If this is Darcy Sheppard," Marie said, her voice rising, "this would be the most powerful piece of Scopelliti evidence I've ever seen." Scopelliti evidence is similar-fact evidence used by an accused arguing self-defence. If the accused was responding to an act of aggression, then self-defence is basically established, if that reaction wasn't wildly disproportionate to the threat. The Supreme Court of Canada, in a case called *R. v. Scopelliti,* allowed the defence to introduce similar-fact evidence establishing that the victim of a self-defence tended to be an aggressor. In plain English, in my case, "Scopelliti evidence" was important to my defence. It showed that Darcy Sheppard was probably the aggressor during our 28 seconds.

ELEVEN

My Elder; His Widow

There are a lot of famous gaits, famous entrances, that have stuck with me. Early in my term as Minister of Aboriginal Affairs, I went to the Assembly of First Nations annual general meeting. As National Chief Phil Fontaine entered the room in which I was waiting, it was akin to the entrance of a rock star. He *was* a rock star—surrounded by a half-dozen aides and advisers, his long hair flowing behind him, a strong smile, and a crusher of a handshake. His first words to me were: "How's your father?"

Phil Fontaine is the most successful aboriginal politician in the history of Canada. Getting re-elected as a national chief is a rare occurrence. Only once has a chief served three terms. Fontaine did so amidst a time of enormous hope and turmoil. His success was based on lowering expectations and building consensus. His grasp and his reach were as one, and for that he was respected.

Fontaine, like a good politician, remembered details about people that often shocked and always impressed. Chief Fontaine had indeed worked with my dad during the formation of the First Nations Financing Authority. My dad was the General Counsel and drafted and negotiated most of its terms. As my father lived in Victoria, it was not obvious that there was a connection between the General Counsel and the Ontario Minister of Aboriginal Affairs. It was one made instantly by Fontaine, however.

We immediately hit it off. We shared very personal stories about our political challenges, and our families. Susan and I hosted Fontaine and his partner Kathleen Mahoney, of the University of Calgary, for dinner one night. We kept in touch by phone when each of us left politics in 2009.

Fontaine called me several times after the 28 seconds. When I finally got around to answering him, he arranged to come to my house for a visit. At some point, there was a knock on my front door, and I opened it to see the National Chief standing there, alone. He'd taken a cab to my house, and joined me inside for coffee.

He offered many words of support and made it clear that he'd do anything to assist. At one point, he suggested that I meet Fred Kelly.

I looked at him, unsure of the name, but my brain was wobbly. Fred Kelly sounded familiar, nonetheless.

"Fred's my Elder. He's my spiritual ... leader. He's one of the most respected Elders in the country. And he has been of great help to people facing challenges like yours."

I never imagined that I'd face a challenge that would be worth the time of a First Nations Elder. He'd no doubt counselled survivors of Canada's residential schools, wherein children were taken from their mothers, made to assimilate, and often abused in schools far from their communities. Fontaine himself had been a product of residential schools.

I was immediately attracted to the idea of meeting with a First Nations Elder. Firstly, I'd always felt a kinship with aboriginal spirituality during the many rituals performed while I was an MPP. In my riding, there was an aboriginal men's residence designed to help some transition out of poverty or prison into society. I attended many of their gatherings. After all, I'd studied and practised aboriginal law, and Canada's history in this area had deeply affected me as a young man.

In government, I'd attended dozens of smudge ceremonies, drum ceremonies, and powwows. Figuring out how to dance around a room to the drum beat, while all eyes are upon you, was more difficult than participating in a drum ceremony—an enormous honour I enjoyed twice in my life, as Minister of Aboriginal Affairs.

Most meetings with First Nations Chiefs or Métis leaders began with a prayer and the burning of ceremonial tobacco, usually led by the words of an Elder. There was something about those words, the voices of the Elders, the feel of those ceremonies, to which I felt a connection.

What made Fontaine's offer more poignant was Darcy Sheppard's heritage. While he'd never sought official status as a person of First Nations descent, he would have qualified. Sheppard did identify himself as Métis.

After Fontaine completed the introductions, I exchanged emails with Fred Kelly, who was extremely warm and articulate. He invited me to join him in Ottawa, and offered an address that I handed to a taxi driver at the Ottawa airport. I'm not sure what I was expecting, but it wasn't his home. The day was rainy, blustery, and chilly, sometime in December, a few months after the accident.

Kelly was strikingly handsome and fit, with the hair of a movie star. He offered me some coffee. We sat at his kitchen table to discuss what would happen that day.

It began with a smudge ceremony, and sharing a peace pipe, each of us taking a turn inhaling the ceremonial tobacco. I'd brought some tobacco with me, and offered it to him in a formal gesture often expected when greeting an Elder, and sometimes a chief. (I had some leftover from my Aboriginal Affairs days. About a half-dozen little sacks of cloth, containing special tobacco, and tied with a ribbon or a string. My chief adviser Douglas Sanderson, a Cree, had helped me keep a number on hand—like a business card for an aboriginal affairs politician.)

What happened next is considered sacred, and not to be shared publicly. Kelly did say that I could recount some highlights. I spent the day there, six hours or so, before he kindly drove me to the airport. There was a mini sweat-lodge set up, many prayers, much talking, plenty of silences. At one point I shared a recurring dream with Kelly, who was quite startled by the details, and it prompted him to hold a naming ceremony. After several rituals, he presented me with a feather and named me Eagle. It's one of my most prized possessions.

Elder Kelly was very clear about a few things. Firstly, he conveyed to me that Darcy Sheppard was in "a better place." Secondly, he said that I was now bonded to Kelly eternally. We were, as he put it, "brothers." Lastly, Elder Kelly went out of his way to address my own feelings—of shame, and of course the grief I felt regarding Sheppard's death. I can't say much more about what happened that day, but afterwards, I was changed.

Occasionally, we get together and visit, particularly when he is in Toronto, and keep in touch via email and Facebook. In the spring of 2010, we met for a coffee at a downtown hotel. After exchanging pleasantries, and then catching up at length, I told him of a dream I'd had, watching a killer whale, severely wounded, its fin gouged and moving tentatively, coming toward me. He replied that I was healing.

After a time, he sat back and started speaking about an experience he'd recently had. I could barely believe my ears.

"A few weeks ago, I was meeting with a young woman who'd been sent to me by a good friend. She had lost someone in her life, and I was to perform a ceremony that would assist her in letting go."

Fred paused, sipped his coffee, and continued.

"I asked her to write a letter, to the man who'd died, but either she misunderstood or understood well what she wanted. When she handed me the letter, I was shocked. It was a letter addressed to Michael Bryant, asking for help. Here it is."

The letter was from Darcy Sheppard's widow.

When Darcy Sheppard was 20, he married Tracey. (Tracey speaks openly about her life, online and otherwise, but I'll omit her last name to protect her children's privacy.) They had two children, then separated, and in January 2000 Tracey lost custody and access to her three children, two of whom were Darcy's. Initially, Darcy gained custody of his two kids, but eventually Tracey's mother came and took the children away, with the help of the Children's Aid Society.

A recovering addict, Tracey had been off her narcotic of choice for some time, while continuing on physician-supervised methadone treatment. (Properly dosed, methadone patients can reduce or stop altogether their use of heroin or morphine, but it's supposed to be a means to an end—namely, abstinence from all drugs and alcohol.)

Tracey wanted help getting supervised access to her children. So she wrote a letter to the only lawyer, she said, "who might actually help me." How she knew that giving that letter to Fred Kelly would mean I would read it remains a mystery to me.

I was initially elated. The opportunity to help Darcy Sheppard's children and their mother seemed like a divine gift to me. Moreover, I was being asked for help, which is always a gift to be returned in kind. Or so I'd learned from my time in recovery from alcoholism, where helping others, rather than oneself, is a blessing of the highest order.

My wife was not so ecstatic. In fact, she was fearful for me, for her, and for anything having anything to do with the 28 seconds. It was no doubt wise counsel, but I couldn't accept it. And so getting involved in Tracey's child access proceedings drove Susan and me apart still further.

The summer of 2010, I drove out to meet Tracey and her boyfriend (now husband) in a town near Brockville. We met in a little park on the grounds of a community college, across from the Tim Hortons. Standing beside Tracey was her boyfriend, whom I'll call Jack, and one of her college teachers, who was also a social worker.

Tracey wore a huge smile and gave me a hug. Her hair was pulled back from her face in a ponytail, blondish hair, large eyes, sweatshirt and jeans. To me, she looked like a mom with young children—in her late twenties or so. A very hyper mom: Tracey spoke very fast and enthusiastically. She was bursting with energy and emotion.

Jack was a few years younger than her, which she joked about. He was tall, lanky, quiet, and boyish. Of the pair, they were quite different on the outside, but clearly shared a common struggle against their demons on the inside.

Jack had purchased a large double-double and a donut for me. "Hope the coffee's still warm," he said.

"That's his disposable income for the month, Michael," the college teacher said, allowing me to appreciate the generosity. Jack was of First Nations descent, so I knew not to insult his greeting gift by offering to reimburse him.

They were rich in spirit, poor in income. Both were recovering from addiction and attending doctor visits regularly. When I asked to exchange telephone numbers, Tracey told me she didn't have one this month. They were surviving on welfare alone.

"Congratulations on your grades," I offered to Tracey. She'd sent me a copy of her recent transcript. Straight A's. She seemed rightly proud.

She spoke fondly of Darcy. Tracey had seen him in the weeks before he died. He was squatting at her place, with another woman, until Tracey told them to go back to Toronto, because of all the partying.

At one point she wept quietly, wiping away her tears as she spoke of Darcy and me, the 28 seconds.

"I'm sorry for you and for your family.... *Dammit* ... He was going to die, Michael," she said. Tracey was trying to comfort me, and I found it uncomfortable. I was here to help her. Not the other way around.

That said, I just accepted her kindness. I didn't want to push her, or ask her a bunch of questions about him, although she said some things in passing about him that I hadn't known.

"Darcy's father's name was Bear. Indian. He died, run over by a car. How crazy is that?"

"Oh, Darcy," she exclaimed at one point, "he always talked about his crazy dreams. About making some money. He'd pay back all the support he owed me, he always promised," and she laughed. "Never paid me a cent, that.... Well it wasn't his fault, really. He just couldn't get his life together."

We talked about her old life, her new life, about Darcy, and her inability to manage the legal system. I said I'd do everything I could to help. We agreed to keep in touch through the college teacher. As I drove away, she seemed to be weeping, overwhelmed. I literally prayed that I could help her, in some way.

Through Marie Henein, I paired Tracey up with one of Canada's most famous family lawyers, Martha McCarthy, whose firm took on the file pro bono. I agreed to cover some out-of-pocket expenses of her law firm—the disbursement costs of filing and serving and travelling by the lawyers.

"Now you need to let go of this," Martha said to me. "I don't want you involved." So I did.

Then, in early 2012, Tracey and I spoke on the telephone. We spoke about the non-profit foundation she was working on, to help parents facing the challenges of having lost custody of their children. And she shared with me a couple YouTube videos of her kids that had been posted. Her daughter's singing voice was pretty stunning in a cover of a familiar hit. Darcy's child.

TWELVE

The Defence

A fter criminal charges have been laid, and a lawyer is retained, the next thing that happens is referred to simply as "disclosure." Prior to the *Charter of Rights and Freedoms,* the obligation on the police and prosecutors to show their cards was minimal. The prosecutors could spring a witness or a wiretap on the defence during trial, leading to a lot of scrambling by the defence to address the damning evidence. However, a year before I began clerking at the Supreme Court of Canada, a landmark decision was released, called *Stinchcombe.* It was written by one of Canada's greatest barristers, Mr. Justice John Sopinka, and a majority of the Court agreed with him.

Ever since *Stinchcombe* was rendered in 1991, there has been an obligation on the prosecution to disclose to the defence all the information it has—whether it helps or hurts the prosecution's case—in order to allow the accused to prepare a defence. This has to happen early in the proceedings. If it's discovered that the prosecution withheld some information, then the charges can be thrown out.

The "disclosure package," as it's often called, is provided to defence counsel usually in dribs and drabs, as it comes to the police and prosecutors. In my case, disclosure came in several instalments.

In the first batch, Marie noticed no reference in the disclosure to the people who had contacted us about Darcy Sheppard.

This seemed odd because sometimes the people said that they'd contacted the police first to alert them of their stories, but no such reference was made in the disclosure. As I learned, sometimes the police need to be specifically asked for certain evidence for it to be discovered. This was not the first time my unqualified confidence in our justice system was deflated.

Moreover, Marie knew that many people might have called the police, but never shared their stories. We kept hearing, second- or third-hand, about someone who had contacted the police and received no response.

So Marie asked for the contact information for anybody who had contacted the police regarding *Attorney General v. Michael Bryant*. And with that, we struck gold.

Over a dozen people had contacted the police with information helpful to my case, but the police had failed to investigate any of these witnesses' stories. If their evidence was exculpatory, it seems that the police were uninterested in it.

As each name and telephone number or email address came in, Marie and our legal team would follow up with an interview. We gathered some very compelling evidence demonstrating that Darcy Sheppard had attacked people before, and done so increasingly during the month leading up to my encounter with him. It appears that he was getting more and more aggressive.

To be fair to the prosecution, they were learning of this exculpatory evidence at the same time as we were getting contact information from the police. Later, the prosecution would work with the police to review all that evidence, all those witnesses. The prosecution, in other words, did a thorough job.

However, just as the case was shaping up, another bombshell dropped. This time, it wasn't good news for the defence.

MARIE HENEIN is notoriously skeptical about all her cases, even the very strong ones like *Attorney General v. Michael Bryant*. She immediately sees the pitfalls awaiting her defence of a client, and then, as each hour progresses and she builds her case, she sees more challenges, and more, and then more. Marie sees them all, and it's like a weight upon her. So many pitfalls, so little time, so much to do. Her preparation, for herself and her clients, is like nothing I'd experienced before.

Her adversary in my case, the prosecutor, was himself an enigma, a different sort. Richard Peck, a B.C. lawyer, just happened to be in Ontario when the accident occurred. Peck was in Brampton in September as the special prosecutor in the corruption trial of an OPP officer, so the Ontario Crown's offices were already aware that they had a special prosecutor in town when Darcy Allan Sheppard died. Peck was a defence counsel, most of the time. His most famous case was probably the Air India trial; his clients were acquitted.

By 5 a.m. on the morning of September 1, 2009, Peck's services had already been secured—presumably by the Ontario chief prosecutor, or otherwise by the Crown Prosecution Service. I don't know whether the Attorney General, Chris Bentley, was consulted. Bentley had 25 years of experience as a criminal lawyer before he ran for MPP in a London constituency. We'd become fast friends during his first four-year term in office, my second. I sometimes consulted with him on criminal law matters when I was Attorney General. We were both too busy to continue that practice after he succeeded me. Besides, he didn't need my advice, and kept his cards close to his chest. We'd had a coffee in 2007, when I was shuffled to Aboriginal Affairs and he to Attorney General. I gave him all the best advice I could, and thereafter we rarely discussed his business. Sometimes I needed to pester him about a matter involving aboriginal affairs. But that was it. We would have chatted a few months before the 28 seconds, when I left politics to join Invest Toronto.

We wouldn't speak again for about a year, and never exchanged a word during the time that I was charged.

My bet is that Bentley and the Deputy Attorney General would have agreed that he couldn't be involved in the prosecution of his predecessor and friend. I'll never know those details. I've never asked him.

Special Prosecutor Richard Peck was highly esteemed by his colleagues, in B.C. and across the country, for his intellect, knowledge, and ability. A 2008 cover story in *Canadian Lawyer* magazine called him "Mr. Congeniality." His grandfather had been a Klondike pioneer and was eventually a Member of Parliament, leaving his seat for World War I, then returning with a Victoria Cross to reclaim it. Peck's father was head of B.C.'s industrial relations commission during heated battles between labour and former Premier Bill Bennett's Social Credit government. Peck's inquiring mind was such, the *Toronto Star* reported, that he wrote a paper in 1991 dissecting the trial of Christ. It was, he concluded, a travesty.

Richard Peck was 61 years old. Marie was about 20 years his junior, but she had done enough famous cases that no one doubted her experience. Nonetheless, going up against a lawyer who had 20 years on her would normally make one the underdog. Not so with Marie. Her confidence carried no arrogance and no doubt. It was a fact: she was a remarkable lawyer. The only question was how bad was the evidence. She had that Reggie Jackson straw-that-stirs-the-drink look. *When*—not if, *when*—the pitch came anywhere near the plate, it was going to get knocked clean out of the park.

It's not quite right to imagine prosecutor and defence counsel as adversaries, but often that's the case. In theory, the defence counsel is an officer of the court, who is there primarily to ensure that the accused receives a fair trial, and to hold the prosecution to account. It's not supposed to be personal, and the relationship between defence and prosecution isn't supposed to be acrimonious.

Nor is the prosecutor supposed to be fighting tooth and nail for a conviction. I should know: prosecutors are all agents of the Attorney General, which is what I used to be. I felt like a part of that team of 900 prosecutors during my four years with that ministry. During that time, we often repeated publicly, and to ourselves in internal discussions, that the prosecutor's job is not to "win," but to discharge the Crown's duty. This mantra comes from a 1954 Supreme Court of Canada case that described the prosecutor's unique role: "It cannot be over-emphasized that the purpose of a criminal prosecution is not to obtain a conviction; it is to lay before a jury what the Crown considers to be credible evidence relevant to what is alleged to be a crime ... The role of the prosecutor excludes any notion of winning or losing; his function is a matter of public duty...." To be sure, Richard Peck fit that description. Objective, dignified, and duty-bound.

That said, the duty is not to roll over. It's to present the evidence forcefully, to make the case for a conviction. Perhaps just as importantly, a prosecutor has to be seen by the public as doing his or her job effectively and fairly. That doesn't mean a prosecutor is swayed by public opinion, but there is no question that part of Peck's job was not just to be fair, but also to publicly manifest that objectivity. People were watching this case to see whether the prosecution was in cahoots with me. Was I getting favourable treatment because I used to be the Attorney General? The answer had to be no, and part of Special Prosecutor Richard Peck's job was to ensure that the prosecution was objective, with no favourable treatment blowing my way.

Of course the reverse was my own concern. I presumed that Peck, intellectually, understood the challenge as well as anyone. But I'd been in situations, in politics and in the courts, where the pressure to fulfill one's duties comes with a level of public scrutiny that's unsustainable for some. Some people just crumble in the crossfire, and the moment of crumbling might be a last-minute, panicky, underslept, hands-thrown-up-in-the-air moment. The path of least resistance, for Special Prosecutor Richard Peck, was to toss the hot potato of my prosecution over to a trial judge or a jury (the accused gets to decide whether to be tried by judge or jury). Peck's job was to determine whether there was a reasonable prospect of conviction, but the easiest route was to just take the case to trial.

The same was true for my defence counsel, Marie. Nothing would have showcased her talents so clearly and so thoroughly as a two-week trial defending the charges against me. As much as I, too, wanted the charges dropped, I salivated a little at the prospect of Marie shredding the prosecution's case. I relished the thought of her interrogating certain witnesses, especially the investigating officers.

But we knew exactly how the trial would go. Some days are good days for the defence, but inevitably some are bad. In the early days, the prosecution would present its case, including witnesses with perhaps damning testimony; sometimes there would be a break between the witnesses' examination on the stand by the prosecutor and Marie's cross-examination. If one of those breaks was at the end of the day, or before the noon-time broadcasts, then the news the next day would be the damaging assertions, only later dismantled by Marie. For those who tuned into the trial randomly, that day's news would be all they remembered about the trial.

I was always sure that I'd be acquitted, but just as confident that a trial would be an excruciating and damaging exercise. But that was my opinion. The more uncontroversial option, for both prosecutor and defence counsel, was to hold a trial. One of the reasons, if not the main reason, that I retained Marie Henein was that she was fearless. The uncontroversial option was of little interest to her; it was the option that best served her client that mattered to Marie.

Undoubtedly, Marie is the best barrister I've met. (I still think that my ex-wife is the best solicitor, or transactional lawyer—negotiating deals on behalf of clients—but that's for another book.) But meeting with Marie, as a client, was rarely a pleasant experience. I always left it feeling like I'd survived another day of boot camp. My brain was exhausted and I was physically drained. "Tough day with Marie," I'd often say to Susan, if I was quiet in a corner at night. "She's too much, sometimes."

Like every great barrister, she quickly formulates a theory of her case, then devises a strategy and executes it, knowing that it will require some adjustments, but never so much as to stray from the clear target, the clear strategy. Marie and I agreed on a basic strategy within ten days of my release from jail. But executing the strategy became complicated the next month, when the prosecution delivered some devastating news.

"I've got good news and bad news," Marie said, over the telephone, in mid-October.

"Bad news first."

"I've just been advised that Richard Peck is considering adding new charges."

I knew immediately that this was a terrible development. The charges he was considering adding were dangerous driving (a felony) and/or, potentially, careless driving, a misdemeanour offence. These were so-called lesser charges open to the judge to make a finding of guilty, even if they weren't explicitly one of the charges laid. However, typically for a serious matter like this, it was all or nothing. Either I was guilty of killing Darcy Sheppard, or I wasn't. And if I wasn't, then lesser charges would not bring any more justice to the matter.

However, in my case, adding charges would have been a disaster for me personally. There would have been an implicit suggestion of guilt had charges been added. Most people wouldn't get the nuance of the fact that they were lesser and therefore inclusive of the original charges. They would come to the conclusion that I was somehow the author of my own misfortune—that somehow I'd done something wrong during those 28 seconds.

"We stick with the original strategy," Marie said, "but first he's got to agree to not add any charges until he hears me out on the main charges. If he does, I say we just show him our case. It's risky but he needs to see what I see."

My only question was how quickly this could be done.

So the strategy itself was straightforward: in exchange for waiving all the pre-trial advantages that a defendant holds, we presented our entire case, with a view to convincing the prosecutor to drop the charges.

Dropping the charges is a decision within the sole discretion of the Attorney General's agent, the Crown attorney on the case. It's not for the police to decide. They can lay charges, but only the Crown can withdraw them. Nor can a judge interfere with that decision. I knew this well, and as Attorney General had worked with prosecutors to make some very difficult decisions to drop charges. I'd sat across from the daughter of murdered parents, to try to explain why the person we were all convinced assassinated her parents was not going to be prosecuted by the Crown. (More on that later.)

My legal team consisted of not just Marie, but also her juniors, who were hardly junior. Margaret Bojanowska, Jordan Glick, Matthew Gourlay, and Danielle Robitaille are superb criminal lawyers. They all played a pivotal role in my defence, albeit Marie was extremely hands-on throughout. But I learned something about the criminal defence bar in Toronto. They stick together and work together to help each other, even if they're not retained on the case. This doesn't apply to every lawyer, but amongst those who reciprocate, there is a small group of colleagues who advance the interests of the accused, at large. So Marie was able to consult with any number of senior criminal lawyers including a couple of my own supporters, who happened to be strong legal minds.

The strategy was simple, as good strategies tend to be. The two key potential "witnesses" were Susan and myself. Hardly ideal, since spouses and accused are rarely disinterested parties. That said, Marie made it clear to me that I should not discuss what happened with Susan. Doug Hunt, Susan's lawyer, said the same thing to her. After all, as a witness, we'd be asked if we discussed the case so as to ensure our stories matched. Few would believe that we had not discussed what happened, but some might. It would become self-evident, Marie said, if narratives had been discussed, one contaminating the other.

So we took her advice. It turned out to be great legal advice, and terrible advice for our marriage. Not being able to discuss the single worst half-minute of our lives prevented us from providing the other with a level of support that was desperately needed. In hindsight, invariably as late as it is clear, I regret following that advice. But it's too late now.

Besides, he said/she said testimony will only go so far. When it came to getting charges dropped, obtaining watertight expert evidence was the linchpin. The prosecution could drop charges only if we could present irrefutable forensic evidence from the finest experts we could find, backed up by peer-reviewed expert analysis, and bolstered by additional expert evidence surrounding it.

That was Marie Henein's strategy. One major challenge, I learned, was the cost. Marie generously agreed to defer charging me for her legal fees until I could start affording them. I was unemployed for months after the arrest, and even thereafter my employment income reflected my productivity, which wasn't much.

But the experts weren't governed by principles of *pro bono publico* (the public good) that are supposed to guide my legal profession. The experts needed to get paid in full, every two weeks, or they would stop doing their work. If the delays in accounts receivable stretched too long, they'd just refuse to work the case. In other words, they operated as they should: as a business requiring compensation for services rendered.

This meant that I required a lot of money to pay for expert evidence at premium rates, in order to meet Marie's extremely tight timelines. The experts all worked overtime and were told to put my case at the front of their line, at whatever cost was necessary. This is how Marie works. On every single case.

And that required a cash flow that I couldn't generate. I did not have anywhere near that capacity. I'd been a politician most of my professional life, and there is no pension for Ontario MPPs elected after 1995. The entirety of my severance from the Legislature was swallowed by these costs within a month. I had to borrow very large sums, and a quarter of the cost was defrayed by the stunning generosity of friends.

In any event, for my defence, Marie Henein assembled a dizzying array of forensic engineers and video-pixel analysts and biomechanical engineers and forensic pathologists. The forensic evidence required a back-and-forth between lawyer and expert, and lawyer and client, to ensure that the expert evidence matched my imperfect sense of what happened. Moreover, witnesses for the defence needed to be met, interviewed, and cajoled to swear an affidavit. Meanwhile, Marie took lessons to learn how to drive with a stick-shift, so she could better comprehend those critical seconds involving my Saab's manual transmission.

(All of this was done amidst Marie's extremely busy law practice

with dozens of clients and dozens more coming in, plus her supervision of her associates, plus the conference speeches, volunteer
work, and demands of her personal life: being a wife and a mom.
In fact, the only thing that could interrupt Marie working with a
client was her family. When they called, she dropped everything,
every time, which was not infrequently, no matter how serious was
our meeting. So every so often a conversation flickered between
her work ["the new engineer's report jives with—*Michael! You with
us?*—the video expert's timing on 2nd brake stop—"] and her
family ["the hairbrush is in the top drawer, *left* corner"].)

But that was only half of it. Her boldest decision was to disclose
everything we had to the prosecution, rather than hold it back for
the trial. The element of surprise is an important tactical advantage
for the defence. Whereas the prosecution must disclose the entirety
of its case, the defence need not, since otherwise the prosecution
can work with police to discredit the defence in anticipation of
trial. The risk that Marie was taking, which I fully supported, was
that the prosecution would fail to drop the charges, at which point
it would be too late to take back all our cards.

In October, Special Prosecutor Richard Peck agreed to meet
with Marie in the coming weeks to discuss his adding new charges.
He wouldn't do so, he undertook, until he gave Marie an opportunity to talk him out of it. What Peck didn't realize was that Marie
was going to overwhelm the prosecution with the full force of our
case.

So Marie interviewed all the many exculpatory witnesses, and
assembled the forensic evidence. The latter was the engineering
reports setting out the movements of my Saab during the 28
seconds.

But the seminal expert was the video expert. He took what the
police had provided—all those videos of shadows and figures and
the Saab and its headlights—and made sense of it. He was able to

break down the event to 1/100 of a second. It was through that process, using all the expert reports, that Marie was able to determine that the entire incident, from Sheppard pulling in front of my car to the moment when his skull fatally hit the curb, took up 28 seconds. Marie was able to, in essence, paint a picture of every second of the 28 seconds. It was the art of the defence.

Then she went a step further. Marie took all that expert evidence and had still more experts peer review our video expert's report, to ensure that the evidence was unassailable. The combination of expert, peer-reviewed videotape evidence, combined with the other forensic experts, gave her the tools she needed to box the prosecutor in. Faced with this seemingly watertight defence, the choice to drop the charges would be, the theory went, inescapable.

We knew, however, that the prosecutor could proceed to trial in any event. Once the charges are laid, there is no moment in the criminal justice process where the prosecutor has to formally explain why he or she is proceeding with the prosecution. (A procedure called a "preliminary inquiry" also exists, which presents a logical point for the prosecutor to review the prospect of conviction, but again this lies within the discretion of the prosecutor himself.) In our case in particular, the pressure on Peck to avoid favourable treatment of the former Attorney General meant that all the evidence in the world wasn't necessarily going to prevent a trial.

The last part of the strategy required Marie to be an effective advocate, and that didn't mean barking demands or making idle threats. Though the totality of the forensic evidence was powerful, the real genius of her advocacy was how she came to earn the trust of her adversary, the prosecutor, Richard Peck. Marie Henein is known for being tough, but she can also be charming, respectful, funny, candid, humble, and attentive. But being likeable isn't enough to earn an adversary's confidence. Marie had to conduct herself ethically as both acting in my interests and as an officer of the court. The prosecutor ought not be misled by defence counsel, albeit the line between being a good defence counsel and a learned colleague is a fine one. At times, the work between prosecution and defence counsel might appear to be collaborative, but it's not. Nonetheless, cooperation, collaboration, debate, and fact-finding are difficult to distinguish when both counsel are working as they should.

Marie Henein went into a meeting with Peck and his Ontario agent Mark Sandler in December 2009, a few months into the prosecution. At that meeting, she disclosed much of what we'd assembled about the 28 seconds—a bold and unprecedented tactic. It worked. Peck decided to hold off on adding charges, and permitted Marie to make a full presentation once we had our case ready for him to consider whether charges ought to be dropped.

That presentation happened in March 2010. There were many questions, and Marie, I'm told, did a masterful job. But still, no signs of which way the prosecution was leaning were forthcoming. In fact, the risk taken by Marie, the overall strategy to give the prosecution our entire case, was agonizing for her. I felt confident that it was working, but she did not. The prosecutors agreed to be open minded, but never offered any initial impressions in December or March, when the evidence was fully disclosed. Everything that we presented, in other words, was *with* prejudice. It would either lead to the charges being dropped, or they would spend all their resources and time on blowing holes in our case. Again, we were confident there were no holes, but that didn't make the decision any easier for Marie.

After the March presentation by Marie, Sandler suggested to Peck, who agreed, that perhaps it was time for Susan and I to make a statement. We had declined to do so with the police, which was unquestionably the right decision. The police, in my case, were simply trying to build a case against me. Anything I said that was exculpatory would have been discarded. Anything that could be construed as incriminating would have been used against me. As I learned, that approach was typical of most police work today. The police are your friends, no question, if they perceive you to be at risk, or otherwise a victim. But they can be your adversary otherwise. My advice to people under investigation is to speak with a lawyer before making a statement to the police.

We decided to make a statement to the prosecution, in my case, as part of the police and prosecution's full review of all evidence, and reinvestigation, flowing from Marie's presentation in December 2009. It was risky but a good-faith commitment, consistent with our full disclosure of all the evidence in an effort to get the charges dropped.

In early April the interview took place. If I looked worn out, it wasn't from nervousness about the interview. It was a result of Marie's preparation.

As a lawyer at McCarthy Tetrault in the late 1990s, I had the opportunity to watch lawyers conduct very effective, sometimes vicious, cross-examinations. One of my mentors, Tom Heintzman, was said to have put a witness into an emergency ward with a heart attack. Another, the late great David Little, made my ears buzz afterwards, like after an overly amplified concert, from his bellowing voice.

Yet Marie was in a different category of inquisitors. She seemed to channel Hannibal Lecter, so able was she to find a person's deepest frailties and exploit them. As grateful as I am to Marie Henein, the experience was at times as pleasant as a burst appendix. She was relentless and, as the job sometimes demands, seemingly heartless.

Once, we were reviewing a pathologist's report, which detailed the injuries of Darcy Sheppard and speculated upon exactly what happened at his time of death. Contemplating my own role in Sheppard's death was usually emotional for me, but Marie would have none of it. When I asked to take a break, and walked outside her office to the water fountain down the hall, she followed me. Pulling me into a conference room, she proceeded to chew me out.

"If you need some therapy, go to a therapist, but I'm your *lawyer*, not your fuckin' therapist. *You've got to get over yourself and get it together*. Stop getting so emotional. Start getting seriously more helpful. Get your shit together."

This sort of pep-talk/brow-beating was tough to take, but I never doubted that Marie was in my corner. Nobody knew more about what happened that night than Marie—more than I did, for she knew, as a result of her fact-gathering and analysis, more than any mere memory-holder could muster. So her insistence on my innocence gave me great comfort, offering an unspoken blessing of tough-love, *à la Henein,* to this day.

In any event, Susan and I made separate statements, under questioning from Mark Sandler, at a court reporting office in downtown Toronto. Sandler's demeanour was professional and inviting—of the truth. The questions were meticulous and exhaustive. The level of detail he sought seemed, to me, as much a test of my credibility as a rendering of the facts themselves. No one can be expected to recall everything, and I was no exception.

Sitting beside Sandler was a detective, who was ever present throughout the investigation and prosecution. He was always congenial, and made a suspect feel as if he were quietly on your side. I doubt that was ever actually the case. When he finally agreed that the charges ought to be dropped, I'm told, he was the last hold-out amongst the police and prosecution. Although the prosecutor had sole discretion to drop the charges, a dissenting police officer was to be avoided, and his input was crucial to any final decisions.

I wasn't present at Susan's interview, obviously, but she said that it went fine. As it turned out, she remembered little of what had happened. It was clear that she hadn't discussed the case with me, Marie said, observing the interview. (Susan had separate representation from former Ontario Chief Prosecutor Douglas Hunt, Q.C.) My interview was also straightforward. No surprises. I answered the questions and nothing more. If I didn't know the answer, I didn't speculate.

Except when asked what I'd do with the benefit of hindsight. "I never would have left the house."

THIRTEEN

Uncomfortably Numb

"**N**ext stop, next stop, next stop, next stop, next stop."
I repeated these words over and over to myself. I'd
missed my stop again. Bus stop—or, technically speaking, Toronto
Transit Commission (TTC) streetcar stop. Toronto's municipal
government owns the transit system for the city. As a politician,
I'd been a member of a provincial government that invested a lot
of tax dollars in the transit system for Toronto. But it's never quite
enough, and inevitably we were making up for the negligence of
governments past, federal and provincial.

Compared to other world-class cities, the transit in Toronto
at times can be embarrassing. The "streetcars" look like museum
pieces: old—really old—beasts of metal that rumble along tracks
laid out on certain main thoroughfares, like the one near our house.
In fact, the system was being updated, finally, and so-called rapid
transit lines (aboveground subways) that were faster and sleeker
and more efficient were scheduled to replace the old streetcars in
a few years. For now, it was the streetcar, and I'd managed to miss
my stop—again.

The missed streetcar stop, it seemed to me, summed up
all that was distracted and messed up with my personality. I
drove some people bonkers with my incapacity to focus on the
moment. I'd go to get popcorn at a movie theatre and return
half an hour later, unable to explain where I'd been. I was late for

everything—everything—no matter how important. I'd fail to call people, email people, meet people, meet deadlines, work on projects, work through a to-do list.

I had boarded the streetcar at Yonge and St. Clair. My stop, Avenue and St. Clair, was one full city block away, barely enough to justify taking the streetcar rather than walking. But it was -10°C, so I got on the streetcar with my trusty weekly pass. Why not take the streetcar, I thought. Faster and warmer.

Not so much, thanks to my own version of tunnel vision.

I'd missed that damn stop so many times because I'd get on that streetcar and forget where I was. Whatever distracted me at the time absorbed all my attention. A tornado could not bring me back to the present. I had tunnel vision, unable to see anything but what was in front of me in that tunnel.

From Yonge to Avenue Road on the streetcar was four stops, or about four minutes. If I were to get off at Avenue Road, I had to concentrate on getting off and only on that. If I started reading, or observed someone who reminded me of something, or got on my BlackBerry, or eavesdropped, or listened to the music playing through a nearby iPod's earphones, I'd miss the stop.

I'd wake up sometimes miles down the line, and have to get off and get on the streetcar heading back the other direction. It didn't matter if I were heading east or west, I missed it all the time. Getting home, finding home, was the hardest thing.

This time, I had managed to miss the stop going west, got off at Spadina, a half mile too far, and got back on the streetcar heading east. And managed to miss that one too, ending up at Yonge Street again. I'd missed my stop *twice*. So this time, I started talking to myself from the moment I got on the streetcar. *Next stop, next stop, next stop, next ... stop.*

"YEAH, WHAT HAPPENED?!" my son Louie was asking me, for the third time.

I was trying to explain to him and Sadie what was happening in our lives, a couple days after I'd returned home from jail.

The day after the accident I had called Marie Bountrogianni. Marie was elected as a Liberal MPP in Hamilton in 1999, the same year I was first elected. She was a child psychologist who became Minister of Child and Youth Services during the first McGuinty government in 2003, before retiring from politics in 2007. It's hard to think of anyone who would have been better equipped to advise the terrified parents that Susan and I were.

Dr. B came to our house soon after I called her following the accident. She was great. She told us not to be emotional with Sadie and Louie. We were to tell them the facts, just the facts, to try to be as objective as we could.

So I told them, in as generic a way as I could, what had happened that night. I didn't go into details, in part because I had a hard time describing it in any way to anyone. Louie kept saying, "I don't understand. What happened? Did you run him over? Did he crash his bike into you? What happened?"

My brief explanation to the kids about "the car accident" that involved "a man dying" perplexed them. And no wonder. I couldn't get into details, for fear that my kids would get subpoenaed to testify. That might have been a little paranoid.

A few things stuck out for them: the man who died was drunk, he was on a bicycle, daddy was driving, mommy in the passenger seat. I left out the part involving police charging me because I didn't want them worrying about daddy going to jail. Thereafter, they referred to Darcy Sheppard as the "drunk guy"—which had its own ironic twist. That's one of the things that's stuck in their heads ever since. They now think that anybody who's drunk is very, very dangerous and nothing but trouble. And I suppose they are not far wrong.

We also talked to their teachers and their school principal to make sure they weren't taking heat from any other kids about my situation. The school staff were remarkable. The principal and teachers would discreetly monitor conversations from time to time. So far as we know, there was never any problem from other students. This may have been a reflection of how the parents behaved at home.

Through much of it, the kids just saw my picture in the paper and assumed it to be business as usual. That's one reason to be grateful, I guess, for a little routine celebrity of the sort that political life offers. The one thing Sadie and Louie didn't like was when I resigned from Invest Toronto. They thought it was a big deal to be *president* of something. They still ask, "When are you going to be president again?"

Finally, they gave up after getting their questions poorly answered, and asked to build a fort in the basement. About an hour later, I was upstairs in my bedroom, when I overheard the two of them playing in Sadie's room. They were playing a game called "car crash," each taking turns being either the driver or the "dead guy."

This was called processing, Marie Bountrogianni told me later. It was very positive, she said. Uh-huh.

When they spotted me at their doorway, Louie asked: "Daddy, will you play car crash with us? You can be the driver!!"

MY MOM AND DAD had come to Toronto from Victoria soon after the accident. They had been very frightened for me. When they arrived in Toronto, I made the mistake of being too much the lawyer and too little the son when I spoke to them. I spoke as if there were no emotions at play. I tried to explain how things were going to unfold, almost like a technical briefing. Meanwhile, they were generally shocked over all the changes, so my odd demeanour was just another item on the insanity menu.

We sat down at the kitchen table, and I started going through the possible criminal proceedings and processes—trial by judge, trial by judge and jury, Ontario court of justice provincial court or superior court, indictable charges versus avoiding a preliminary inquiry. Very procedural stuff.

"So, in other words, if we opt for a preliminary inquiry, then ..."

Having sat with rapt attention, her eyes betraying confusion and compassion, Mom just burst out crying.

Here was her eldest son, the boy who'd gone to Harvard, gotten elected, married with beautiful children, the son who'd been nothing but a source of pride for her. Now, I was in a very serious predicament.

She had thought that I'd never be a source of worry, by this stage in my life. At a certain point, moms want to be able to ease up on the worrying; they just want their kids to be okay. And now I'd been arrested and, from her perspective, the mother's perspective, that dreadful perspective of imagining all the things that could go wrong, I was maybe going to jail.

It was awful for her. Awful. When I saw her crying that day, it was the only time that I felt really angry about what had happened to me. Not for me, but for her. *Police make decisions that can save people's lives, that can end people's lives, that can destroy people's lives,* I thought, watching my mom weep. *The power to break a mother's heart, because of a rush to judgment, because of timorous souls, too lazy or too nervous to conduct a proper investigation, to face a little heat from the media....*

All that was too much to expect of them, as I've said often: one cannot build a justice system around how to charge an ex–Attorney General. The system is going to slip a disk bending over backwards to avoid the appearance of lenient treatment, necessarily rendering a bizarre process and result. The hours logged into this case by the special prosecutors were likely 10 or 20 times the amount of time a Crown would normally put into a case. The two dozen Toronto Police Service officers involved in a case spanning 28 seconds was hardly standard procedure.

I will say this once and not belabour the point, but I'd be remiss not to repeat what's been said to me again and again, by police, prosecutors, defence counsel, and judges: normally, particularly in traffic situations, the police need to conduct an investigation, obtain a reconstruction report, speak to witnesses, and gather all evidence *before* charges are laid. It is not unusual for Toronto Police Services to wait weeks (or even months) before deciding how they will proceed with such charges. In my case, the police couldn't wait a news cycle. I got the opposite of special treatment. I was disadvantaged by virtue of being a former Attorney General, but so be it. I'd not trade in those four years as Attorney General for standard treatment by the criminal justice system. I'd not trade in those four years for anything. And the point remains that a justice system cannot be designed for such exceptional cases. One just has to hope that the system eventually works it out.

I furiously knocked over stuff to find Mom a Kleenex, thinking: *I know, I know, I know: I waived my rights to receive typical treatment by the justice system, by the media, by virtue of putting my name on an election ballot. No matter that no one gets to actually waive that right explicitly. Supposedly it comes with the territory. I get it. I get it. But don't expect my mother to get it, and don't expect me to like it.*

After that, I stopped explaining to my parents how the system worked and just started telling them everything was going to be okay.

THERE'S NOTHING LIKE the image of another person's body rising out of your own to make you appreciate the transcendental possibilities of yoga. Or make you really appreciate pigeon stretches—the equivalent of twisting your body into a hairpin folded back on itself. Particularly if the image of the body rising out of your own was someone you'd been accused of killing, and who was most definitely dead.

It was a freezing evening in Toronto, the last week of December 2009. At Moksha Yoga Uptown, I tried the Pranayama for the first time, in a smaller room, which meant holding postures for a long time, breathing a lot (as opposed to?), and barely breaking a sweat. At the time it happened, I almost didn't think it odd, didn't reflect on it much. I was in pain, my body folded over in a position heretofore unknown to my anatomy. The yoga instructor was saying that the pigeon stretch was excellent at "opening up the hips." When she first said it, I thought this was an analogous description. But at that moment, with my body twisted into a hairpin folded back on itself, I realized that she meant it literally. This stretch was like placing my hips in a nutcracker and pushing the lever down until there was a loud crunch.

"This will open up your hips. If you're struggling, if you feel stuck, it's often emotional blockage. These stretches will open up your hips and unblock some emotions that are stuck," she said, with a soothing voice that made it hurt less.

Oh, this will be good, I thought. I've got plenty of blockages. Plenty. A marriage collapsing, a soul searching, a head cracking, a heart breaking, enough repression to hibernate a bear into the next century, and everything that comes with being a former Attorney General who has been charged with two felonies for the death of someone last seen alive by the 43-year-old man in a pigeon stretch.

Stretch. Creak. Ouch. She came around and gently placed her hand on my lower back. Whereas most in the class were comfortably flat on the floor like a hairpin folded on itself, I looked like a hairpin after a long ride in the garborator. So she carefully extended my stretch with a soft push down on my back.

A few seconds later, I saw an image of Darcy Sheppard.

He seemed to be hovering there, floating for a few seconds.

I can't remember what happened except that it seemed as if he exited my body; he just rose up and left.

"So. How was yoga?" Susan asked me, when I got home, about an hour later. I was a novice at yoga; had only been a few times. It was a new hobby in a new life of hobbies *du jour.* Her question was a major effort to sound civil and friendly. She might have said: "Hope your solitary excursion was all you wanted it to be, because I'm so lonely I could ..."

But she didn't say that.

"Well, thanks for asking," I said quickly. This was something we were learning through various audiobooks on therapy for couples: master couples versus disaster couples. We were the latter, seeking the status of the former. So you needed to show affection and compliment your partner for things you sincerely appreciate. Like asking how yoga went.

"Good."

Pause.

"I think during ... What's that pose where you—" I started doing it and she helped.

"Pigeon stretch—"

"HI DADDY!! I LOVE YOU!!" Louie, age 5, plowed into my hip and stomach, pinning me against the counter, rearing back, and crashing his pillowy fist into my solar plexus. Hugs were exchanged, and we went off to watch him play a video game. An hour later, at dinner, sitting across from Susan, my eyebrows curled upwards.

"Did I tell you that during my pigeon stretch I think I saw Darcy Sheppard rise out of my body? At yoga. I saw him—"

"Wow. No, you hadn't told me. Describe." This painfully formal extrapolation of Gottman Institute master marital techniques made us both cringe invisibly. I did describe, and then we conversed on anything but that.

The mistake would be to imagine that Sheppard had somehow exited from my life, that I'd gotten over my grief or fear or shame or pain involving him. The experience of what happened that night welded Sheppard to me forever. It's always there. He's always there. This does not mean that I await the day that he's not somewhere in the constellations of my thoughts. I can pretend he's not there, or hide from him, or distract myself from him. Or try to do something less fearful.

"So," I said to Susan. "I'd say that the dark part of Darcy maybe rose up out of my body. But he's always there, somewhere."

Susan just looked at me. "Okay. I think I understand what you're saying," which was her post-counselling way of saying, kindly, that she shared comprehension, if not entirely believing or grasping my feelings. We were extremely post-modern at this point.

Suddenly, she appeared. Or maybe we just suddenly noticed her standing there. Sadie, the 7-year-old, had been listening to our conversation. She had either hid behind the wall or just stood there in plain view, making herself invisible. This was her latest trick.

Susan said, softly: "Do you understand that Daddy doesn't mean that a real, living man came out of his body? You understand that—"

"No, I understand. He was like a ghost. The man who died in the car accident. The dark ghost left Daddy's body.... But it could come back, Daddy, so be careful."

I nodded my agreement, very slowly.

"I KNOW THAT EVERYTHING will work out for you."

"I am sure things will work out."

"I hope that things will work out for you."

"Do you think everything will work out?"

These four comments were said very often to me, and I reacted very differently to each. During the nine months between being arrested and the dropping of the criminal charges, I was rarely angry (albeit mostly dysfunctional, mostly depressed, occasionally happy). With my pride hollowed out by the experience, there wasn't much to be angry about. But there was ego detritus left behind. I resented greatly those who seemed to question my innocence, just as I welled up when they supported me.

I privately awarded gold medals to those who said, "I know that everything will work out for you." It represented a judgment of me as unquestionably good and innocent. Their prognosis was positive, without qualification: they "know" that I will be exonerated by the criminal justice system.

Silver went to those who expressed confidence in that result of exoneration, but they hedged their bets. Perhaps it's just Canadian semantics, being not overconfident: "I am *sure* things will work out."

Bronze medals are impressive only if there is high drama involved: an athlete's mother has just died, or someone has suffered a crippling injury. Or if it's a miracle they were even able to compete and finish: think rower Silken Laumann's 1992 Olympic bronze for Canada.

But for me, for the first six months after Sheppard died, I was not a big fan of the bronze medallists. They were a distant third, from my haughty perspective. "I hope that things will work out for you." They'd only get a medal because they expressed hope for me. Otherwise, I'd disqualify them altogether.

What the f#k do you mean you HOPE I'm innocent! Of course I'm innocent, you *&^%--!*

Now, they were probably talking without any intention of expressing doubt about my innocence. But the fact that they just "hope" it, rather than being "sure" about my innocence, got them only a bronze.

The Goat award went to those who dared question my innocence. They didn't hope for it, it seemed to me, nor could they muster up confidence in me. They actually asked me a question about my innocence. Goat: "Do you think everything will work out?"

Even though these people were trying, in their way, to express solidarity with me, I reacted badly. Ungrateful shit that I can be, I'd always reply the same, with differing emphasis, depending on their medal status.

"*Of course* I will be exonerated!" I'd reply to bronze medal winners.

"Yes, I will be exonerated," I'd say, nodding, shrugging, stating the obvious to the gold medallist.

Or "I *know* there will be exoneration," unlike you lazy hopers-not-knowers (silver).

For the goat, just "of course," then, with a look of dismay and hurt, I'd make an escape, looking to find someone to commiserate on the goat awardee's utter lack of judgment.

Judgment is tricky business. Judge not lest ye be judged is quite right, but it's not a prohibition on judgment. The tricky part is finding the righteous judgment. Here I was, judging people's powers of empathy and confidence in me, when all they were doing was trying to make me feel better. Or maybe they were curious and wanted to know my opinion and feelings on my future.

The truth. Judgment is not truth and it's not untruth. Judgment is apart from truth, more mechanical than soulful. Every day criminal court judges hand down sentences to people perhaps also judged innocent of heart by that very same judge. Such judges are executing their legal duties, applying the due process of the law. This is the stuff of textbooks and cases and logic. I'm convinced much of this could be done via computer software. X plus Y equals guilty. Not guilty means no X or no Y.

But I would learn to judge not, lest I be judged. Most people that I came into contact with did not judge me as anything but Michael. They'd say I was a "good person" or "one of the good guys," and I'd be flattered and sometimes astounded: *how would you know?*

The first step in learning the lesson of judgment is found within, I learned from others. This sounds like words from a fortune cookie but it would be a good one if you got it. Judge yourself as you would be judged righteously, the little Cookie Torah reads. Without that, I would keep judging myself wrongly and others unfairly.

Harry taught me that. An elderly Dutch fellow with a medium thin moustache and heavy accent—let's call him Harry—whom I knew from my fellowship of recovery shared with me that he had been jailed years before, and that he resented his prosecutors and judges for years, to no avail. Before I could leap to a defensive posture, he poked his finger in my chest.

"The law is not yer true judge, Mister," and he poked my sternum, softly, three times, then left it there. "You are yer own judge and love is yer judge and God is yer judge."

The skin on my forehead drew lines horizontal but more accurately curling like question marks. I was straining to open my mind, my forehead pulling open its doors with all its weight.

Eyes widened and eyebrows raised, Harry threw his hands back: "How do you judge me, young man?"

"I judge you to be a good soul, probably a great father and grandfather and husband. But *goodness.* You're good, Harry."

"But I was found guilty by de court. I was guilty under de law—"

My forehead relaxed as I closed my eyes and shook my head with a paternalistic affection.

"No, Harry. I don't judge you harshly at all for that. You got drunk and hurt someone in a fight, you said. It was a mistake.

There was lots of fault to go around, under the law. But it doesn't rob you of your goodness."

Harry's chest started heaving and his lower lip curled up, touching his moustache. Out came the poking finger. He roared:

"What do you mean!? I was guill-tey! Guil-ty!!"

"No, Harry. You are innocent. You're one of the good ones, Harry. Whatever you did. The law's judgment is different. The law is there for a decent purpose, but it can't take everything away from you."

Harry pulled back his shoulder to really get behind this last poke: "So who can take every-ting away from me, if not dat judge sitting on dat bench, if not dese people looking up or down at me? Who?"

And I felt a poke in my sternum that seemed to crack me in two. His hands were thrown back now, eyes wide again, asking that question.

After that conversation, from then on, I got it. I didn't always remember to get it, but when I remembered Harry, I was fine. The law would do what it would do. The prosecutor would do what he would do. If it came to trial, the judge would judge me under the law, but probably like me just fine, regardless.

After that day, I tried to stop persecuting myself. I tried to. Being rigorously honest with oneself doesn't mean defaulting to self-pity, martyrdom, hand-wringing, shame. And I stopped judging others. Or I tried to. Only *I* could take everything away from me, and I wasn't going to do that to myself.

ROOT VEGETABLES are grown in hot climates, mild climates, and cold climates. If you've only had carrots grown in California or Texas, you don't know the sweetness of a carrot. Carrots grown in comfortable climates don't convert starch to sugar, or at least not to the degree that root vegetables grown in cold climates do.

A plant physiologist would explain that the hard frosts, the bitter freezing, over and over, demands the conversion of starches to sugars to survive. The sweet carrot—and it can be so incredibly sweet, 13 percent of that carrot can be pure sugar—is telling us that it wants to live. For if ice crystallizes in that carrot, it dies. That harsh freezing, maybe several, pushes that carrot towards death. But if it doesn't crystallize and die, if it can fight that near-death experience and survive, the carrot is left immeasurably sweeter than its carrot cousin sunning in Florida.*

Some people confront that frost in life, and they fight, or they give up, and if they let the darkness crystallize, they die inside. Or at least they're cold, perma-frozen. We all know someone like that. Their souls are frozen. And of course there are many people who opt for moderate climates, warmth, even heat, over near-death frostbites. Perhaps they faced a coming cold front, and they headed for the hills, or sand-dunes, or suburbs.

I've had a few hard freezings. Certainly, I've had one serious deep freeze. And I didn't head for the hills because I couldn't. No hills were within sight. So I had to devise some survival techniques.

When in a foxhole, under fire, be a fox.

When something terrible happens, there is an aftermath. Even death surely has an aftermath, but I'm just guessing. I don't have to guess about what happens after you've allegedly killed somebody, and the cuffs get burned into your wrists, taken off only once you're ensconced in a jail cell. That aftermath of the truly terrible—in my case, 28 seconds that ended with the death of Darcy Sheppard—affords the opportunity for reflection and conscious action.

Yes, you're in shock. But still, it's nothing like the terrible

---

* The analogy came to me listening to a podcast: American Public Media, Krista Tippett, *On Being*, "Driven by Flavor with Dan Barber," December 9, 2010.

event itself: a moment of tunnel vision that is driven not by one's consciousness, but by something deeply primal and perhaps metaphysical. The whole fight-or-flight phenomenon, which I suppose is what happened to me during my deadly 28 seconds, seemed, in retrospect, driven by another spirit. I have never felt more or less in control of my actions.

Foxholes were military constructions, places where people fought during wars, particularly in World War I. In the foxhole, people would shout sayings that persist to this day. "Incoming!" "Fire in the hole!"

Sometimes you're in a foxhole alone. A battle rages above and you know that survival is the best you might do. You can panic and jump out of the hole and start shooting crazily at the enemy until you're shot down. You can freeze and do nothing at all until you're bombed, burned, or rooted out. Or you can behave like a fox, using all of your wits, cunning, and fortitude.

Sometimes the aftermath of a tragedy can seem what it is not. Upon learning of the death of my grandfather, my 11-year-old self immediately seized upon the idea that it was my fault. The night before, my tired parents had told me, after another evening at his deathbed, to pray that "Papa will go to a better place where he won't suffer anymore." So as an 11-year-old who basically did what he was told when out of his depth, I just went ahead and prayed that my grandfather would die that night.

And he did.

I'd killed my grandfather, I thought to myself.

When I was told by my mom that, indeed, my grandfather had died, she did so while putting down a laundry basket in the hallway outside our kitchen at the house in Gordon Head. A red plastic oval laundry basket. My father closed the door behind him as he walked slowly up the stairs to tell his mother that her husband of 50-plus years had died.

I ran to the bathroom and locked the door, weeping wildly. We had those 1970s mirrors in that bathroom—half a hexagon of mirrors: one faced you directly, the two adjacent mirrors were angled out at 45 degrees. If you pulled the two together, you had a triangle of mirrors. As anyone knows who has tried this, if you put your head at the apex of the triangle, pulling those two mirrors tight against your cheeks, the reflection is dramatic. There are countless reflections of your face in that triangle, stretching to infinity, it seems.

It seemed an excellent means by which I could communicate with God, to advise him of the terrible mistake that had been made, and to demand a retraction, by way of a miraculous recovery. I'd killed my grandfather, it seemed to me, so now it was time to unkill him. God, help! I didn't mean it!! You are way too literal, God! I meant give him a bit of Demerol, not cyanide!!

Blubbering into a million mirrored reflections of myself, I sought a long-distance connection to God that went unanswered. I was panicked and responded in a very panicky way to what I perceived as a tragedy.

I embraced the reality of his death like someone chugs a pitcher of beer. Not surprisingly, I became overwhelmed. I did not behave like a fox.

But the tragedy may not be as it seems. Eventually I began to realize that maybe I hadn't killed my grandfather. Indeed I had not. Maybe it wasn't a tragedy but just the circle of life. That man had to die at some point. Time would eventually allow me to begin soaking up the wisdom and love to be found from his death. But I suffocated that process by trying to gang up on God. All those reflections of me in a full-on God-ambush that went nowhere.

Perhaps it's too much to ask of someone that he or she take time to patiently reflect in the immediate aftermath of a tragedy. Some people freak out, as I did when Papa Bryant died. Some just go into shocked immobility and delay the aftermath. Some instead find themselves able to be cunning when meeting a cunning unreality. I'd not killed my grandfather, after all. That was not reality. It was unreality.

So what I did as soon as I was arrested, cuffed, and bent down to sit in the squad car was to suspend belief, suspend disbelief, levitate amid the chaos. I did the same thing when they put me in the cell at the Traffic Division station. When I was released from the police station, I affected the same stance. Upon seeing a demonized photo of me in a newspaper looking like a deranged road rager, I did the same thing again. The gods, or maybe just an overactive mind, were playing tricks on me, tricking me into assumptions that were unfounded and misguided. Rather than accepting or rejecting them—impossible, as long as one is caught up in the chaos—I just embraced the trickery with a few of my own tricks. Sometimes the aftermath of a tragedy, itself a moment of tragic consequences, requires astute trickery of the self, by the self, to the self.

Is that really *me* in that photo in the newspaper, or is this not quite real? Am I really being arrested for a homicide, or is this an illusion? Am I really the first former Attorney General to sit in a jail cell for allegedly killing someone, or is this not quite a bad dream? This is not a trick that can be performed by an 11-year-old after committing imaginary euthanasia. But a sober 44-year-old can do it sometime around midnight in a jail cell.

> I'll lay me down and bleed awhile,
> and then I'll rise and fight again.
>
> —*Richard, first Earl of Cornwall (1209–1272)*

There is no way to turn trauma around quickly. Delude yourself all you want, if that's how you outfox insanity. But delusion and repression should be used sparingly, for they are boomerangs that come back to whack you, no matter how far or how hard you throw them. The harder the boomerang of delusion is hurled, the longer you repress, the harder the whack at the end of the cycle.

Repression is a technique that my mother uses spectacularly in her battle with multiple sclerosis. That effort prolongs her life, decades after being told she would die young from the disease. She has outfoxed the disease throughout her life, never fully accepting its pain and incapacity. But outside of ducking a mortal illness, repression is a really bad idea. After the 28 seconds, I deluded myself that I could make my experience an exclusively positive one. I refused to entertain the notion that it was painful.

My wife, Susan, was the opposite: she wanted to familiarize herself with the tragedy before us. She sought to write the screen-play for the horror flick to come; a pre-screening was a necessary part of her recovery. She wanted to think through all the worst-case scenarios.

"Life imprisonment?"

"That's ridiculous to think about," I replied. "I won't be convicted and therefore I won't be sentenced."

"But anything can happen—"

"No. Nothing bad will happen like that."

"Will we go bankrupt paying legal fees?" she asked.

"Impossible. I'll go into debt and pay it off. It's just money."

"How much money?"

"Not too much. It will be fine."

"But what if it isn't?"

"It will be. And I can't talk about this anymore."

And that was that.

I went through a few weeks of this. And then one day I woke up and put on a suit. It was the first week of October. The sun was still warm, but I wasn't too hot in a jacket. The shirt was pale blue, the tie was tasteful: green and blue, no big polka-dots, no fuchsia stripes. Just green and blue and thin white stripes, like your dad wears. The socks were boring: navy blue. The shoes were brown, matching the belt. A light-coloured suit with tan and mauve and some lime. A little boxy for my liking, but I didn't want to look ... good. Just properly dressed.

I came down for breakfast.

Susan stared at me.

"What are ... Where are you going?"

I was unemployed. I'd resigned as CEO of Invest Toronto the day after I'd been charged. Now here I was, less than a month later, looking extremely employed. Except that I wasn't. I was extremely unemployed, looking extremely employed.

"Where are you going?" Susan repeated.

"I don't know. I just thought I needed to get busier today. Look the part."

She looked very sad, suddenly. She was dressed for work, and she was going to work. In fact, she'd gone to work the day after I was charged. She had to, I understood. In a life suddenly without any order, and an unemployed husband, her employment, her brilliant law practice, had to continue. It just had to.

"If you want to help, send me work," she'd emailed her clients, who'd all offered to support her. They did.

I had no clients, however, or office from which to serve clients. This was the zenith of my repression. My delusion. That all would be well. I'd just put on a tie and a happy face. Then off I'd go. Nowhere.

So, Lesson Two: minimize the repression of the direness of your trauma. If it floats your boat, repress away for a few hours or days. But then stop. Lay down and bleed awhile. To paraphrase Joseph Campbell: once you're falling, might as well dive. It's the only way to rise and fight again.

How does that work? Well, I spent time with people, thinking that I was helping them deal with the 28 seconds. Friends told me they'd lost a lot of sleep, were worried sick about me, and found themselves having a minor existential crisis. I thought that I was doing pretty good (I wasn't), but I'd nothing to do with my day, so I'd hang out with them. Help them out, I thought. Show them how okay I was.

Just being with people, even if for delusional reasons, is a way of surviving one of life's hard freezings. The other thing I did, already mentioned, was write thank-you notes. Hundreds. I thanked people who'd sent me letters of support, or food, or emails, or for having Facebook friended me. I went through a lot of stationery. As I said, everything I did took ten times longer than it needed to, so this filled up a lot of my days.

Otherwise, I don't really know what I did with my time, other than the time spent in Marie Henein's office. I do recall, however, being aware, every day, that I was alive and Darcy Sheppard was dead.

Thy will be done, not *I* will be done.

The hardest part of a traumatic life event, for the egomaniac, is the complete destruction of one's will. It's also the best part, assuming one is an egomaniac with an inferiority complex.

About six months after Sheppard died, I was discussing this subject with a close friend, whom I'll call Mack. Mack was an alcoholic and an addict, recovering. He'd not touched the stuff for more than 20 years. We were drinking tea, as part of my World Tour. I was the solo act on the tour, visiting the living rooms and nearby coffee shops of friends and strangers wanting to talk to me about the nightmare of August 31st.

"For people like us," he said, "the ego is the enemy. The ego needs to be crushed, really, killed, in order to find serenity. Peace comes not from our own will. The prayer says 'Thy will be done,' not 'I'll figure it out.'"

I was entranced. So right, I thought. I wanted me some of that ego-killing potion. It seemed like an antidote to insanity.

"How do I do that? Kill the ego. How—"

"That's what has happened to you. Your ego has been killed, under terrible, terrible circumstances."

And this was quite true.

Not that I hadn't tried an egomaniacal approach, for a short time in the jail cell, when Darcy Sheppard's death had barely been confirmed to me. In that cell, I'd gone through all the stages of grief—fear, anger, denial, etc.—in a tidy few hours.

At one point, I'd gamed out a comprehensive strategy—a 360, in the consulting parlance. I thought very clearly and then a wave of murky, dirty, kelp-filled water washed over that clarity. I'd plotted how perhaps I could manage this. But I couldn't. It would take lawyers and experts and a prosecutor and a judge or a jury. And that was just the leading cast members. There would be people who came to my rescue: friends and family and strangers, loved ones and people who'd not liked me so much before August 31st. Besides, I'd no choice in the matter of my rescue. I'd been laid low. I was inoperative, incapacitated; batteries removed.

I couldn't will my way out of the trauma, the tragedy. There would be brief flashes of ego in the coming months, but they probably added up to a total of less than an hour of egomania. The rest was out of my hands, and I came to accept that as my fate.

This was, for me, new territory. I'd willed success, I thought, in the past. God hadn't written my LSAT, it seemed to me. Nor had He wooed a Supreme Court of Canada judge for a clerkship. Nor had He knocked on thousands of doors to get a nomination, then win an election. I'd made all that happen, I'd always thought. The cast and crew along for the ride were very much supporting actors, not the headliners.

In hindsight, it wasn't that way at all. Yes, there is a role to play, for the self. One has to show up, as Woody Allen says, to succeed. But beyond that, maybe Woody's right. Maybe one just has to show up. Maybe success is a collusion of forces beyond our control, and we fool ourselves into thinking that it's about who you know, what you know. Without my mom and sister, without my profs and a handful of librarians, and my father, I'd never have learned how to write a good essay, a good exam. Without the hundreds of volunteers, I'd never have tasted political success. Without the confidence and appointment by the Premier, I'd never have become Attorney General.

So in the aftermath of Sheppard's death, I handed everything over to others. My criminal defence was undertaken and executed by my lawyer. Employment came after a coffee with John West, the managing partner of Ogilvy Renault's Toronto office, set up by someone else (Richard King). An opportunity to teach a class at the University of Toronto arrived as dessert during a lunch with Professor David Cameron. A phone call from Ryerson University opened up an empty office for me to go to just weeks after I was charged. Recovery from post-traumatic stress disorder came thanks to supervision by my therapist, Dr. Sutton. My relationship with Susan was governed by our caretaker and marital therapist, Dr. Cohen. All this help was originated by or provided by others. The path was written by a Thee, not by me.

Be humble.
Embrace humility. When faced with a nightmare, the best strategy is humility before, during, and after. When in doubt, on your knees.

In war, surrender involves a crossing over to the winning side. When I admitted I was powerless over alcohol, and that my life was unmanageable, it was a complete surrender. I'd lost my war on booze. I crossed over to the winning side. In my life, that lesson of humility, a giving over of oneself, and a surrender of my will, best prepared me for the 28 seconds. That said, I'd lost much of that humility between the time I stopped drinking and the night that changed everything.

The corollary to surrender is humility. Having handed over my will to the care of others, what was I to do? The answer was to embrace humility, as if I had no choice. As it turned out, during the first couple of years after the 28 seconds, I really was powerless and humbled. I embraced humility out of an incapacity to embrace anything else.

"Whatever truculent means, if it's good, then I'm that," Muhammad Ali responded to Howard Cosell. The sportscaster was verbally sparring with Ali, as ever, with Cosell seeking to demonstrate his superior intelligence (low humility) with an ornate vocabulary. Heavyweight champion Ali was riffing off his "I am the Greatest" rap (no humility), to which Cosell said: "You're being extremely truculent." But Ali, the undereducated boxer, outsmarted the overeducated commentator through mock humility: "Whatever truculent means, if it's good, then I'm that."

That always stuck with me. At the time, as a teenager watching the highlight clip of Ali–Cosell exchanges on a Betamax cassette, I thought it was riotous. Muhammad Ali's immodesty combined with cornball humour. I would think of this when watching clips of Senator Sam Ervin Jr.'s "simple country lawyer" routine during the Watergate Commission, notwithstanding Ervin's status as a Harvard graduate. Ali and Ervin were engaging in mock humility, I thought, with Ali being explicit about his irony: *I may not have a big vocabulary but I'm a great boxer, and you're a pompous poser.*

Faux humility, of course, is vanity squared; it's über-pride plus a bonus put-down. And yet Muhammad Ali would know humility better than most human beings. Once America's greatest athlete, now Ali can barely lift a finger due to Parkinson's disease. Decades earlier, an Olympic gold medal around his neck, he couldn't enter some restaurants in the South because he was a "Negro." Later he was charged with crimes, stripped of his heavyweight championship, and of his boxing licence, his very *raison d'être,* it seemed. All for refusing to be drafted. He said his Muslim faith prohibited him from fighting in a war. "I ain't got no quarrel with them," he said. "No Viet Cong ever called me nigger." For the best three and half years of his boxing life, he couldn't fight.

When the U.S. Supreme Court vindicated Ali, he must have been a changed man. He must have tasted humility and grown from it. Physically, he was not the same fighter, yet in many ways, he had become more formidable. He used his noggin, often literally—by taking punches in order to tire out his opponents, the so-called Rope-a-Dope—to outstrategize his opponents at a level never seen before or after. And yet Ali's routine didn't really change at all. It was the immodest stuff, mixed in with faux humility, the mocking kind, the boomerang kind, the kind full of pride.

Long ago, I decided to adopt the Muhammad Ali style because he was my hero, both for being a superhuman boxing icon and for his courage to "face machine guns ... before denouncing Elijah Muhammad and the Religion of Islam. I'm ready to die." I still get chills when I see that clip. I'm ready to die. Who doesn't wonder what we'd die for? Even if Ali's hyperbole could be questioned as just that, the man did walk away from his world and forgo much in the name of his faith and his conscience.

Ali was loved and hated but mostly loved. Those who hated him, I bet, didn't understand the part of him that actually was humble, the part that was ready to die for something greater than himself. They only saw the "I am the GREATEST" routine.

Or, the shortest poem in the English language, authored by Ali: "Me, Whee!"

And yet, what would happen to this man in his latter years? A reckoning. He would be rendered all but mute and physically almost catatonic, as a result of Parkinson's disease. No doubt it was partially caused or exacerbated by his physical beatings, by the boomerangs he launched against himself, taunting his opponents to pound him on the ropes, tire themselves out, only for Ali to spring back and finish them off in a knockout.

So can it be said that Ali was humbled? Did these physical ailments render a vain man humble? What of his pride, in this radically altered state? The physically perfect boxer reduced to the mute mummies he used to mock as his opponents. (Ali called George Foreman "The Mummy" for his plodding, frightening, quiet attacks. Foreman would later express gratitude to Ali for not hitting him when Ali had a free shot to hammer the already falling Foreman, en route to being knocked out. The Mummy was falling slowly like a tree—timber!—yet Ali had the humility and the humanity to not overdo it.)

Or was Ali always a humble man who put on an act intended to fool people, engage people, enrage people? The Vanity Fair that was Muhammad Ali perhaps was just that. Maybe he was a humble man, all along. Or maybe an insecure man, fearful, who projected his fear through a façade of bravado.

In any event, I've learned that humility is the most serene, happy place to be, for me. The Ali Act, on the other hand, I find exhausting, anxious, and unreal. I feel almost hungover afterwards. The best advice I got when I needed humility, and wished to shake the darkness, was to stop focusing on myself, and instead focus entirely upon others. Be outwardly focused, I was told. Engage in service to others. So I did.

I learned the meaning of true altruism from my brother, Alan.

He helped people without taking credit for the help, and if he could help people without them discovering the source, that was ideal. He did it for the joy of helping, not for his ego.

So it would be wrong-headed to brag about my new life's altruistic activities, if any could be described as such. I've come to see that I need everyone, to reach out to everyone, to connect with people, to help them, in order to find humility and serenity in my own life. In so many ways, as the French poet Paul Claudel puts it, "There is not one of them I can do without."

All of which stands in contrast to where I was before the 28 seconds, and explains, for me, why I left politics when I did.

Don't fool yourself.

As one recovers from something dramatic in a life, sometimes we cling to familiar platitudes rather than grow. Our capacity for repression, denial, and mendacious thinking ought not be underestimated. I learned not to trust my first thoughts, my knee-jerk reactions, my instincts. Building the muscle of self-appraisal, the ability to take a moral inventory of oneself, also allowed for some sober reflection upon my past.

In hindsight, I think that I came to fool myself about my political motivations. To be sure, many of my intentions were laudable. But not all, and the failure to be rigorously honest with myself led me astray from the best original reason for entering politics: to help others. Being rigorously honest with oneself is easier said than done. It requires a level of skepticism of one's own instincts, which we're typically told to follow. For the recovering alcoholic, however, our first reactions are usually the ones not to follow; we learn to look before leaping. It's called "the next right step." That said, some people in recovery find themselves facing more of a blank slate than they ever imagined. I had to reach back, often, to second-guess many of my assumptions.

So I now see that I went into politics because it seemed like a glorious calling. I went into politics because my dad was my hero, and politics had been his calling. And I went into politics for reasons that defy logic and description. I also went into politics with a host of solutions, looking for problems. And that was arrogant.

Sometimes a mixture of intentions can land one in a very good place. And that's what happened with politics and me. I learned that the only way to get elected, truly, was to do it yourself, and then get people to help you help others.

Between February 1998 and June 1999, when I was first elected, I must have knocked on thousands of doors. I spoke with thousands of people. I signed up over 1000 of them to the St. Paul's Provincial Liberal Association (the Ontario Liberal Party division for my local riding, called "St. Paul's"). Millions of words were exchanged, thousands of hands shaken. The experience of entering politics had been the most exciting and rewarding one of my life. And then I continued that grassroots work in my constituency office where, five days a week, people would visit, call, email, or write me seeking assistance with a matter involving a public service. On weekends I would attend events in the local constituency, during which more people would ask for more help.

Most of the people who approached me for help received assistance in some fashion. Perhaps all we did is tell them who to contact to get assistance, or maybe we told them that their matter was in fact private, not something for an MPP to solve. But even the private matters—divorce, credit rating, unemployment, workplace troubles—sometimes included public assistance in some form. So we assisted.

Imagine a job where people respected your office enough to approach you for help, and then you helped them. Now multiply this feeling exponentially and you have a happy MPP.

But some MPPs get appointed to Cabinet, and some cabinet

ministers think that the most important part of their job is the work done in government, where the most bang for the buck is obtained. Rather than assisting the woman from Balliol Street who had cockroaches in her apartment, which she'd helpfully brought along in a resealable plastic bag and placed on my desk, I could work with my cabinet colleagues to fashion legislation and a process that was more tenant-friendly for thousands, perhaps millions of tenants.

The trick is to not let the latter impede helping the former; to not let the work of high utilitarian value preclude helping that lady with a purse full of cockroaches. Someone has to help her. And if it's not me, it might not be anyone. Or, even if someone from my office helps her, for which I'm usually rewarded with a vote at election time, I miss out on life's gardening. Predictably, the longer I was in politics, the less I got my hands dirty.

No wonder I wanted to leave by decade's end. I had originally been thirsty for human connection, but over time bought into the algorithm for popularity and public works. I mistook ego hits, via media coverage, for human connection. I got a rush from reading my name in a newspaper, or seeing myself on television. It was ego at its worst, and believe me, attracting media coverage makes the life of a media harlot a veritable rat race, an endless sprint on a wheel to nowhere.

If I ever find myself involved in politics again, it will be for the original reasons: human connection and service to others. Now, this is not to feign modesty; I was associated with many good works. But that was as much the result of the service and offerings of others as my own doings. Hillary Clinton is right that it takes a village to raise a child. But that doesn't mean that leading the village is the goal. The goal is better children and a better village.

FOURTEEN

Attorney General
v. Michael Bryant

After her presentation to Special Prosecutor Richard Peck, Marie Henein, my lawyer, received no signals from either Peck or his Ontario counterpart, Mark Sandler, as to whether they were inclined to drop the charges or to proceed to trial.

"Rollercoaster" is how she often described it to me. One day the nature of Peck's questions suggested that he was preparing to dismiss the charges. The next day he would seem hell-bent for a trial.

Throughout March, April, and May, Peck and Sandler conducted their own investigation, with the police, of every aspect of the case. They interviewed our own witnesses, checking their accounts with the affidavits filed by Marie from the March presentation. They re-interviewed the Crown witnesses—those relied upon by police in laying the charges.

And Peck himself, accompanied by Marie, inspected my Saab, which was held as evidence in a garage somewhere in Vaughan, Ontario. He scanned the marks on the hood, and witnessed first-hand the traces of Darcy Sheppard's blood specks on the inside of my windshield, demonstrating just how far in the car he was during the 28 seconds.

He sat inside the driver's seat, to get a sense of my perspective, imagining Darcy climbing in the car. The driver's seat was quite low to the ground, and Sheppard was above me, leaning in, climbing in, such that I had zero leverage against him.

"It was like sitting in a bathtub," I told Marie, "while trying to defend yourself against a giant climbing in the tub." Pushing him off, when the car wasn't moving, just wasn't an option for me.

Peck and Henein spoke almost every day during the week. Increasingly, Marie was able to anticipate Peck's concerns, to read behind the questions, pinpoint the evidence he needed, either from the videos or from a witness or an expert report. And for each piece of the puzzle Peck needed, Marie Henein had to deliver. If there were too many pieces missing, we knew, the case would go to trial.

The problem was, she told me, that the puzzle seemed to grow bigger with time. How complete did this growing puzzle need to be for Peck to have the confidence that there was no reasonable prospect of conviction? Every time it seemed that the puzzle was almost complete, another branch would form, leading to more inquiries, more puzzle-assembly. March, April, May. On it went, as the expanding puzzle was assembled: some pieces large, some tiny, intricate, elusive.

"WE NEED TO MEET," Marie said on the morning of May 21, 2010. She'd uttered those words a thousand times to me. It could mean anything. There was rarely a typical day during those nine months after the charges were laid. I was employed by now, but I always made Marie's requests a priority over my law practice. I was at her office within an hour. She asked me to sit down.

I suddenly had a feeling of dread, and I don't know why. That Marie was sporting her poker face was nothing new. But I'd known for weeks now that the Crown prosecutor was very close to a final decision as to whether or not he'd proceed to trial. Given all our efforts to have him drop the charges, simply proceeding to trial would have felt like a setback. I prepared myself for the worst.

"This Tuesday morning, May 25th, at 9:15, the prosecution will withdraw the information.... Drop the charges.... It's over, Michael. It's over."

I just stared at her, as she allowed herself a grin. She was clearly enjoying this moment, and deservedly so. This was as great a bit of lawyering as she'd ever done. Regardless, she'd saved my life, and I hope she knew it.

I put my face in both of my hands for what seemed like an hour. I felt void of thought. Just as the new normal had become Michael as Accused Felon, it changed. Michael as Officially Innocent was a new feeling I wasn't used to. My face was covered not to disguise tears—there was nothing I wouldn't do in front of Marie Henein—but because I didn't know who I was now. I didn't know what I'd look like. I stopped breathing for a few long seconds. Then I put my elbows on my knees and stared into the floor, my face only half covered now. Marie waited. I'm sure she'd seen this reaction before.

I hadn't noticed that she'd closed the door to the office, which only happened if something extraordinary was going on. There were no secrets in that law office, or the few secrets kept behind those closed doors were never meant to be shared. In this case, she was delivering good news to a client. Marie deserved to savour this one alone.

I thanked her, I know, but don't remember much more of what I said. Marie, though, needed no magic words from me, being that rare soul who needs no affirmation from others to find satisfaction in life.

"Now," she started to say, and I knew she was going to warn me against prematurely disclosing this news.

I cut her off. "I know, Marie. I know. I won't do anything to compromise this. Let's talk about who I can tell."

"Good," she said. "No one. You can tell no one, other than Susan."

Fine. I didn't care. I just wanted it to be Tuesday. I wanted it officially over. I'd suddenly grown as skeptical of the outcome as Marie had been. In fact, I was terrified about a syllable leaking. At the best of times, anything could happen to undo such arrangements between the time they were agreed to by lawyers and the time they were presented before a judge. Given the potential consequences, I wanted to do nothing that might displease anyone in any way.

"You're going to have to figure out what to do with the media afterwards, but let me help you. It's not my expertise but you're going to need some help. Maybe get Nikki involved at the last possible minute."

I agreed that I'd have to appear before the media. Otherwise, I'd be savaged. *What does he have to hide?* Moreover, a press conference would allow me to be presented on TV in a controlled environment, without protesters or couriers or pit bull breeders heckling me. And once I'd answered questions, I could go back to doing no more media. I had zero appetite for public *anything,* at that moment.

I knew from experience that a press conference could be organized in a few hours with an experienced group of people. Alone, I had no clue how I'd do it. I just needed to be sure that Nikki was available that morning. Plus I wanted Jan Innes's help on everything, especially my remarks. As it turned out, Jan was able to clear her morning at the last possible minute, and she ran the presser like she had for Premier David Peterson, and for the great Canadian telecom giant Ted Rogers.

Indeed, Nikki and Jan were able to get a room at the Sheraton booked first thing Tuesday morning, then order all the equipment needed for a press conference, then get the word out that I'd be available to the media after the court proceedings were over. Then Nikki called my former staffers from my political days: Sandra

D'Ambrosio, Rod Elliot, Emily Bullock, Sarah Roberts, Beth Hirshfeld. They all came out, somehow.

WHEN THE SUNNY SPRING Tuesday of May 25, 2010, arrived in Toronto, the morning rituals in our home might have seemed entirely normal, but they weren't. Anxiety and fear should probably have vanished from my heart, but they hadn't.

I had a date at 9:15 a.m. in a courtroom at Old City Hall to hear the outcome of the two charges against me: criminal negligence causing death and dangerous driving causing death. We'd kept the news to ourselves over the weekend. I'd spent it redrafting some brief remarks for the presser.

We were so paranoid about locking down the result that we didn't even share the news with our parents. Within an hour of Marie telling me that the charges were being dropped, the previous Friday, I was on the front lawn of our house, where media had camped out nine months previous, telling Susan the news. I can't remember why she was on the front lawn, but I remember her looking panicked at the odd look on my face.

"What?! What?!"

I fixed the odd look into a smile. "It's over."

We embraced, then ran in the house, for fear that someone could hear us discussing the prosecutor's decision.

By Tuesday morning, Susan and I felt it was safe to tell our parents who, along with us, had spent nine trying months wondering what would become of their children and grandchildren. It was time also to tell Sadie and Louie that not only had their father been in a car accident involving a man's death nine months ago, but that the police also had charged me with killing the man. The kids were going to have to learn this in any event. I didn't want them hearing something on the playground.

Just before Sadie and Louie were to leave for school with Sarah,

I took them aside. As any parent would understand, our biggest concern through all of this had been the possible harm it would do our children. I hadn't told them I'd been arrested because I was worried they would just assume that it meant I was going to jail. So as I talked to them on the morning of May 25, I was able to finally address my arrest and charges.

"Guys, before you go, I have something to tell you," I said.

They had their backpacks on, Old Navy sweatshirts, Pink and Blue, standing side-by-side, looking up at me, wondering what I was going to say. Their eyes seemed to grow bigger as I knelt down and spoke as clearly as I could. I told them that the police had arrested me, but that they had changed their minds.

When I said the police arrested me, Sadie's eyes went wide and she sucked in her breath. Almost in the same sentence, I said, "But they've changed their minds and they are unarresting me," and she exhaled and breathed out a sigh of relief. I explained that I might be in the newspaper again and warned Sarah, as she took them off to school, to keep an eye out for reporters or cameras and if she spotted any that it might be a good idea to "lose your capacity to speak English."

Susan called her parents and I called mine to tell them the charges were being dropped. For my parents, it had been a long nine months. Nothing like this had happened to our family—death, criminal charges, public castigation. My parents had enjoyed being the annoying couple with the envious family narrative. Their youngest, Alan, had an exotic job in an exciting location—working at a professional sports franchise in the city that gave us Elvis. Their daughter had been named one of Canada's Outstanding Principals, and her children and husband had brought nothing but joy to the proud grandparents. I'd had my political success, of which they were insufferably proud; they loved Susan and their grandchildren in Toronto. Then, in their seventies, the unexpected: the prodigal son on the front page of the Victoria paper, charged with killing someone.

And on the glorious morning of May 25, 2010, I was able to phone and tell them that, barring some procedural snafu in the next couple of hours, it was over.

They both just wept. No words. There were just no words to say. Until finally Dad asked me to repeat again what I'd said. And Mom said "thank goodness" over and over. It was a short phone call. I prayed that the 28 seconds hadn't taken too much off their lives.

A couple more calls to make. My sister Janine, also in Victoria, choked, wept, and seemed to collapse. She repeated "oh Michael, thank god," a few times. I got my brother Alan's voicemail, and he called back, with a catch in his voice. He had checked in regularly from his workplace in Memphis over the past nine months. Little did I know, I would have the opportunity to watch over him too, soon enough, in another terrible ordeal to hit my family. More on that later.

Susan's father, Henry, had also been quite indignant and defensive of me, which was uncharacteristic, and her mother, Arlene, had always been great to me, so they were also relieved to get the news. From across the room, and up the stairs, I could hear Arlene's reaction through the telephone. Something between a sigh and a whoop and a little Yiddish.

So the day of May 25th began with a mix of domestic routine, the cautious spreading of relief and happiness, and preparation for what was to come. In short order, Marie Henein arrived to pick up Susan and me, and the three of us drove to Old City Hall and our date at the Ontario Court of Justice. On arriving there, we did that stage-managed walk the media require for their shots. Marie whispered to me, "Take your wife's hand" as we headed to the court. As usual, I was kind of lost in my thoughts and was oblivious to stagecraft.

There were a couple of people from the fellowship of recovery, folks who had shown up completely unsolicited, to support me. Professor Pina D'Agostino, a friend of Susan's and mine from Osgoode Hall Law School, was there as well for moral support. She must have heard the news story and raced from the law school to Old City Hall, in rush hour. When we greeted Pina with surprise, she just shrugged her shoulders and said, "I'm Italian," like that should explain it.

I was still worried. I knew that anything could go wrong. I knew of Judge Paul Bentley, although obviously I hadn't appointed him. I remembered he had been in a very serious bicycle accident and had had to take a long leave of absence. He was highly respected as the founding justice of Toronto's Drug Court.* But I wasn't sure if he'd been involved in a case with this kind of profile. I knew that sometimes judges could unknowingly, almost subconsciously, behave differently with cases with significant profile. If the judge was paranoid about appearances, paranoid of being misjudged as biased, then he or she could lean too far the other way, to the detriment of the accused. All this stuff was running through my head. Anything could happen.

I was also worried about bike couriers making a scene and some kind of protest overtaking the legal proceedings. I had read very little over those nine months, especially not the blogs that had sprung up angrily denouncing me, which I learned about only later. I'd had very little contact with or awareness of the outraged community of bike couriers—with a couple of exceptions.

One of the exceptions arose a couple months after the 28

---

* Mr. Justice Paul Bentley pioneered addiction treatment courts in Canada, and established the International Association of Drug Treatment Courts. He was the founding and presiding Justice for Toronto's Drug Treatment Court, commencing in 1998. Justice Bentley died of cancer in June 2011. Suffice it to say, my trepidation regarding the presiding judge was paranoid, irrational, and foolish.

seconds. For a time, I kept seeing couriers giving me double-takes as they rode by, whenever I went to Marie Henein's office, which I visited probably three times a week. But that was the extent of it: some recognition, and nothing more. I wondered if I was imagining the double-take. Paranoid, maybe.

One day in late October, I came out of Marie's office and was walking through a downtown alley toward a friend's office. I became aware of a female courier following me. Was she? Was I being paranoid again? I sensed that maybe I'd seen her before.

When I came outside again after my visit, about ten minutes later, she was still there. Waiting.

She said, "Michael Bryant?"

"Yeah?" (It never occurs to me to just lie in those situations. Maybe I'm reflexively hoping that my ego will get stroked by the recognition.)

She said, "I'm a real admirer of your work." Bright smile, bright eyes.

"Oh, that's nice ... thank you." Bright smile returned.

"How do you do it?"

Then I noticed that the smile was forced, constipated, painful. And her hands were trembling.

"How do I do ... what?"

"Get away with murder!... How do you do it, you motherfu—!!"

I spun on my heel and walked away from her, toward King Street, where it was always busy.

By now her horror-film growl had turned into shrieks.

"Murderer! Murderer!" She asked me if I took Murder 101 at Harvard. A few people walked past in the wide alley, barely looking up at the scene, as I moved quickly away from her.

A repeat of that performance was what I prepared myself for as we walked toward the courtroom on May 25th, seven months later. I wondered if the court security was nervous too.

As 9:15 approached, Susan and I entered the court and sat at a table behind Marie and her team. Darcy's father Allan was in the courtroom and so was Misty Bailey, Darcy's girlfriend of a few months. She was surrounded by victim services staff from the Ministry of the Attorney General. Allan Sheppard just looked alone.

I looked over at them a lot. I wished there was a way for me to make Mr. Sheppard, in particular, understand how deeply I regretted what had happened. Misty continued to weep, but never looked in my direction. Mr. Sheppard sat still, weighed down by a composed, resigned, quiet sorrow.

Marie had already told me that on the way in I wasn't to acknowledge Special Prosecutor Richard Peck or Ontario Prosecutor Mark Sandler. Don't nod at them. Don't wave at them. Don't shake their hands. Stay away from them. She wanted no perception of friendliness between the prosecutor and me, or anything that would look as if some fix was in, which obviously it wasn't. I wasn't planning on yukking it up with them, anyways.

Just before proceedings began, Sandler spun around and grabbed a chair from one of the tables. He put it in the well of the court, the middle of the room, and asked me to sit on the chair. I looked over at Susan and moved away from her. She seemed to swallow hard. Sitting down on that chair, I felt very exposed. The table had served as a cloak of sorts. Like a podium for a speaker. Something between the orator and the audience. But that was gone now. I was sitting there, fighting the impulse to squirm, for my leg to shake (as it constantly does), and tried not to look around. I still don't know if the purpose of that was to give me a clear view of the judge, or because the accused should be seen to be sitting on a dock.

And then it began. Richard Peck began speaking. And the words I was waiting for were almost the first that he uttered: "Your Honour, I am asking that the information before the court be marked as withdrawn."

So formal, these words, so technical. The "information" spoken of by Peck was the charges laid against me on August 31, 2009. Those charges were to be "marked as withdrawn." He wasn't asking the court to withdraw them: that was not within its jurisdiction. It was only within Peck's jurisdiction to drop the charges, and with those words he'd done exactly that. Done, as in past tense. My nervousness drained away.

But of course the extraordinary show had just begun. It was stranger than fiction that a former Attorney General in Canada would be charged with such serious crimes. It was exceptional but appropriate that the Crown (represented by the Attorney General of the day) had appointed an independent prosecutor from another province. It was unprecedented that Marie Henein had opened her defence case to prosecutors and police before trial. And it was unusual that the prosecutor would give the reasons for withdrawing charges in open court. Usually, the prosecutor just drops the charges unceremoniously, phoning defence counsel, and that's it. The discretion lies solely with the prosecutor, and the judge need not approve anything. It's like a police officer laying charges, or a parking constable writing a parking ticket.

But as Marie often said: "There's nothing ordinary about this case."

That morning, Peck set out in detail the reasons for the withdrawal of the charges against me, a move that was widely praised, by lawyers and newspaper editorialists, for the transparency and credibility it gave the process. Since the laying of charges, "a great deal more has been learned from the ongoing investigation," Peck said. The case "falls short of the standard" needed to sustain a reasonable prospect of conviction, he said.

"I wish to emphasize that this decision is mine and mine alone. I wish to note that officials of the Ministry of the Attorney General in Ontario had no input into this decision whatsoever, and that includes the Attorney General himself.... That approach is consistent with the independence demanded of me in this exercise."

AS PECK SPOKE, I drifted between listening closely to his remarks, and observing other people in the courtroom. From my vantage point in the middle of the court, I occasionally looked around, and behind, and upwards. Everyone seemed to be focused on the front of the court, to Peck's submissions. There were two levels to this courtroom, with seats on the same floor as counsel and judge, and then a second floor, like a balcony, where there were still more seats. Probably a hundred people or so.

The courtroom used to be the Toronto City Council Chamber, where the council met between 1899 and 1965, after which the grand, Romanesque space was converted into a courtroom, and a new City Hall was constructed. But the room, like most in Old City Hall, retained its grandeur. The spectators' gallery for council simply became overflow for court observers. There were many details in that room that caught my eye.

I'd been in that courtroom as Attorney General, for various formal ceremonies, including the swearing in of the current chief justice that I'd appointed. I'd also spoken there at the graduation of the Drug Court participants, discussed in another Chapter. I'd been newly sober when I'd addressed those fellow travellers, with whom I shared much, notwithstanding that I was the attorney, and they were the accused.

Now I too was here as the accused. The room looked entirely different for me.

I felt that I was in that room for the first time, even though I'd last been there about a year previous, gowned up in the formal attire worn by barristers sometimes, speaking exuberantly about Ontario's first ever female chief justice of the Ontario Court of

Justice. I'd posed for photos with Chief Justice Bonkalo, and also with my hero Ian Scott, who had appointed her as a Crown prosecutor when he'd been Attorney General.

This courtroom was different now, to me. I wasn't there as an officer of the court, but as an object of the court's attention. I wasn't to speak, but nor was I a spectator. Whereas before I'd been a headline star of the show, now I felt nothing about stardom. I felt rightly humbled in that courtroom, for the first time. I was no more or less special than anyone else in that room. Yes, that courtroom felt different to me. Everything did.

Peck began chronologically, taking the court through the early events of August 31, 2009: Sheppard's intoxication, his visit to his girlfriend's apartment, the 911 calls by neighbours reporting Sheppard assaulting his girlfriend, and then "a homeless man, possibly with a bicycle lock," in Peck's words. Then Peck brought Sheppard to the point of no return, as it turned out, with him crossing in front of my car. The next question, Peck said, was whether Sheppard had been the aggressor.

Here was the part of the proceedings where Peck would outline past instances of Sheppard attacking other people—the so-called Scopelliti evidence. I looked over at Allan Sheppard, to see if he was offended by this part. There's no question that this information was legally relevant to establishing who was the aggressor. But I've no doubt that this was very hurtful to hear, yet again, for anyone who wanted to grieve Darcy's passing, rather than dwell on his demons. Allan Sheppard continued to sit very still, expressing little other than the deep sorrow I sensed, but only he knows what all that felt like. I've got a son too, and I wouldn't have wanted to walk a mile in Allan Sheppard's shoes, especially on this spring morning in this hallowed courtroom, hearing a chronicling of the painfully unmanageable life of Darcy Sheppard.

Peck outlined six separate incidents of violence involving

Sheppard. Marie had another half-dozen that could also have been included, but the point was made. Peck referred to each witness who'd come forward by their initials. "A number of citizens who had had incidents with [Sheppard] recognized him and believed that they should turn this information over to the police, or to the defence, for further investigation. All of the incidents described were investigated by the Crown and/or the police."

I looked over at Susan, who was riveted, trying to make sense of all this, and needing more facts to do so. I looked at Misty, weeping still. At Allan Sheppard, watching Peck, and occasionally just looking down—blinking slowly, it seemed to me.

"J.M." was a grandmother, in her late seventies, who was in her car alone when suddenly confronted by Darcy Sheppard at a traffic light. "He started swearing." He demanded that she get out of her car. "He was angry, she could not figure out why." She tried to drive away from him, but he caught up to her and "slammed his bicycle right in front of her. He was trying to stop her car. He was now standing ... feet apart, he started advancing toward her, yelling at her to get out of the car." She "gunned it," in her words, driving across the street, onto a sidewalk, to escape. "She described him as being like a madman."

Some of these stories I was very familiar with. Some I had heard only fragments. At a certain point, the litany of stories that came forward amounted to one story: Darcy Sheppard could get very angry, and violent, with drivers of automobiles, who more often than not were unaware of what prompted Darcy's anger, and who described him as raving, mad, and extreme; people who feared for their lives, so much so that they contacted police or the defence to tell their stories (sometimes repeating the stories told to the police).

As I listed to the J.M. incident, of course I imagined the terror of a 70-year-plus woman, thinking of my own mother. At that age, the face of their fear is like a child's; they're so astonished, for elderly people tend not to throw themselves into violent situations, wary as they are of their own frailties.

But I also imagined Darcy Sheppard's own fear. In his mind, perhaps, the burning indignation of yet another person disrespecting him, another moment of chaos heaped upon a life out of control, leading him to dangerously will the situation under control, a control framed by rage, and yet again that became impossible as the drivers sought to escape him, his futile efforts at control, his justice. It was gasoline on his lit fury. So furious that the senselessness of attacking a grandmother did not deter him.

If you've never experienced such rage, you are fortunate. I'm not justifying his actions, but the time I've spent in recovery has taught me that for every injustice, for every resentment, there are a host of contributors, some people from the past, some imagined, some rational, irrational, some just hellish memories that can't be shaken without divine intervention.

When I heard J.M.'s story, I was obviously grateful for her courage to come forward, and subject herself to interviews and re-interviews and the pain of reliving a frightful memory. I felt an instant connection to her astonishment and need to escape this wild and inexplicable spectacle of Darcy Sheppard on that attack. And there was also a fleeting moment of recognition, of the demons at work in Darcy Sheppard's own hell.

After all, for several years now, I've sat in rooms and heard tales of terror from men just like Darcy. Exactly like him. And often they shared an incident on the streets of Toronto that had triggered the terror, given and taken, by the speaker at one of these weekly meetings. That terror lived by these men (and women too), however, could be somewhat managed, more often than not, as long as they were sober.

Typically, the imperfect end to these fellow alcoholics' stories was one of progress. Not perfection—few happy endings arise when that kind of terror is in the air. But progress: a slowly learned capacity to not repeat past bursts of anger, or to not allow it to so escalate. This progress, I hear almost every week as I sit on those chairs to be stacked eight-high at the end of the night, this progress demonstrates hope—to the speaker, as he tells it, and to all of us, as we live it with him, often with a weary nod of the head.

Many, many miles have been walked in the shoes of our brothers and sisters in this fellowship of recovering alcoholics, men and women who connect with each other's failures, *our failures*, in facing some version of the hell that Darcy could not manage, but which we've learned together to manage a little better than we had in the past. And so we reflexively nod our heads, in communion with the hope of that progress, and the miracle of one man's survival, one woman's survival, for one day, in sobriety.

"A.P." was a salesman crossing the road, in the wrong place, at the wrong time, Richard Peck began with the second instance of Scopelliti evidence. Darcy Sheppard shaved the tiger, "zoomed by" A.P., and exchanged expletives with A.P. on Yonge Street. What followed might not seem remarkable, except that A.P. was not alone in his confrontation with Sheppard. He was larger than Darcy Sheppard, which would have made A.P. a very, very large man, and he was accompanied by four co-workers. None of that slowed Darcy's anger, "swearing and shouting loudly ... spitting" and, wielding a bike lock, yelling "You want to go, let's go." A.P. said he "could smell alcohol on his breath."

That happened in June of 2009, Darcy's last few months of life, and a time of increasing anger and violence, as evidenced by the string of reports that came in to the police and to Marie Henein. The next incident Peck reported on, involving "C.C.," a 23-year-old woman, happened in late July 2009. Just over a month later, it would end for Darcy Sheppard.

C.C. was driving downtown. "A cyclist was swerving in and out of traffic in an aggressive way." As single-lane traffic was merging, Sheppard felt that he'd been cut off by C.C. There was yelling, then something happened with which I was familiar: "The cyclist passed her and pulled in front. He did a half-turn parallel to the front bumper of her car. She had to slam on her brakes to avoid hitting him." For me, this was an eerie re-enactment of the 28 seconds.

Peck continued: "The cyclist threw his bike on the ground and came at her. He was completely enraged. He called her a whore and a stupid bitch. She was scared, panicking, completely terrified, in her words. He repeatedly spat on her vehicle and her through her partially open window. She rolled up her window. She reversed her car, drove to the right. At first, the cyclist pursued her, but soon was diverted—his attention was diverted to another driver.

"When she saw his photograph in the newspaper, she burst into tears because she knew this was the cyclist who had attacked her. She contacted the police."

Next was the incident of August 11, 2009, which was photo-graphed by David Wires from his office window. These photographs were "remarkable," Peck said, as he tendered them as exhibits for the court and stated, ominously, that "the probative force of that type of evidence cannot be denied." Put another way, those photos, and the story behind them, were perhaps all that was needed for Peck to drop the charges.

As Peck told the court, "D.T.," in his BMW, was confronted by a shirtless Darcy Sheppard, on foot. D.T. was a foot over into the oncoming traffic lane, which had lit Darcy's fuse. "The situation escalated. The man kept screaming, yelling, taunting, delivering expletives. He reached into D.T.'s car and tried to grab for the keys but it was a keyless model. He tried to smack D.T. in the face and grab the earpiece for his Bluetooth from his ear." When D.T. pushed Darcy's hands out of the car, he responded: 'Get out of the f'ing car and I'll beat your head in.' He spat all over the car and was banging on it, grabbing the car and jumping on it."

And this part gave me chills: "The car had a narrow running board. He was holding onto the window. When D.T. tried to roll up the window, he backed away and then jumped back onto the car. He would not back off. D.T. tried to back the car up, but the individual jumped on the car and rode with it backwards." Peck himself seemed taken by this incident, as he said: "At some point, Mr. Sheppard is the person we're talking about, had his attention diverted by another person, and it was then that D.T. was able to drive off and go home and wash the spit off his car."

There were two additional incidents. One involved "B.S." and also happened in August. I've told that story already. The other involved "L.S.," on August 31st, the same day as the 28 seconds. In fact, this happened only a few hours before the 28 seconds—at 6:20 p.m. L.S. was driving downtown, and spotted "a cyclist who was weaving in and out in front of cars and doing figure eights in the intersection. She was frightened. The cyclist was acting erratically" and his "actions were preventing cars from driving."

This story I hadn't heard before, or maybe I didn't want to hear it. Of course, Marie had shared it with me but her words hadn't sunk in, for me. "She had to slam on her brakes a couple of times to keep from hitting him.... She observed the cyclist put his hand through the open driver's side window of a BMW ... to reach for the steering wheel or scare the driver. The cyclist had been banging on many car windshields and was yelling at drivers."

I looked over at Susan, listening to Peck put the pieces of the puzzle together. Her eyes were particularly wide open. She'd previously heard tidbits about Darcy Sheppard's similar incidents of attacking motorists. But to have them detailed by Peck—Susan was shocked, she later told me. Shocked at the terror wrought by this one man upon so many.

Peck went on to state the obvious: "These would appear to reflect an escalating cycle of aggressiveness toward motorists in the days leading to the fatal interaction with Mr. Bryant." It may have been obvious, but its implications had not before been the subject of my many internal symposiums of regret. I'd considered what might have happened that night, but not what might have happened had Sheppard not chosen Susan, me, and the Saab to confront that night.

If Sheppard's inner turmoil was reflected in "an escalating cycle of aggressiveness towards motorists," then his demons must have been multiplying and moshing. As I inhaled deeply, then stared down at my shoes, Peck's description of Darcy Sheppard's life was ironically sobering. Flashing before my eyes were frantic looks from friends and loved ones, Marie Henein in particular, saying something to the effect that Darcy Sheppard was not going to leave Bloor Street alive that night of August 31st. Or, at least, someone was going to the hospital that night at his behest, they said, hoping to comfort me.

I shook my head imperceptibly. That wasn't the point, to me. The point was that Sheppard was steadily cracking up in a universe that was chaotic enough, for him. I'm familiar with a few of Darcy's demons; familiar with the vacillation between sense and nonsense; familiar with the sulphuric winds of madness. But at its worst, I can escape to an inner sanctuary, that cave within a cave that I sought out in my night in the cell; that quiet place, deep under the turbulent Pacific Ocean, where everything went more slowly. However, that exit was blocked, for Darcy. Likely it was blocked because he was drunk. Or maybe he'd just reached a point of such mania that the only exit was destined to be violent. In any event, those 28 seconds on Bloor Street were the end of a long road for him, like a diver doomed for the bends, who'd started way too deep, and rose way, way too fast.

I looked over again at Allan Sheppard, who was poised but clearly pained by this part of the prosecutor's explication. "These facts that I am outlining here again are being mentioned because they have significant legal relevance," Peck emphasized. "They are not to demonize Mr. Sheppard, nor as the basis for anyone suggesting that he somehow deserved his fate."

Demonize? I thought, blinking again toward his father. *Impossible.* Darcy had enough demons, for which I judged not, and for which he deserved more compassion and aid than ever offered or received in his life, at least from our criminal justice system. Allan Sheppard had done all he could, I thought. But here we were, in a courtroom, yet again, dealing with the ravages of Darcy's addictions, nightmares past, and his unrelenting demons. At least the Crown, Richard Peck, had the decency to pay homage to the darkness that was not Darcy himself, but the living hell in which he resided.

This was all cold comfort to my wife. I didn't always share these thoughts directly with her. My obvious and great compassion for Susan's suffering, at Darcy's behest, was poorly expressed. That I could empathize with Sheppard's suffering was a product of my recovery in sobriety, itself an ongoing mystery to Susan. But it was a singular journey for me. Just as my connection to his afflictions could be shared only by someone in the fellowship of the addicted. Somehow it all just sounded like I felt more for him than I did for her, which wasn't true at all for me, but that's how it felt sometimes for Susan.

What a mess. What a mess.

Then Peck provided a few comments on Sheppard's "criminal record going back many years," and provided some detailed background on Darcy Sheppard's life. (More on that in a separate Chapter.)

Finally, the prosecutor described the 28 seconds. For the first time, I felt very anxious. Reliving that night was something that I'd done, and Marie had tried to elicit from me, but I'd never heard someone describe what happened, objectively, based on the evidence. It made it all feel, to me, too real.

Nothing he said differs from the 28 Seconds Chapter, as far as I can tell. In any event, here were some of the key findings: "One of the largely consistent themes [arising from the evidence provided by witness accounts and the videos] is that Mr. Sheppard was acting loudly and aggressively, confronting Mr. Bryant, while he and his wife remained passive. Ms. Abramovitch, in her statement, described Mr. Sheppard as terrifying."

Peck then turned his attention to the 2.5 seconds that became the focus of many a YouTube video, usually doctored up to make the scene look menacing. It's basically the only time Sheppard and the Saab came into contact, prior to his own efforts to climb into the Saab as I tried to get away. It was the 2.5 seconds that became the focus for Peck in determining whether to prosecute the lesser charge of dangerous driving (as opposed to dangerous driving causing death, or to criminal negligence causing death):

> At this point Mr. Bryant's car has stalled again, and he describes himself as being in a state of panic. He was trying to get his car started and concentrating on that task. The Saab had a sensitive and tight clutch, as confirmed by the investigation.
>
> When the vehicle restarted it accelerated into Mr. Sheppard causing him to land on the hood of the vehicle. At the point of this third movement forward of the vehicle, Mr. Bryant states that he had been looking down while engaged in his efforts to restart the car. When he looked up he saw

Mr. Sheppard on the hood of the car and immediately hit the brakes.

The expert evidence demonstrates that approximately 2.5 seconds elapsed from the time the vehicle started its forward motion to the time it came to a stop. The brake lights were visible approximately one second into this forward movement. There is a little bit of debate among the teams of experts on that. One expert has it at 0.8 seconds, and the other has it at 1.4 seconds, it's a flash.

... There is no evidence that the third movement at a relatively low speed caused any serious injury. It was brief in duration.

In other words, Peck looked at prosecuting me for dangerous driving, based on actions that took place over the course of between 1.1 seconds and 1.7 seconds. The laws of physics alone would make it impossible for someone to commit the felony dangerous driving from a stalled car in one-and-a-half seconds. The charge would not be pursued.

The prosecutor continued to work through the 28 seconds, meticulously. A few remarks stuck out, for me, as I sat through his submissions: "Mr. Sheppard then leapt onto the vehicle as the vehicle began to move away.... The accounts of the eyewitnesses, coupled with the forensic examinations, confirm that Mr. Sheppard was attempting to attack Mr. Bryant at that time. When he leapt onto the car, his hand or hands were inside the vehicle.... Impressions consistent with having come from Mr. Sheppard's jeans were found in the rubberized area on the top of the driver's door. This latter finding is consistent with the witness who described Mr. Sheppard as being in the car from the waist up."

The thought of him growing out of the door and into the

car, smothering me, reminded me how close Sheppard had got to Susan—a couple feet away. All along, her presence had driven my actions. It was one thing to try to get out of the car to defend myself. It was another when she too was at risk. Now it was clear to me, in that courtroom, how it might have been for her.

Remember, Susan and I had never discussed her perspective on what happened. She never told me how close she'd come to being potentially struck by Darcy Sheppard. As it turns out, it's all blacked out for her. She remembers none of this part of the 28 seconds.

How fast was the car going? "Expert analysis of some of the video has determined that the average speed of the vehicle during this drive was somewhere in the range of ... 21 miles per hour. It appears that the vehicle may never have left first gear during the course of this drive."

What of the media reports that I was bashing Sheppard against trees and a mailbox? "A forensic examination of the vehicle and the curb demonstrates that the Saab did not rub up against the curb or mount the curb at any time during the portion of the drive."

Was Darcy dragged down Bloor Street for a kilometre, as reported? "The total distance from the point where Mr. Sheppard jumped onto the car, to the point where he fell off, was approximately 100 metres."

How did Darcy Sheppard actually die? Was he run over by the Saab? Did the car crush him? "The vehicle was travelling on the south side of the eastbound lane. A fire hydrant was located close to the south curb in the area of 131 Bloor Street. The side cap of the fire hydrant pointed toward the curb, that is toward the north. The distance from the side cap to the curb was one foot. This side cap caught Mr. Sheppard on the left torso, on the exterior of his torso. This caused him to dislodge from the car, striking his head either on a curb or on a raised patch of asphalt. The mechanics of his death involve an impact to the right side of the head that caused fatal damage to the brain stem."

As those words were spoken in court the air hung still; not one of the more than a hundred people in the courtroom stirred or shuffled or coughed. It was as if everyone were holding their breath.

How long did all this take to unfold? "Based on an analysis of the elapsed time from the various videos, it appears that only 10.5 seconds elapsed from the time Mr. Sheppard blocked the Saab to the time he was thrown from the hood in that third forward movement.... [T]he time from when Mr. Sheppard first pulled in front of the Saab, until he was dislodged from the Saab at 131 Bloor Street when he fell off the car and died, was less than half a minute. Slight disagreement, one expert has it at 27.5, and one has it at 28.5 seconds, less than half a minute."

This was the first time that the exact number of seconds had caught my attention. I'd always been aware that it was under half a minute, at least since Marie had told me as much. But the phrase 28 seconds started flashing before my eyes. *28 Seconds.*

Peck then outlined the law of dangerous driving causing death, of criminal negligence, and of the lesser charge of dangerous driving. I had tuned out by now, even as he was speaking the critical words: "The Crown must evaluate the totality of the evidence. Having done so, there is no reasonable prospect of conviction on these or other *Criminal Code* charges. Accordingly, I have asked that these charges be marked as withdrawn."

All I could think of was: 28 Seconds.

As I heard the words "charges be marked as withdrawn," I awoke from wherever I was. Charges withdrawn. 28 Seconds.

In closing, Peck put aside formalities, and made one final observation about this case of "extremely tragic consequences." He said: "One man's life has been ineluctably affected, while another's has been taken. Almost 400 years ago John Donne said that every person's death diminishes us. Those words, true then, resonate today in the solemnity of this courtroom." As they did with me.

And with that, the special prosecutor sat down, his work completed.

When my lawyer Marie Henein addressed the court, it was, for me, anticlimactic yet deeply moving. If anyone had awaited her refutation of his words, they would be disappointed. She simply confirmed what the prosecutor had found, but with some powerful perspective. I felt profoundly supported by Marie Henein at that moment, as if all along she had been roughing me up, testing me, preparing me, gutting me, for this moment of great advocacy and compassion. If I had been at times detached and distracted during Peck's presentation, I was not when Marie spoke. I looked over at Susan again, who sat up, shoulders back, breathing more deeply.

Marie said that what happened on August 31, 2009, was about "one thing and one thing only. That the commonplace decisions that each of us make every minute of every day can put us in a situation that, in our wildest dreams, we would never have imagined. It could have been any of us driving home in that car on August 31, 2009, and it is this that resonates with, and has struck a chord with, the numerous members of the public, many of whom have actually taken the time to contact me and to speak about these events and how they have impacted them.

"Tragedies are rarely expected or intended. The little decisions we make daily, meaningless and quickly forgotten at the time, can have a life-altering impact."

Her submission alone, she noted, had taken much longer than this particular life-altering 28 seconds.

"None of us think of our lives changing in twenty-eight seconds. Twenty-eight seconds and you are in the criminal-justice system. Twenty-eight seconds, you are in the back of a police car, twenty-eight seconds and you do not get home to your children, twenty-eight seconds of heart-breaking tragedy for everyone. It is twenty-eight seconds that Michael and Susan will live with for the rest of their lives. It is twenty-eight seconds that has saddened us all."

Most important, as far as the court was concerned, she said, it was 28 seconds that investigators had spent months dissecting and analyzing and researching. And at the end, the only conclusion that was available from the evidence was to withdraw the charges.

Justice Bentley spoke at the end, affirming the proper role of a judge in a prosecution: pursuing or dropping criminal charges "is totally up to the Crown." He rightly complimented Henein, Peck, and Sandler, then spoke the words I'd awaited since the night I spent in jail, nine months previous. These words made me choke up, and dissolved a great weight upon me. "So at the request of the Crown, the charge is withdrawn. Adjourn the courtroom."

I exhaled, and turned to Susan.

She offered a curious look, and blurted out: "So that's what happened!"

The astonishing truth is, she didn't know, until that morning, exactly what had happened. She remembered only about 10 of the 28 seconds. And we'd been ordered by our respective lawyers not to discuss what had happened, in case we went to trial and were summoned to testify. It would be bad if our accounts looked as if they'd been, for lack of a better term, matched and married so as to provide mutual support. We were such pious officers of the court that we did as we were told.

Susan wiped away some tears. She'd been elated all day, and since we'd learned the news that the prosecutor was dropping the charges. Peck's presentation was fascinating to her, as she had felt completely in the dark about the events, and about the defence efforts and activities over the past nine months. Perhaps that's because I too was disconnected from a lot of details, or perhaps because I'd failed to loop her in, for whatever reason: to avoid perceived collusion regarding her potential witness testimony, or because I was simply dysfunctional.

In any event, Peck's presentation was revelatory to Susan. Her intellect was stirred, not her emotions. But Marie's presentation had been both intellectual and gut-wrenching. It had deflated Susan's pink cloud, at least momentarily, and the crash to earth left her turned inside out. Susan was also angry at Marie's conciliatory words toward the police.

And this is an important distinction that Susan would often make, in her own personal narrative of the 28 seconds. For Susan, it wasn't about how anything could change in a New York minute. It was about the power of the police.

"I can be an upstanding citizen," she said to me at our kitchen table one night, "who does nothing wrong, but who can still have my life ruined by a police officer, *just like that,*" snapping her fingers, "because they've got tyrannical powers.... Okay, fine, the prosecutors and the judges can clean up the cops' mess. So the charges got dropped against you. But just look at us. *Look at what they did to us.*"

So Susan bristled at any kind words about the work of the police in my case. Her fear, her outrage, at the current state of police powers in Canada remains the same today.

But now, at Old City Hall, we were done with the police. We hugged for a long time. We were swarmed by friends. Then Marie Henein appeared suddenly before us. She looked pleased, content, in a fashion I'd not seen before. A grin, neither enthusiastic nor surprised.

It was time to thank her.

"Marie. Thanks for saving my life."

"You're innocent, Michael, and I just did my job." And she shrugged. That was it.

I watched people hurry out of the courtroom. Some more hugs

were exchanged with well wishers, but they were awkward and rushed, on my account. I was agitated, nervous about what would happen next. I knew that others had done their work, and rendered the just result. But now I had to go face the media. Now it was my turn to say something, *do something*, for the first time since summer had passed from autumn, to winter, and finally spring.

We lingered, as the courtroom buzzed with conversation, so as to let Mr. Sheppard and Misty Bailey leave. Then, Marie, Susan, and I left Old City Hall through a back door, where one of her associates was waiting with a car, and we drove over to the Sheraton hotel for the press conference.

I read a statement that I had worked on over the weekend. I wasn't really on my game. I was still out of it. A former staffer, Sandra D'Ambrosio, told me later that I came across as someone who was pretty messed up. "As you should be," she said. "I wouldn't have changed a thing." In this case, perception definitely was reality.

What I told the media was that I would never forget the unnecessary tragedy of that night. "A young man is dead and for his family and friends that remains the searing memory. To them I express my sympathies and sincere condolences. I have grieved that loss and I always will.... This has turned out," I said, with more knowing than anyone really understood, "to be a tale of addiction, mental health, an independent justice system, a tragic death, and a couple out on their wedding anniversary with the top down. It is not a morality play about bikes versus cars, couriers versus drivers, or about class, privilege, and politics. It's just about how, in twenty-eight seconds, everything can change. And, thereafter, time marches on. And so will I."

Afterwards, Marie and I took a few predictable questions, about my future, and about facts that Peck had addressed.

After that, as I was leaving, a reporter shouted out to me, "Are you going to get another convertible?"

In the old days, I would just open up my mouth and let some typical quip come out. But I just bit my lip and said, "We'll see."

That response may have provided the glimpse of a more subdued, restrained Michael Bryant. But it also gave me an idea.

Susan and I got dropped off outside her office at First Canadian Place. Waiting for us there was Stephen LeDrew, a former president of the Liberal Party of Canada, a former Toronto mayoral candidate, a lawyer, and a personality on CP24, with his own popular show. He'd been clever enough to figure out that we'd probably go to Susan's office and was there seeking to arrange an on-air interview. He left graciously after I declined.

I'd spent a lot of time talking with Jan Innes about whether or not to do any media. The main story was to be told by Peck, she said, and anything I said would just muddle that result. Doing a bunch of media would look self-serving, she thought. True enough. Besides, I wasn't interested in moving public opinion about myself. People would think what they'd think, and that wasn't for me to change.

Jan convinced me to do none except that one news conference. That afternoon, Amanda Lang from CBC called me up—she's a good friend—and said Peter Mansbridge wanted to interview me for *The National* broadcast. I was tempted. In fact, very. I had to call up Jan and say, "Tell me why, again, I'm saying *no* to Peter Mansbridge?"

Once I'd said no to Mansbridge, however, I knew I could say no to anybody. I had many requests from the media in the time after the charges were dropped. Matt Galloway from CBC Radio's *Metro Morning* said he'd have me on for a week, if I wanted to take that much time. (I think he was exaggerating. When he ran into me, near the CBC Studios in Toronto, months after May 25th, he was gracious and extremely convincing.) *Toronto Life* invited me to every social event known to Toronto, presumably to snap a pic to accompany a piece Leah McLaren did, *sans* interview, for that magazine. Every media outlet offered the moon: covers, pre-arranged questions, a lot or a little time. But soon it became clear I wasn't going to talk, and the requests tapered off. (Some friends in the media, however, kept in touch, offered generous personal support, and never once requested an interview, or shared what we'd discussed.)

I said no that day to Stephen LeDrew. And to Mansbridge, and Galloway, and I would have said no to Jay Leno, Jon Stewart, and *The Huffington Post*. Then I said goodbye to Susan as she went back to work. I got on the subway. I took it north, up to the Hertz at Bloor and Yonge.

And I rented a convertible.

I hadn't driven a car for nine months. I put the top down. Then I went straight into a traffic jam for 45 minutes, wondering what it was exactly I had missed. I got a phone call about an hour later from a friend, saying she'd heard I was in a convertible. I said I was. She told me to pull over, put the top up, and go home. So I did. Some people might have seen that as the old Bryant chutzpah. But it wasn't. It was much more than that.

When I was drinking, I was like a vampire. I couldn't stand the sunlight. Hangovers were painful in the daylight. I hated being outside. I loved cloudy, rainy days. That's why Vancouver is a good place to be a drunk. I used to literally hate it when I woke up and the sun was shining.

Sober, it was the opposite. I always felt that I'd deprived myself of sun. Part of my love of convertibles was a celebration of my sobriety and my capacity to celebrate the day and revel in the light. I also wanted to get back on the horse. I didn't want to be afraid anymore in a car. I didn't want to be afraid to live my life.

I knew that almost everything in my life had changed. But I wanted to see what hadn't.

FIFTEEN

Darcy Allan Sheppard (1975–2009)

During the nine months that criminal charges hung over my head, Susan and I attended her 25-year high school reunion in Montreal. At it, I was introduced to a man I'd never met before. His eyes glowed bright upon hearing my name and recognizing my newfound notoriety. He leaned in toward me, his whisper growling with attitude and machismo. "Anyone jumps onto my fuckin' car," he declared, "ain't gonna get off it alive either!"

Err, nice to meet you and how do you do?

I realize and appreciate that some people were just trying to comfort me by demonizing Darcy (or vice versa, for those seeking to comfort Darcy's friends and family).

But still, so many people got so very much wrong during those nine months. So much wrong about what happened that night, about Darcy Sheppard, about me, about Susan. So much wrong about the unbridgeable two solitudes we were purported to represent.

That anyone, as that man in Montreal apparently did, assumed I had intentionally done harm to Darcy Sheppard shocked me every time I heard it. And I heard it more than once.

Someone once assured me—by what obscure calculation I have not a clue—that "90 percent of people would have done the same thing." *Only 90 percent?* I thought. Wouldn't any man have tried to escape harm and protect his wife in the same way?

But it's true. Whatever the breakdown, some people would surely have done otherwise. They might have done nothing, sat waiting for the storm that was Darcy Sheppard to blow over. Or they might have jumped out of the car to confront him and fight. And, just maybe, doing either would have got them badly hurt or killed—because Darcy Sheppard's modus operandi was by now well established.

I don't know how most would react in such a situation. But many presumed to know how it would unfold. I doubt that they'd have the faintest idea what they'd do if they were ever faced with what I had faced. Just as I had no clue until it happened.

All I can say for sure is that I never hated Darcy Sheppard. There really wasn't time in the fleeting but calamitous moments in which our lives intersected. Oddly, I wasn't even particularly angry with him—not then or since.

I was, on that night and for those terrible seconds, simply afraid of him; terrified, actually, for both myself and my wife. I wanted only to get away from him. What those who grieve his loss and pour their anger at it out on me might be surprised to know is that at another time, in another context, perhaps at a meeting of the fellowship of which I am a member, I might have poured Darcy Sheppard a coffee, as I have done many times for men and women much like him. As others have done for me, and as I've been taught to do, I might have introduced myself, shook his hand, told him a little about my own life, my own struggle with alcohol, what I had done to get sober and he, in turn, might have reciprocated. Because that is what we do there. We share our stories, share the solution we have been blessed to find, and know—above all—that none of us is any better than any other of us.

The great Canadian theologian Jean Vanier said that finding kindredness with others—especially those lost or broken in body or spirit—was the life undertaking of all of us.

"It can be a long and sometimes painful process," he said. "It involves a growth to freedom, an opening up of our hearts to others, no longer hiding behind masks or behind the walls of fear and prejudice. It means discovering our common humanity."

Vanier's establishment of L'Arche, the international network of communities for people with intellectual disabilities, had taught him a lot about loneliness, he wrote, about "the inner pain that springs from a sense of rejection." Beyond doubt, Darcy Sheppard surely suffered that pain. His restlessness and seeming insatiability—like that of so many addicts—was once aptly described by Hunter S. Thompson, who said: "All my life my heart has sought a thing that I can't name."

That pain can trigger violence, or it can inspire. Johnny Cash wrote of the beasts of addiction being caged by brittle bars. For Darcy's final weeks, those bars turned to dust under the breath of alcohol. Exit beast.

For Jean Vanier, the healing from the pain of rejection, the restlessness of mind, body, and soul, the desperate pursuit of false gods can be found only in meaningful relationships. And that's where I have found it.

The 28 seconds shared by Darcy, myself, and Susan has been portrayed as rich vs. poor, influential vs. marginalized, privileged vs. oppressed. However, since regaining sobriety in the years leading up to August 31, 2009, and in the years since, I have been a member of a niche of society where such distinctions carry absolutely no weight at all. We are all no better and no worse than the other.

Alcoholism, as with addiction of any kind, is utterly democratic. It disregards celebrity, social status, bank balances, club memberships, political office. In the rooms of recovery, people with Order of Canada pins on their jacket lapels sit beside men who have done hard prison time. You will find women who are accomplished actresses or CEOs, and those who worked the streets as prostitutes or drug dealers. You will find men and women who arrive in high-performance automobiles, and those who come straight from hostels by foot or on the subway. You will find people of every conceivable race, background, religious creed, and sexual preference. You will find people 40 years or more from their last drink, and those still under the influence. You will find people just like me. And you will find people just like Darcy Sheppard. And you will find them talking, one with the other, or, at meeting's end, briefly holding hands in a prayer for serenity.

That is why I've never harboured anger or resentment toward Darcy Sheppard. I know men just like him. I know the charm and delight and wisdom of them, when they are well. I know the horrors of their lives—and the lives of all those they touch—when they are not. There is nothing dignified about an alcoholic life. There is nothing pleasant about an alcoholic death. I know that none of us, no matter what our background or walk of life, choose such a lot. And I know that neither did Darcy.

Nor is Darcy Sheppard the author of his own misfortune. For nightmares, brief or endless, can be visited upon any of us, notwithstanding all our efforts to the contrary. I like how author David Foster Wallace puts it. "Both destiny's kisses and its dope-slaps illustrate an individual person's basic personal powerlessness over the really meaningful events in his life."

And the most astonishing aspect of the life of Darcy Sheppard is not that he behaved for most of his 33 years in the angry, self-destructive way that he did. The marvel, given the appalling story of his life and the monstrous odds stacked against him, is that he managed to do as well as he did.

No one would approve, obviously, of his history of violence, some of which was chronicled by the special prosecutor, Richard Peck, or of his failure to financially support the children he fathered.

But few fiction writers would have invented the ghastly circumstances of Darcy Sheppard's childhood. It's hard to believe that Darcy's was a Canadian boyhood, not a hellish tale from the Third World.

Darcy was born with fetal alcohol syndrome, to an alcoholic mother, on October 11, 1975, in Edmonton. He was aboriginal and would be the eldest of nine children. His biological father, a status Indian, had attended a residential school and was killed when, drunk on the road, he was hit by a car. Darcy was about 2 years old.

As so often happens in the hideous cycle of damaged psyches and souls, the son would take up where the parents left off. And his plight was worsened by the very social safety net that is supposed to catch those orphaned by addiction.

Darcy lived with his mother until he was 2 years old. Then, he, a younger brother, and baby sister were taken into custody by Child and Family Services in Alberta. He and his brother were kept together, but they were separated from their sister.

And here is the gruesome part. I'll quote from the court proceedings in case you think I'm exaggerating or dramatizing the facts. "Over several years, from about the time he was three or four until the time he was six, Darcy Sheppard and his brother were placed in over 30 foster homes." Richard Peck, who would read this excruciating biography to the court on May 25, 2010, had one word for it: "Staggering."

The two boys moved regularly between foster setting and their mother's care, Peck said. They were subject in some of these homes to "shocking" maltreatment. The worst kind of trauma he experienced over and over. (Some details were provided in sentencing reports regarding Darcy Sheppard. His brother is still alive and deserves his privacy, so no detailed disclosure of his brother's circumstances is intended.)

When Darcy was 6, he and his brother were adopted by the Sheppard family. Eventually, the Sheppards divorced and Darcy and his brother remained living with Allan Sheppard Sr. In court materials from past offences, Allan Sheppard described his boy as intelligent, resourceful, imaginative, creative, and persuasive, but deeply scarred by his life experiences. At 11, Darcy ran away from home, then was placed in the Glenrose Rehabilitation Hospital in Edmonton. At 12, he overdosed on his medication and was placed in a psychiatric hospital for observation. Until he was 17, he was admitted to a number of residential facilities and group homes that dealt with youth who have psychological and behavioural problems.

He began using marijuana at 10 and began drinking when he was 16. At 17, with a Grade 9 education, he set out on his own. That was when drug use and drinking were becoming almost daily habits.

Darcy did not seem to lack a work ethic. He laboured at various times as a disc jockey, a construction worker, a bicycle messenger, a window washer, a club promoter, and a comedy street performer. He also raced competitively in off-road bicycle races for six years and was good enough to gain sponsors for such events. Over the years, he suffered a number of concussions as a result of bike-racing, and the injuries seemed to affect his memory.

When Darcy was 20, he met and married Tracey, with whom he had two children. Darcy and Tracey separated, and in January 2000 she lost and he gained custody of the children for a short time. Eventually, Tracey's mom took the children to Toronto. After the loss of his children, Darcy began using crack cocaine daily. That led to the loss of jobs and of bike-racing sponsors.

In 2001, he fathered a third child, but lost contact with the child and mother one year later. He fathered a fourth child, born in 2004. In 2006, while incarcerated, Darcy Sheppard began attending 12-step meetings for recovery from alcoholism and addiction. In November 2006, he applied for residential treatment at the Rainbow Lodge. "It is self evident from a detailed review of available records that alcohol and drug use, as well as psychiatric issues imperfectly understood, contributed" to his conduct, Peck would say.

"Given what we know about Mr. Sheppard, it is not surprising that he would go into a rage from time to time, and you know, it is quite an amazing story. Most people are ill-situate [*sic*] to overcome the obstacles this man faced."

Sheppard had a criminal record going back years. In 1996, he was convicted of assault and breaking-and-entering. Less than a year later he pleaded guilty to assault, failing to comply, and failing to attend court.

In April 1997, he had assaulted his common-law partner at the time. Alcohol was identified as a significant issue. A conditional sentence was imposed. By August 31, 2009, Sheppard had more than 60 outstanding warrants in his home province of Alberta, mostly for fraud and property crimes.

His life was full of 28-second life bites, most of which ruined him, again and again.

In 2007, by which time he'd moved to Toronto, Sheppard was convicted, as a result of offences committed in July 2006, of uttering a death threat, possession of a weapon (two air pistols) for a purpose dangerous to public peace, and using an imitation firearm while committing an indictable offence of threatening death.

What happened? He had entered a cab near Church and Wellesley Streets, told the driver he had "killed someone and I'm going to kill you." He pulled out the imitation guns and directed the cabbie to another location. En route, he threatened to shoot a woman on the street. Darcy would tell the court he was drinking heavily and using crack cocaine at the time. During pre-trial custody, he attended 12-step meetings and acknowledged that his problem was alcohol, that alcohol was the trigger for his using crack.

In a pre-sentence report, Sheppard reflected that he had a lot of opportunities at age 23 and lost it all once he developed a crack addiction. He said he was addicted to crack cocaine for years. By his later twenties, he used alcohol daily, he said, beginning the moment he awoke in the morning. When his time was not structured, he drank. He was assessed as a high risk to reoffend.

In Toronto, Sheppard had joined the subculture of bicycle messengers. There, he apparently found a community where he was liked and valued. Various of his friends have described him as a troubled spirit, but a comic, generous, boisterous sweetheart. To those who got to know him, there was the attractive side of so many addicts and alcoholics, the charm and sense of humour, the resilience, the energy, the potential.

His friends have told journalists that his challenges were massive, that his efforts to deal with them had been inspiring. They said he would offer friends his coat if it were cold, fix other people's cars when they needed repair, stop to help strangers on the street.

Over the years, he reportedly maintained a good relationship with his adoptive father, Allan Sheppard. Darcy had apparently told friends he would have been dead in his teens without Allan Sheppard Sr., who had seen Darcy only a week before the accident and had urged him once again to deal with his addictions.

Beyond a doubt, Darcy Sheppard hit all the markers for a predisposition for addiction. He had the genetic inheritance of alcoholism in his family. He had the egregiously ruinous childhood, the abuse, the abandonment, the displacement.

It's been said that alcoholism, among many other things, is that voice that comes to you in the middle of the night telling you that you're detritus, a piece of garbage, one of God's mistakes. And for much of Darcy Sheppard's life, he must have felt that the world and most of those in it believed that to be so.

For some like Darcy, alcohol and drugs can be a bid to still that voice, to fill the great big hole inside, to provide brief respite from loneliness, torment, loss—something to alleviate the accumulated pain of his lifetime.

I sometimes wonder if I ever actually crossed paths with Darcy Sheppard when we sought recovery in the same rooms. If I didn't, I have met people who say they did, and men and women from backgrounds much like his. For there is almost nothing in the dreary recitation of the details of his life, or in his death, that would be shocking, or even terribly unusual, in the fellowship of recovery.

There, we are frequently reminded that untreated addiction ends in a predictable, and predictably awful, way: in either jails, institutions, or death. And anyone who spends any amount of time in recovery programs sees the truth of the axiom played out over and over again.

After the accident, the community of bicycle couriers rallied repeatedly in Darcy Sheppard's memory. It is an underclass and a counterculture that renders a lot in metal: their bikes, their piercings of face and body. Their uniform often includes camouflage pants, which the dead man was wearing that night.

While Sheppard and I did come from different beginnings and different worlds, and while I have no way of ever understanding the pain and consequences of his past, there was more intersection of our life experience than any of those so quick to grab at a *Bonfire of the Vanities* narrative might have imagined.

We are told in recovery that alcoholics are probably destined to spend a portion of their lives in the company of other alcoholics. The only question is whether they will be drinking together while they do so, or helping each other to stay sober. It has been, to date, and one day at a time, my great good fortune to be among the latter.

We are also told that all our experiences, no matter what they are, have value when shared with others. They serve either as examples when we do succeed, or as warnings when we don't. In that sense, and in others, Darcy Allan Sheppard, whose friends called him Al and whose name will be linked to mine for the rest of my days, stays with me always.

SIXTEEN

The Elephant in the Room:
Criminal Justice Reforms

If anyone got the short shrift from our criminal justice system's
blindness to addiction, it was Darcy Sheppard. His tale is littered
with opportunities for intervention and support for someone clearly
needing aid from the health-care system. Maybe for a time he was,
like many, unwilling to face his demons. But the system did not offer
him a mirror, nor did it seek to treat his addiction when his willingness did arrive. Darcy Sheppard is a poster child for the failure of
our criminal justice system to aid the sick through health care.

Compared to other governments, the Ontario government
I served with, led by Premier Dalton McGuinty, did more than
most. But we never fully opened our eyes to the harms wrought
by substance abuse. Simply put, the human carnage and financial cost are monumental. Five years ago, the Canadian Centre
on Substance Abuse estimated the costs of substance abuse on the
health-care and justice systems, along with lost workplace productivity, at $39.8 billion annually in Canada. Three years ago, the
Centre for Addiction and Mental Health (CAMH) estimated that
alcohol abuse alone costs each Canadian $463 a year and that direct
health-care costs for alcohol abuse exceed those of cancer. Let me
repeat that: direct health-care costs for alcohol abuse exceed those
of cancer.

An extensive study done for CAMH—*Avoidable Costs of
Alcohol Abuse in Canada, 2002*—suggested that implementing six

recommendations could, even under conservative estimates, save 800 lives a year, save more than 88,000 acute care hospital days a year, and save $1 billion a year across the country.

"We should take alcohol way more seriously than we currently take it," said CAMH senior scientist Dr. Jürgen Rehm at the time. "It is one of the main costing factors within our health sector and it is preventable."

The harm ripples on and on, into homes, into wombs. Alcoholism blackens eyes, breaks noses, and worse. A separate research study by CAMH established a link between drinking and domestic and partner violence. In the chapter on Canada in a book called *Unhappy Hours: Alcohol and Partner Aggression in the Americas,* international researchers found that the level of alcohol consumption was strongly associated with being both the perpetrator and victim of partner violence.

Alcoholism harms newborns, ruins their lives. A 2006 report for the Institute of Medical Science at the University of Toronto estimated that 3000 babies are born each year in Canada with fetal alcohol spectrum disorder (FASD). At the time, best estimates put the annual costs associated with those under 21 affected with FASD at almost $350 million. Darcy Sheppard was one of those babies.

Alcoholism is in your home, or on your block. According to a 2004 Canadian addiction survey, while most Canadians who consume alcohol drink in moderation, about 16 percent of those who reported drinking in the previous year admitted consumption levels associated with an elevated risk of alcohol-related problems.

Alcoholism is cunning and baffling, not only for alcoholics, but for everyone else, lulling all of us into thinking it's someone else's problem. Studies also suggest that Canadians' perceptions of the relative seriousness of substance abuse are out of whack with the actual costs they impose on society. Total costs associated with alcohol are more than twice those for all other illicit drugs (according to the 2002 data), yet the public consistently rated the overall seriousness of illicit drugs (in the Canadian Addiction Survey of 2004) as higher.

This is neither stupidity nor mere perversity. Researchers have found there are strong psychological, social, economic, or cultural incentives that serve to conceal or downplay the true nature of certain hazards in society. After all, alcohol is readily and legally available to all adults.

Being legal, alcohol is still the drug of choice, the Canadian Centre on Substance Abuse reported in a 2007 study that compared the perceived seriousness against actual costs of substance abuse. "As such, [it] commands a somewhat privileged position in our society," the report said. "Data on the significant costs of alcohol to Canadian society, however, suggest that it is appropriate to confront this position and expose alcohol as a significant yet relatively under-recognized social risk."

In sum, substance abuse is everywhere, it's right in front of you, it's wreaking havoc, it's hurting, it's killing, and it's costing you, the taxpayer, a lot of money.

Worse still, the consequences of substance abuse get too little attention, too late, at the back end (the justice system), rather than the front (as a chronic health issue). One scholarly report reviewed federal spending for 2005, finding that of the tax dollars spent dealing with illegal drugs, 73 percent is spent on enforcement, 14 percent on treatment, and the remainder on harm reduction, prevention (3 percent), and research.

Not surprisingly, many alcoholics and drug addicts run up against the criminal justice system. Some crimes are perpetrated merely to feed addictions, as in the junkie who robs, steals, or defrauds in order to fund a habit. Other crimes have possession or consumption of drugs or alcohol as an element of the offence: narcotics possession and trafficking, driving under the influence of alcohol or drugs. Some arise as a consequence of intoxication: nuisance-related offences, usually involving drunken revelling or vandalism; but also assault, sexual assault, and murder.

As the Ontario Legislature's Select Committee on Mental Health and Addiction said in its August 2010 report, fully half of Canadian offenders reported substance abuse as a cause of their offence and 36 percent of those in custody in Ontario suffered from some form of mental illness.

Yet, "far too many Ontarians experience their first contact with the mental health system through the justice system," the committee said. "These are obvious signs that mental health and addiction care needs to be transformed in Ontario."

The lessons I have learned through legal and political experience and personal calamity support that argument. Darcy Sheppard's story is the only exhibit needed to prove my case. In a nutshell, our justice system ought to have early on recognized that young Darcy needed help from the health-care system far more than he needed warrants, countless court appearances, and dead time in the bucket.

The criminal justice system is blind to addictions, even though that's what drives most crimes. Police, prosecutors, judges, corrections officials, and those accountable for the system—politicians like me in a former life—are often oblivious, willfully blind, or simply ignorant of the role that drugs, alcohol, or mental illness plays in a crime.

For Sheppard was like most in the criminal justice system who wind up in the back of a squad car drunk or stoned, thanks to intoxicated violence, or intoxicated driving; or accused of a property or financial crime, the motivation of which was feeding an addiction, or paying its debts. This group of people might be thought of as the addict-accused. It is not too difficult for them to self-identify, nor for the police or correctional authority to verify that identification.

These people populate the criminal justice system at levels best described as epidemic.

The Canadian Centre on Substance Abuse states simply that "the majority of offenders show evidence of some kind of substance abuse problem." How big a majority? In my view, getting the exact number is splitting hairs. The point is that most of the people in the criminal justice system share one thing: it's not the colour of their hair, or where they're from, or whether they were dropped as a child, or whether their high school was public or private, or even their upbringing. The one thing that most offenders share is a substance abuse problem.

In Saskatchewan, up to 93 percent of provincial offenders are identified as having a substance abuse problem. Approximately 80 percent of prisoners in prisons in England and Wales have a substance abuse problem. An assessment of the entire prison population in Maine found that almost 90 percent of prisoners had a substance abuse problem. In New Zealand, 80 percent of offenders used alcohol or other drugs immediately prior to committing their most recent offence(s).

In fact, if all these addict-accused were treated differently than those not in this category, there wouldn't be much left for the criminal justice system to do. Substance abuse fuels the criminal justice system like smoking fuels lung cancer. Or, more to the point, addiction is to the justice system what lung cancer is to health care: chronic, expensive, and screaming out for prevention over treatment. The difference, of course, is that addiction treatment *is* the prevention; the treated alcoholic has a good chance of staying sober, which means all those costs of his addiction disappear upon achieving sobriety. It is as if there were an antidote that actually cured lung cancer, provided that the patient didn't ever smoke again. Wouldn't the health-care system, on behalf of the taxpayer, want to get a hold of that antidote?

I am personally accountable for many of these shortcomings, to be sure. I could have done more, I could have done better. After all, I was an MPP for a decade, in the provincial Cabinet for six years, four as Attorney General, literally accountable for the justice system in my home province. Consider my A.-G. duties, helpfully set forth in a statute. The breadth of these duties was daunting and inspiring for me when I first read them: "The Attorney General, (a) is the Law Officer of the Executive Council; (b) shall see that the administration of public affairs is in accordance with the law; (c) shall superintend all matters connected with the administration of justice in Ontario; ... (e) shall advise the Government upon all matters of law connected with legislative enactments and upon all matters of law referred to him or her by the Government; (f) shall advise the Government upon all matters of a legislative nature and superintend all Government measures of a legislative nature; (g) shall advise the heads of the ministries and agencies of Government upon all matters of law connected with such ministries and agencies; (h) shall conduct and regulate all litigation for and against the Crown or any ministry or agency of Government in respect of any subject within the authority or jurisdiction of the Legislature; (i) shall superintend all matters connected with judicial offices."

Pretty serious job description.

Looking back, I have considered how I "superintend[ed] all matters connected with the administration of justice in Ontario" with respect to addiction and mental health treatment. I have re-thought my approach and think that I had it backwards.

Our approach perpetuated a justice system too often blind to the addicts and mentally ill people within the system. On the one hand, we expanded the niches within the system that actually addressed the unwellness, through a hybrid of health care and justice. Thus we expanded significantly the Drug Court in Ontario, and helped start a Mental Health Court. On the other hand, the vast majority of those addicts and mentally ill in the system were treated solely by blunt penal tools, without regard to what was often keeping them in a life of crime.

A Drug Court, on the other hand, provides court-supervised treatment for individuals addicted to cocaine and/or opiates who have been charged with possession of, or trafficking in, small quantities of crack/cocaine or heroin, or with property offences in order to support their drug use, or with prostitution-related offences. The participants, heretofore criminal defendants, participate in what amounts to judicially supervised addiction treatment. Upon successful completion of the program, which lasts approximately one year, participants receive a non-custodial sentence, rather than incarceration. The latest studies show that 97 percent of Drug Court graduates do not return to the criminal justice system. Ponder that for a moment.

I spoke as Attorney General at one of these Drug Court "graduations," full of family and friends in the courtroom. People cheered and clapped. I was in my early months of sobriety, making it a pretty emotional moment for me. Thankfully, our government had made significant budget increases and expansions of the Drug Court and its jurisdiction. I'd also appointed the veteran prosecutor for the Drug Court, Mr. Justice Kofi Barnes, to the Ontario Court of Justice; it was my first appointment.

The niche courts are excellent and, like niche courts in the U.S., have had significant success in lowering recidivism. The most rigorous and conservative scientific estimates have all concluded that drug courts significantly reduce crime by as much as 35 percent compared to imprisonment. In addition, drug courts produce US$2.21–US$3.36 in avoided criminal justice benefits for every US$1.00 spent on them. Up to US$12.00 (per US$1.00 invested) is saved by the community on reduced emergency room visits and other medical care, foster care, and victimization costs such as property loss. Similar figures are found in Canada.

However, these niche courts are just that—exceptions within the broader system that is blind to addiction and mental health. If someone is fortunate enough to have the opportunity to enter a Drug Court or Mental Health Court, then their prospects are improved. But what about the vast majority of the accused and convicted people in the system?

An unintended effect of the niche courts is to create the illusion that the criminal justice system is doing something about addiction and mental health, when in fact it is barely paying lip service to the issue. The annual federal budget for Drug Courts in Canada, for six cities, is $3.5 million, or 0.027 percent of Canada's overall budget spent on criminal justice services.* Much more is spent by the federal government on upgrading luggage security at airports than on rehabilitating addicts via Drug Courts.†

Nor do the Drug Courts address the alcoholic in the system, or the addict who committed a violent crime, or someone with mental health issues. In other words, the vast, vast majority of those in the criminal justice system, either being accused or serving a sentence, do not benefit from the Drug Court approach.

The solution is to adopt the Drug Court approach to the entire system, without limitation. This requires enormous political will, and I do note that I did not do it whilst I was there. I thought that the Drug Court expansions that we initiated when I was Attorney

---

* JustResearch. (2003). No. 12. Ottawa: Department of Justice Canada. http:// canada.justice.gc.ca.

† The 2012 budget allocates "$21 Million over Five Years to Upgrade Baggage Scanning Equipment at Canadian Airports." Government of Canada, Budget Papers, Chapter 4.2: Supporting Families and Communities (June 6, 2011). www. budget.gc.ca/2011/plan/chap4b-eng.html.

General were a good effort, when in fact it was window dressing at best.

The comprehensive solution requires a social services worker in every courtroom, as is done in the Midtown Manhattan Street Court, which transformed that neighbourhood entirely. In that court, the social worker recommends to the judge the best next step for an accused, based upon a professional diagnosis. If the accused broke a window, and he's an addict, then there is a common-sense response from the judge: restitution for the broken window, and treatment for the addiction. That way, the justice system is part of the solution: addressing the harm done to the neighbourhood (the broken window is fixed) and the individual ailment (the addiction). If the addict gets treatment, the chances of that individual breaking another window decline dramatically. All of this is possible because the Midtown Manhattan Street Court is very alert to whether an accused is a substance abuser, and responds accordingly.

However, if the justice system is blind to addictions, then the addict-accused faces an all-or-nothing, lose-lose choice: deny any responsibility, perhaps evade a conviction, and go back on the street to cause more harm; the substance abuse ignored by the judge and untreated by the system. Or, the accused is convicted and faces only a financial penalty or some jail time, wherein the substance abuse likely worsens.

Even more important, a comprehensive solution requires training for police, prosecutors, and judges that they are currently not getting. Police and prosecutors must triage the accused in the system, putting them into different streams. If police and/ or prosecutor sees alcoholism or addiction or mental health as the root of the defendant's alleged evil, then they go into one of those criminal justice streams. It is critical, in my view, that the accused or convicted themselves be afforded the opportunity to avail themselves of treatment, and to create an incentive for them to do so. Only the willing need apply.

Such an approach ought not to be "soft" on crime. It would be wrongheaded if culpability were ignored in all this. I've been taught that the addict-accused ought to take responsibility for any harm done, for the consequences of addicted behaviour. This is an important part of substance abuse recovery—accepting one's role in harm, making amends, and then moving on. The guilt and shame carried around by some makes crime and substance abuse an even more toxic combination for the abuser. The only way out is recovery, and recovery typically requires a measure of redemption—action taken to right a wrong as best possible.

Accordingly, it's common for recovering alcoholics and addicts to attempt to provide restitution, or otherwise reconcile with those harmed by the consequences of an alcoholic life. Fraud, tax evasion, theft—these brave people come forward to make amends for past harm done, usually in cold cases long forgotten by the victims or the authorities.

In short, the justice system can continue its traditional role of finding culpability and fashioning a sentence, but all that ought to treat substance abuse as relevant. Most importantly, however, is that the justice system goes further, to work with our health-care system to help the substance abuser recover. To help that person get better.

There is no point reconstructing what Darcy Sheppard's life might have been like had he been qualified to voluntarily participate in a Drug Court. Or if the Toronto Police Service officers on the scene at George Street in the early evening of August 31, 2009, speaking with Sheppard less than an hour before his death, had not allowed him to drive off on his bike, badly intoxicated. Regardless of whether they made a grave error, my question is whether there is a systemic issue with police correctly identifying substance abusers and having tools to respond appropriately.

"At the time, I believe a good decision was made," Staff Sergeant John Spanton told the *Toronto Star*. "In terms of his sobriety, the officers made the decision that he was okay. And I would stand behind that."

"I asked for the police to give him a ride home," Misty Bailey, Sheppard's girlfriend, told a *Toronto Star* journalist soon after he died. Another published report said that Sheppard's friends "begged" the police to allow him to stay at their place, rather than hit the streets drunk.

"They [the police] said 'No, he's going to [take] himself home,'" Misty said.

Under questioning by reporters, one Toronto Police Service constable snarled that they weren't a taxi service, after all.

Perhaps not, but there are street workers and social service workers that can work with police to intervene and direct someone like Darcy Sheppard to a detox centre, or otherwise to a safe haven. Or police ought to be trained to manage substance abuse as if it's an ailment, rather than a nuisance to be shooed away down the street.

In Canada, government jurisdictions turn out to be aligned for a comprehensive response to substance abuse within the justice system. Health care and the administration of justice are both provincial matters. I have little doubt that had some of my cabinet colleagues and I stayed behind for a few cabinet meetings, for a few minutes each time, we could have cobbled together a coordinated approach to detoxifying and potentially treating the addict-accused.

There are a number of ways to do it, but it fundamentally requires a hybrid approach: health and justice officials collaborating on a patient/accused, where there is a willingness by the addict to admit and address the substance abuse. This would not displace the entire penal system. Obviously, people ought to be punished by incarceration for serious crimes. Our Canadian democracy will not tolerate anything less.

But rehabilitation is also a purpose of the corrections system. It's called *correctional,* after all. And that work on recovery from an addiction needs to begin as soon as possible for the accused addict. Those detained pending trial are innocent until proven guilty, which means that treatment for those people today is practically nil. And yet most of the provincial prison population are not people serving their sentence, but accused detained pending trial (which ultimately can be used as a credit against a sentence, at a rate of two-to-one or sometimes more). Opening up rooms for recovery to all addicts in contact with the criminal justice system, based on their willingness rather than their alleged or proven offence, would generate opportunities for people to get better, to change their lives, for the better of the many.

Indeed, treatment or recovery for the addict, accused or convicted, innocent or guilty, requires primarily a willingness. Twelve-step groups are permitted to engage with prisoners today (at no cost), but this availability is too random and only for a small proportion of the accused/convicted addicted.

What about the inherent costs of all this? I'm talking about reorienting the criminal justice system into an addiction recovery system of hope, less than a conviction machine. This changes the way that police are trained, prosecutors are trained, and judges are oriented in their courts. It may not require any legislative change, other than using a statute as a policy directive. There would be howls of protest until it all started happening, at which point the common sense of treating the disease rather than its symptoms becomes self-evident.

Is this affordable? I'm not going to offer up the typical answer that we can't afford not to. Or, that the savings from treating the addicted will offset the treatment costs. Suffice it to say, governments hear this argument practically every day, and it rarely cuts the mustard. The parliamentary system requires the executive to justify its spending of tax dollars, and that means budgets that, line by line, account for dollars spent and services delivered. Funding of these programs requires a reorienting of existing programs, expansion of some niche programs, and that all must be budgeted.

There is more than one way to fund this. The massive distillery, beer, and wine industry is a good place to start. Just as tobacco companies have increasingly had to foot the bill for societal costs, affecting their profit margins, the time will come when the filthy lucre has its reckoning. Those profits are huge. Anheuser-Busch InBev N.V. is a Belgian–Brazilian publicly traded company, based in Leuven, Belgium. It is the largest global brewer with nearly 25 percent global market share. Profits for 2010 exceeded US$4 billion. Most of those profits are found in North America.

Meanwhile, about half of the alcohol industry's profits come from underage drinkers and alcoholics. In 2001, a minimum of $22.5 billion (17.5 percent) of consumer expenditures for alcohol came from underage drinking and $25.8 billion (20.1 percent) came from adult pathological drinking (meeting clinical criteria for alcohol abuse or dependence). The combined value of underage and pathological drinking was at least $48.3 billion (37.5 percent) and, as an alternative analysis showed, as much as $62.9 billion (48.8 percent).*

Whether through taxation (of the producers/distributors, not just consumers!), class action, or industry-sponsored programming, those who profit from a legal substance that leads to illegal and harmful activity ought to pay their fair share for the ill effects

---

* *The Economic Value of Underage Drinking and Adult Excessive Drinking to the Alcohol Industry.* (2003). New York: The National Center on Addiction and Substance Abuse (CASA) at Columbia University.

of their products. (Of course, one of the worst offenders is the provinces themselves, most of which own the liquor stores and all the gaming profits. Having negotiated a multi-billion-dollar gaming deal with First Nations on behalf of the province of Ontario, I've seen the possibilities regarding directed revenue sources toward a shared objective.)

The costs of treatment, meanwhile, are less than you'd think. The world's largest 12-step recovery program, and its offshoots, accepts no dues or fees. There are no officials, no official leaders, no trained professionals necessary for a meeting to occur, or for recovery to take place. There are expenses for rentals of space and some coffee, all of which are covered by each group through a voluntary passing of the hat.*

Obviously staffing and infrastructure are needed for a government to undertake a comprehensive approach, but my point is that the treatment itself, the miracle work, is not necessarily a cost barrier. Only the willing need apply, but there is no wait list, and no fees charged to the willing, for local 12-step programs. Some people find that treatment centres, some non-profit, some for-profit, are needed before recovery is possible. This is particularly true for adolescents facing substance abuse.

Regarding the latter, in 2006 I learned about the Pine River Institute when its founder and CEO, Karen Minden, met me in my constituency office. I was her MPP and represented her last resort to save Pine River Institute from a critical funding shortage. The Institute is a residential treatment centre located in a peaceful, forested area outside of Toronto. It's for 13- to 19-year-olds struggling with mental health issues, and specifically addictive behaviours.

---

* Alexandre B. Laudet, PhD, "The Impact of Alcoholics Anonymous on Other Substance Abuse Related Twelve Step Programs," *Recent Dev Alcohol.* 2008. 18: 71–89.

They learn math skills and life skills side-by-side. There's nothing like it in Ontario, and few existing in North America.

As a newly sober MPP, I was particularly driven to assist the Institute. In what amounts to a bureaucratic miracle, we found funding for the Pine River Institute in the Victims' Justice Fund of the Ministry of the Attorney General. I remained an ally in government, as more members of Cabinet came to see this remarkable place help young people save themselves from their demons. After I left politics, I joined the (volunteer) Board of Directors to continue service to the worthy cause.

At some point after first meeting with Karen Minden and her husband, the Board's chair at the time, I found myself up at the Institute getting a tour, and having lunch with the kids. I'd privately asked Karen if it were possible to meet with some kids, to share with them my story, as a recovering alcoholic, and that happened in a bright room with large, comfy chairs, pulled together in a circle.

But then that miraculous thing happened that I'd eventually learn was commonplace: I was learning from them, not the other way around. As we went around the room to share our experiences, each of these young men and women, all about 17 years old, tried to bolster my recovery and congratulate me on achieving sobriety.

Years later, just after the accident, Karen Minden telephoned me to offer her support and comfort.

"We have some young Darcy Sheppards here at Pine River these days," she said, and in the ensuing silence was a prayer for those kids, and for the adolescent Darcy that received all the love in the world from Allan Sheppard, but no doubt could have benefitted from a Pine River Institute had it existed in his time.

But I don't just see Darcy Sheppard in the kids at Pine River, or sitting across from me in a 12-step meeting, leg quivering, eyes darting, jaw clenched. I see him everywhere, and in many people, in some dreams and nightmares. I see him in those camo-green pants, gesticulating outside bars and under street lights, on streets city-dirty and on sidewalks surburban-clean. I see him everywhere but mostly in the shadows. He was a soul, as Claudel would put it—a soul with holy aspirations, which, deprived of daylight, worshipped in the night.

SEVENTEEN

Paying for It

The reforms regarding addictions and the justice system may or
may not have altered the fate of Darcy Sheppard. That is not
for me to say.

What I can discuss—and would be remiss in not addressing—
is my own experience with the costs of a legal defence. After all, it's
not every day that the person accountable for the criminal justice
system gets charged by the system, with its inherent fiscal costs.

Criminal legal defence costs.
Obviously, the vast majority of the population does not have
hundreds of thousands of dollars for legal fees at their disposal.
Nor did I.

This dilemma resembles the health-care crisis for millions of
Americans when suddenly faced with the enormous cost of caring
for themselves, or loved ones (50 million Americans, or 16 percent,
are uninsured; over 40 percent of personal bankruptcies are attributable to health costs). As with the health-care system in the U.S.,
where the government spends more per person than any nation
in the world, the answer to this dilemma for the criminal justice
system in Canada and the U.S. is not simply more government
funding.

The Province of Ontario, for example, already finances legal aid
for the impoverished at a rate that vastly exceeds most jurisdictions

(almost $300 million annually, or the cost of 20,000 new post-secondary spaces in our colleges and universities). People aren't willing to spend a lot more on taxes to fund criminal legal defences, for a variety of reasons. People are innocent until proven guilty, but I bet you'd balk at personally subsidizing the legal fees of the Hells Angels—not because they're presumed guilty, but rather because we live in a democracy. It's just not feasible to imagine that there is a magic bullet for this problem.

Universal coverage for criminal justice defence costs is fiscally a non-starter. Nor is the status quo acceptable to those who consider, even in passing, the unaffordability of our legal system. Nor is the answer simply more tax dollars. I have now personally lived through this public policy issue, as a defendant, and I've lived through the administration of the justice system, as Attorney General. Here are my thoughts.

The issue boils down to the assumption of risks and who pays for what. Currently, our governments, on behalf of taxpayers, make zero contribution to the risk that one of their constituents (unless impoverished) will be confronted by the criminal justice system. Every day you take the risk that you'll be hit with legal bills in the hundreds of thousands of dollars. In hindsight, I wish that I'd insured myself against this risk.

The answer, I think, lies somewhere in that idea of coinsurance or copayment, not unlike the approach taken by the United States when it comes to health care—a similarly imperfect approach in circumstances where universal coverage is unaffordable or just unrealistic. Governments could use their legal aid budget to provide incentives to the private insurance industry, on behalf of taxpayers, to render insurance products for people who choose to insure themselves against this risk. I'm convinced that the amount invested by governments in legal aid every year could be better spent on such a coinsurance or copayment system, governed by a means test. Therefore, Conrad Black would have none of his legal fee insurance—which, by the way, it was reported he had via board directors' liability insurance*—subsidized by taxpayers, whereas the impoverished would have all their insurance covered, with the middle class falling in between.

Such an insurance system would still involve democratic, capitalist choices. For example, I personally chose to take the Marie Henein approach, in circumstances where I knew I was innocent and concluded that a trial was unnecessary. That was an expensive choice. And let me be clear: any financial manager would have told me that I could not afford that choice. I got a second mortgage, in essence (whereas Dalton McGuinty got a second mortgage to defray the costs of his Ontario Liberal leadership campaign in the 1990s, the latest economic crisis turned on personal and institutional choices about financial leverage and risk management—that is, people make judgments about risk all the time, and have to live with the consequences). But one need not pursue the Cadillac defence. A solid defence can be obtained for much less, not unlike the auto insurance system in Ontario and many other provinces, where civil litigation and damages are covered by auto insurance, *up to a point.*

I wish I'd thought of this idea when I was Attorney General, but I am very comfortable defending our record on access to justice. We legalized and regulated paralegals, to allow for more

---

* "An estimated $40 million in defense costs for Black have been covered by the policy of directors and officers insurance for Hollinger International since 2003. The policy was terminated when the company went bankrupt, however, and now Black is on his own in litigation that may test the extent of his wealth, reports *The Globe and Mail,* relying on unidentified sourcing." Martha Nell, "Conrad Black Released on Bond After Some $40M in Legal Bills; How Much More Can He Afford to Pay?," *ABA Journal,* July 21, 2010.

affordable legal services alternatives to a lawyer. We provided the largest increases to the legal aid budget since the heady times of Ian Scott. We provided the largest funding increases to sexual assault centres (10 percent) that they'd ever seen. And we increased the complement of prosecutors and judges (without which the system slows down and costs increase) at an unprecedented rate. But I wish we'd done more.

Prosecutors, not police, should lay criminal charges.

The foregoing reforms address addiction within the system, but what of the system itself? People often ask me what I've learned, as a former Attorney General, from my inside look at how the system works.

Truth be told, one cannot build a justice system around how to charge and prosecute a former Attorney General. So I don't pretend that my experience is typical of anything. That said, I did experience, personally and financially, what it's like when the justice system has you in its crosshairs. Plus, I've attended the University of Marie Henein, with whom I had many long conversations about how the system really works. And this experience has changed the perspective of this former Attorney General.

As Attorney General, I was very familiar with the back end of the justice system: where the final decisions were made—to prosecute, to withdraw charges, to find guilty, to uphold or reverse on appeal. I got to know prosecutors and judges from across the province, at all levels of experience and jurisdiction. From rookie Crown attorneys to the chief justices. I also got to know a number of police chiefs, for whom I have great respect.

It's not the back end of the justice system that I'm worried about. It's the front end: where decisions get made that sometimes have to be fixed at the back end. Along the way, from those early decisions of the police to final outcome, it can be a living hell too easily dismissed for those fortunate enough not to have lived it first-hand. I have come to see, first-hand, that the criminal justice system can be a juggernaut, with a natural path inclined toward a finding of guilt. Once the wheels are set in motion, criminal charges take on a momentum that easily overwhelms an accused. As Attorney General, I was not so naïve as to imagine that all agreements between Crown and defence (so-called plea bargains, as if all are a bargain) were driven simply by guilt or innocence. But I hadn't realized, until I lived it, how steep is the path of least resistance to a finding of guilt. This does not bode well for the presumption of innocence.

For those charged with a criminal offence, the police and some prosecutors appear to be conviction machines. They have checks and balances that allow for corrections of miscarriages of justice, after the fact, via appeals and similar procedures that allow for an impartial second look. But during an investigation and prosecution, the overall orientation of too many police officers is the pursuit of a criminal conviction. That's their job, as they view it. One is theoretically innocent until proven guilty, but it doesn't feel that way at all when you're in it.

So the weighing of evidence done by a trial judge ought not be an academic exercise. It requires an appreciation of what really happened on the ground. What was the orientation of a particular investigation and prosecution: skeptical investigation or a hunt for what is most damning? Is the accused a frequent flyer in the justice system, or is this their first foray? Are the police or prosecutors veterans or rookies? Is this the experienced Guns and Gangs Task Force or the Traffic Division? Does the investigation seem blasé or highly professional? Is anyone going through the motions here, or worse—overly eager for a conviction? Do the players really believe the accused to be innocent until proven guilty, or are they driving up their stats?

Of course, most trial judges ask these questions. The same applies to a prosecutor exercising her quasi-judicial function of determining whether to proceed with a prosecution. The same ought to apply to police when laying a charge, but for too many the knee-jerk reaction is to charge first, ask questions later.

As Supreme Court law clerks, there was something quite abstract about the appeals before us. The human dimension was not fully seized upon by me, anyway. This is particularly awful for an accused when the media present a seemingly comprehensive and authoritative judgment of an accused, notwithstanding that journalism can rarely be comprehensive and authoritative when it comes to guilt and innocence in the eyes of the law. It's not just young law clerks who fall prey to this tunnel vision.

Thus, the Duke University lacrosse players who were assumed to be guilty of a rape in March 2006, a year later turned out to be victims of a "tragic rush to accuse," in the words of North Carolina Attorney General Roy Cooper. In response to the original allegations, Duke University cancelled the remainder of the lacrosse season for the team, and forced the coach to resign. The original prosecutor, who'd been up for re-election, was later disbarred and convicted of criminal contempt. Sadly, there are many other examples from the U.S.

Still, it gave me great comfort, in that jail cell in the wee hours of September 1, 2009, that our Canadian system does not have the perils that come with elected prosecutors and judges, as is the case in the U.S. for some courts. Judges and prosecutors in Canada are independent because they can be unpopular but still keep their jobs. (So, for instance, my former Deputy Minister Murray Segal could stick by his publicly detested plea bargain with Karla Homolka— the "deal with the devil"—and go on to a successful career in the justice sector, because he was doing his job exactly as he should.)

But my observation here goes a step further. People are limited

by their own experiences. Comprehension and compassion for the
innocent person accused of a crime is something best lived, rather
than simply understood.

The presumption of innocence, in other words, requires a level
of skepticism of the system, an outlook that is not always shared by
all. A few police officers have privately told me that I never should
have been charged in the first place. But that wasn't the perspective,
at the time, of the Traffic Division officers, when they saw the body
of Darcy Sheppard, dying on Bloor Street. At that moment, their
compassion rightly went out to Sheppard, and the human impulse
to seek a reckoning was amplified by that emotion. Their working
assumption was "road rage," because they saw a dying cyclist and
an uninjured motorist.

My point is that the decision to charge someone has profound
consequences for the accused. Their liberty is suspended, reputation
ruined, and fiscal resources spent. For an accused, their security of
citizenship—that one can just live life and not be randomly harmed
by the people paid to protect them—is upended.

I might have said "cry me a river" had I been reading such
a sentiment a few years ago. No more. The presumption of
innocence, I've learned, is more a legal abstraction than a reality.
The presumption is often effected when the final verdict is
rendered. Along the way, however, criminal charges carry with
them the unspoken assumption that the accused simply *must* have
done something wrong.

A couple infamous cases bear repeating. Donald Marshall Jr.
spent 11 years in jail for a murder he did not commit. When he was
finally acquitted, the appeal court still called him "the author of his
own misfortune." This phrase has always haunted me, and I could
often see that horrible judgment in people's eyes.

During my final months as Attorney General, Stephen Truscott's
conviction for murder was found by the Ontario Court of Appeal

to have been a miscarriage of justice and he was formally acquitted of murdering Lynne Harper in 1959. Truscott was sentenced to be hanged, but that sentence was commuted to life imprisonment. He served 10 years, then slipped out of the public eye, living with his family under an assumed name, until 2001 when he utilized a federal procedure to review his conviction. The Court of Appeal would review nearly 250 fresh pieces of evidence, before exonerating Truscott. I immediately apologized, on behalf of a system that had changed so much, I'd thought, since 1959. Truscott wasn't impressed with my apology, but I received a generous note from his mother, kindly explaining why no apology would suffice, and rightly so.

Again, these miscarriages of justice teach everyone about the imperfections of the system. It's easy, however, to shrug them off as mere exceptions to a normally glorious record. Not so to the wrongfully convicted. Their lives are ruined, and even judicial correction and exoneration become cold comfort. Truscott and Marshall lost too many years of their lives to prison, and suffered judgments thereafter, by too many, as being the authors of their own misfortune.

The truth is the justice system itself was misfortune's author for these men and others. Yet only the wrongfully convicted bear the lost years, the inevitable shame.

I can't imagine just how ruinous the tragedy is for them and their families. Being wrongfully charged and then exonerated nine months later was more than enough for me.

All of which makes the time between charges laid and charges dismissed a linchpin to the principles of fundamental justice in Canada and the U.S. The delays in the system are taken for granted, notwithstanding the constitutional injunction that there be no unreasonable delays, because that's just the way it is. The phenomenon reminds me a little of the modern health-care system. As new drugs and technologies advance, so does the cost of the system. As new forensic technologies advance, the criminal justice system requires more experts, more money, more preparation, more time. It's a natural evolution.

Indeed, I consider myself an accomplice in this "evolution" in Ontario. The crux of the Organized Justice strategy, as embodied in the Ontario Guns and Gangs Operations Centre and its Task Force, leverages technology and intelligence-led analysis that is the frontier of policing strategies today.* It is fundamentally a response to global organized crime, itself a chilling marvel of technology and illegal commerce. Inevitably, the resources expended in the name of Organized Justice draw from resources that might be directed toward community policing, wherein the police integrate themselves within a community of people who all collaborate to address public safety.

How all this gets reflected in police budgets, priorities, planning, structure, and training is unclear to me, but it doesn't bolster the savvy street work needed to manage substance abuse in our communities. There may be a growing elite of police officers trained in the science of their craft, in intelligence-led policing, and this is a positive development of professionalism.

However, professionalism in investigative tools is quite different from professionalism in the matter of laying criminal charges. There wasn't any intelligence-led investigation before I was charged, within minutes of police showing up at the scene.

Yes, there is obvious value of *CSI*-esque efforts in tackling complicated criminal endeavours. But what of the constables on

---

* Tilley, Nick. (2003). *Problem-Oriented Policing, Intelligence-Led Policing and the National Intelligence Model.* Jill Dando Institute of Crime Science, University College London; The Frontline Perspective: Megan Haynes, "Criminal Intelligence Analysts: Celebrating 35 Years of Service." 2009. Vol. 3, No.1.

the beat, like the ones who watched Darcy Sheppard drive off on his bike, intoxicated at double the legal limit, to his death? And what of those who hastily charge people before an investigation has really started, let alone is complete?

The latter constables operate within a centuries-old police structure that sees police as local adjunct of the military, empowered to guard the innocent from danger, designed to defend against conflict, less than a profession designed for modern due process. Intelligence-led policing bolsters police professionalism, to be sure, but advanced empiricism needs to be matched by an advanced system of laying charges—not just for the expensive *CSI*-esque investigations, but the kind of street incidents like the tragedy of my 28 seconds.

That's why prosecutors, not police, ought to lay criminal charges in Ontario, as is done in B.C. and Quebec. Or at least the more serious crimes, for the felonies. Let the decision be a collaboration between police and prosecutors, as works so well with the Ontario Guns and Gangs Task Force. Let each branch of the criminal justice system be a check against the other, at this critical, too-often-overlooked, early stage—*before* the charges get laid.

WHEN HARM IS WROUGHT, there is a natural tendency to seek comfort, or at least explanation, in finding someone guilty of something. And no doubt some family and friends of Darcy Sheppard felt anger when Richard Peck dropped the charges against me.

Sheppard endured a hard life with no help from a justice system blind to his past trauma, addictions, and immutable afflictions. His life was lost.

That he would die at the hands of someone so identified with that justice system, and its shortcomings, no doubt seemed doubly unjust, probably to the point of cruelty, to his loved ones.

As Attorney General, I was the Ontario justice system's biggest booster, if nothing else. I'd often close speeches at courthouses with the following remarks: "It was the boast of Augustus that he found Rome of brick, and left it of marble. It will be our boast in Ontario that we found a justice system of marble and left it of gold."*

That I would find myself at the other end of the same said justice system—after what was, at best, a cursory investigation, a most ungilded moment—was inexplicable to me and my family.

In this story, there truly were no winners.

---

* I was injudiciously borrowing from the Scottish jurist and politician Lord Henry Brougham (1778–1868): "It was the boast of Augustus that he found Rome of brick and left it of marble. But how much nobler will be the sovereign's boast when he shall have it to say that he found law ... a sealed book and left it a living letter; found it the patrimony of the rich and left it the inheritance of the poor; found it the two-edged sword of craft and oppression and left it the staff of honesty and the shield of innocence."

EIGHTEEN

Another Death: My Brother

To everything, the Book of Ecclesiastes, Pete Seeger, and the Byrds agree, there is a season. And if I had thought, as a result of that awful evening in August 2009, that I'd already lived my season of loss, I was wrong again.

In the early twilight of a Thursday in June 2011, I received a telephone call from my mother. She was hysterical. She said something about my younger brother, Alan, having had emergency open-heart surgery. I caught the next plane to Memphis, where Alan lived and worked.

Alan had been a terrific high-school basketball player in his youth in Victoria. His dream was to have a career in basketball management, and he achieved it. He started in 1998 with the National Basketball Association's Vancouver Grizzlies at GM Place and he moved to Tennessee, along with the franchise, when it became the Memphis Grizzlies.

Big Al was living the life he loved.

He was a fiercely loyal and hilarious senior manager for the Grizzlies. His office, I was told, was always the central hub for team employees. During Grizzlies' games, Alan ran all the music and sound effects at FedEx Forum in Memphis. He didn't make a lot of money, but he saved well, and he owned property in our hometown of Victoria and on Qualicum Beach on Vancouver Island. Alan was also still Canadian to the core, and was utterly thrilled to manage the hockey venue for the 2010 Winter Olympics in Vancouver.

My plane touched down in Memphis on June 10, 2011, the morning after my mother called, and I was driven to the hospital by one of my brother's bosses. When I arrived, I saw Alan's huge body sprawled all over a hospital bed. He was on a respirator and it seemed there were tubes everywhere. On seeing him, I burst into tears.

His two Memphis "brothers," Hark and Pugs, had been by his side since he arrived at the hospital. One of the men had actually saved Alan from dying alone in his apartment, breaking into his place at 3 a.m. and calling an ambulance. He had suffered an aortic dissection—a congenital heart condition, wherein the aorta basically falls apart. Fewer than half of patients with a ruptured aorta survive.

As I sat by Al's side at the hospital, dozens of people came to visit him in the intensive-care unit. It's hard to describe watching your brother's life pass before your eyes over a weekend. But on a certain level, it was an inspiring experience. Alan was a generous friend and his deeds, which I learned of that weekend, consoled and inspired me. Sometimes people stitched together, right in front of us, something that Alan had done to help one or the other. Yet they said he wanted no credit. He just did it for the joy of helping others.

With each passing day, there was good news and bad. That Alan was still alive was the good. The bad news was that the heart medication was being increased at a necessary but alarming rate, as were the painkillers. This was damaging his internal organs, even as his heart seemed to grow weaker and weaker. At one point, doctors had to slice open his calves to allow for the grotesque swelling. It was too macabre for anyone who loved him to watch.

Even so, I enjoyed the visits of Alan's friends and colleagues, some unknowingly saying their goodbyes. One co-worker arrived on my second night, a Saturday, just before 7 p.m., to watch the Vancouver Canucks' playoff hockey game. She pointed the TV at the two of them, sat back in a chair parallel to Alan's bed, held his giant hand, and chatted away to him, as if he were answering her sometimes. She was very pretty and I wondered if Alan had ever fallen for her, never saying anything, happy just to be a friend and in her company. I decided to leave the two of them alone, to watch the game in privacy. He'd have done the same for me, I thought.

But I always cleared out all the visitors at 10 p.m., to allow us to spend a couple of hours together. I'd talk to him, haltingly, at first. It felt like talking to myself, with an audience of ICU nurses and technicians and doctors streaming through every few minutes. Eventually, I spoke to him as if it were perfectly natural to speak to someone who was completely comatose. By midnight, I'd try to sleep in that impossible chair, waking every few hours to stare at the machines and at my brother.

Throughout my vigil, I spent a lot of time talking on the phone to my sister, Janine. She is four years my elder, and over the past few years we'd became as close again as we'd been as little kids. As a little boy, I'd worshipped her. Over time, we grew a little distant, primarily for reasons of geography. By 2006, she had two beautiful children, a wonderful husband, and a successful teaching career. She'd been named one of Canada's Outstanding Principals, and I had emceed the award ceremony in Toronto at which she had been honoured. It was a highlight of our lives.

In Memphis, Janine became my sister like never before. I couldn't have survived the experience without her. She cared for my parents at home in Victoria, but I was never alone in Memphis, with Janine ever present by telephone and by Skype. We had each other, as we were losing our sibling, and for that I will be forever grateful.

In Memphis, in that hospital, I remembered the day that Alan had arrived in my life, not long after he was born and then adopted by our family. I was six years old, but the memory remains vivid: walking in his room and seeing that red hair for the first time, driving home in the car with baby Al in Mom's arms in the front seat, then bringing him into our new home on Longview Drive, in Gordon Head, Victoria, B.C.

It never occurred to me to ask why a child was arriving six years after the last (me). I just knew that Mom couldn't have any more kids herself, after I was born. My comprehension of the female anatomy was such that I assumed they broke the mould after my birth. Perhaps three kids was always the plan, perhaps it was a new plan. No matter: it was the most exciting thing that had happened to me, and I assumed that everyone must have an adopted sibling.

Alan kept scratching his eyes so we put mittens on his tiny hands. Until my own kids were born, that day was the best moment of my life.

On June 13, 2011, at 2 a.m., a neurologist I hadn't yet met began shaking me. Alan was brain dead, he said. Zero brain-stem functions. As much as I'd appreciated all the medical care he'd received, I went into full denial. I demanded further tests to confirm that he couldn't function without a breathing machine.

Later that morning, another neurologist began the tests for brain-stem function. Watching her punch his trachea, poke his eyes, twist his head, made it all quite real for me. I also noticed, quite suddenly, how peaceful he looked. No more gagging reflex from the breathing machine. He wasn't there anymore.

My parents and my sister Janine all agreed that Alan would not want to be sustained artificially. Yet I still hesitated, asking for more tests, needing more time.

On the morning of June 14, a day after our father's birthday, Alan passed away, his heart stopping in front of my eyes as I squeezed his hand. That hand was no longer tiny, the way it was that first day I held it when we brought him home. But it was the same hand, same brother. For 39 years, he had been a joy to our family. And for 39 years, those hands were generous, kind, gentle—and perfect for high-fiving. We'd done a lot of that, the two of us.

After Alan died, I immediately went home to Toronto to hug my kids. Susan was supportive throughout the ordeal, and was herself ripped apart by Alan's loss. She had a brother Alan's age, Seth, and she had also been close to Alan.

During my time in the Memphis hospital, I'd been at peace with the care Alan received and thought I was able to accept the lottery of tragedy as part of life. But for the rest of that summer, I lived through a moderate but very real depression. I was dysfunctional, slow, distracted, and lifeless. It got to the point where I didn't want to get out of bed. My psychiatrist told me to go for a walk for 20 minutes, every day. Apparently, as long as I could do that, we could avoid something more serious. I got better.

Still, over the summer I began to question my faith. How could God allow this to happen? And if God wasn't there to save people, or to decide when they lived or died in a far more just fashion, what on earth was God's role, function, purpose? How do I square a just God with this unjust result of my brother's death? I started to get over the existential crisis, later that year, when I stopped craning my will toward salvation. I can't answer those metaphysical questions any more than a cow can be fluent in Mandarin. I can only tell you what it feels like.

It was through this loss, and the process of trying to fathom and accept it, that I could better understand what it had been like for the family and friends of Darcy Sheppard to so suddenly lose him. I miss my brother, terribly and often.

THE FIRST CHRISTMAS after Alan passed, his biological mother, whom I'll call Judy, Googled "Alan Thomas"—his name, minus our surname. The British Columbia adoption registry has a disclosure veto. When she had requested to contact him many years ago, Alan declined, thinking that it would upset my parents too much.

Nevertheless, she'd discovered his given names through an error by the provincial registry. The Google results put Alan's obituary front and centre. She recognized him immediately.

By reading through a blog I'd created for those wishing to eulogize Al, she learned a lot about the boy she'd given birth to when she was very young. She also discovered the names of Alan's siblings, and as she lived in Victoria, she called Janine first.

At first they agreed to meet later in the week, but then they called each other an hour later to say they couldn't wait that long. They met that afternoon. Soon enough, I was exchanging emails with my brother's biological mom. She announced that she'd be visiting Mississauga, just outside Toronto, in a few weeks. So we agreed to meet.

As I entered the hotel lobby where she was staying, she greeted me with Alan's eyes, and Alan's smile. The last I saw Alan, comatose in the ICU, I hadn't seen his eyes, or his smile.

"I don't know where to start," I said.

"Just start," she replied. Her manner was warm and welcoming.

I shared as many telling stories as I could remember. And then realized I'd been talking for over half an hour.

"Tell me about what it was like at the end," she said. She wanted to know how he died.

"No. I will. But your turn. Tell me—"

"Back then, in 1972, in the town I grew up in ... Well, this has been my secret. A secret I've been holding my entire life. And now ... No more secrets ..."

Judy shared with me how she'd left her home province to have her baby adopted by a family in Victoria. She had ten days after the birth to change her mind. She did not feel old enough to raise a child, let alone by herself, let alone with the birth as a secret.

In fact, despite enjoying being an aunt, she never wanted to raise a child herself.

"All that goes into raising a child ... Just never for me," she said. "I have no regrets."

Judy was incredibly generous and thoughtful with her words, for my mom and for all of us.

I wondered how it felt to discover Alan's identity, to find him, like she did in his obituary, learning of his death.

"For me, I feel like I've found him. Maybe I'd never have found him if he hadn't passed when he did. So it's a loss for you and your family, but it's something else for me. And I feel like I've extended my family. We're family now, if that's okay."

It was okay.

NINETEEN

Home Unalone

B y the time of Alan's death, I was still adjusting to the parade of dramatic changes that seemed to have become my new normal. At some point during our marriage, the two opposites that had formed a vessel of compatibility and support and love started to change, but didn't change together. I had changed dramatically since we married. At times, I didn't recognize my present self any more than Susan did. It's not that we hadn't done the work. We had worn out the carpet in counsellors' offices. Our marriage had been put through too much. We found that, even with the best efforts, we simply weren't able to put Humpty Dumpty back together again.

The comedian Louis C.K. says that "no good marriage has ever ended in divorce," so lamenting a marital split is foolish. It's a joke but we get the point. That doesn't mean there isn't enough guilt and regret to sink a tanker. To me, the end of our marriage feels tragic, sad, mysterious, right, inevitable, hopeful, and bizarre.

On December 9, 2010, we decided to separate. Then, Susan and the kids headed to visit with their grandparents in New Hampshire, while I raced around the city making arrangements for a new life as a single father.

I lucked into a gem of an apartment, thanks to a tip given to my real-estate agent. It's a 1920s building, which has seen little in the way of renovation, thank goodness. Art Deco lobby, large,

12-foot ceilings, expansive hallways, huge windows, and parquet floors.

In double-quick time, I bought and assembled furniture and decorated the children's rooms and the living room. I'd researched the state of TV technology, to determine the largest TV a human could fit through my apartment doorways without requiring a second mortgage. It was The Guilty Father Television, and it would be bigger than the one at their mom's. On this one point, I would be a small person.

We wanted the kids not to fret, about what their new lives would be like. Instead, the plan was to tell them on Boxing Day, then show them immediately the new apartment, their new second home.

Boxing Day came and went. The apartment, miraculously, was ready, including a fresh coat of paint. Not bad for a guy who had no thought of an apartment less than two weeks previous. But I wasn't ready to tell them, and Susan was willing to wait another day before getting on with the rest of our lives.

On December 27, as the kids were eating sandwiches at the kitchen table, Susan and I sat down to tell Sadie and Louie the hardest thing I'd ever had to tell anyone.

It couldn't have gone better, and it couldn't have felt worse. Afterwards, I ran up to the walk-in closet in my suddenly former bedroom, threw myself on the carpet, and buried my face in my hands for the biggest cry since I'd sobered up.

Susan and I had rehearsed the moment several times, after consulting with our now-divorce therapist. The goal was to transmit the facts to the kids, and just the facts, with as little emotion as possible. Then immediately *show* them their new lives.

Susan asked me to speak first. Deep breath.

"You're going to have two homes," I told them, "because Daddy is moving out today, and you're going to see your new apartment in a few moments. It's going to be—"

"What?!" Sadie said, the 8-year-old objecting to this sanitized version. "Are you two not going to be married anymore?!"

"No," we said simultaneously.

"I'm sorry, Sadie," I said. "We're getting unmarried."

Sadie broke into tears. Susan took her in her arms, on one side of the banquette. I was on the side with Louie, who just looked at me, a little grumpy face, and no words.

"You can punch me, if you'd like," I told Louie, so he proceeded to do so, although they felt like love-taps to my cheek. Sometimes when we were playing, Louie would say: "Come here so I can punch you in the face!" and I'd oblige. Now he was doing it not out of fun, but necessity. Sadie crying in Mom's arms, and Louie punching me, repeatedly, in the head.

"I just need a minute to process this," Sadie said, as if she were my mother-in-law rather than my daughter.

"You're stupid!" said Louie.

So they were processing it all, and that was good news. May you never have to go through this in your life. I will never do it again.

We went over to my new apartment, all of us, soon thereafter. Louie ran around, loving the open space, and Sadie gushed over her poster-bed of pink and blue. Louie had daydreamed aloud about having a bed nestled in a hockey net. So I made that happen. It was pretty cool. The gigantic TV was a hit.

When school started the next week, Sadie had show-and-tell the very first day back. She brought her backpack, explaining to everyone that she used it to travel to her new second home, declaring her parents "divorced" like a thing of great drama, even pride. Sadie had also composed a song: "My Parents Broke Up on Boxing Day," replete with a catchy melody.

We soon enough settled into a new routine. Tuesdays and Wednesdays at my place, to allow me to attend my fellowship meetings for recovering alcoholics on Monday and Thursday nights. Weekends were rotated. (The division of property was settled in a five-minute conversation between Susan and me. The papers wouldn't be signed for many months, but only because of my procrastination.)

AN ALARM RINGS at around 7 a.m., the sound of church bells emitting from a mini-stereo I inherited from Alan. (For the Millennial Generation, a deceased bachelor's estate resembles more an electronics store clearance than a garage sale.) Sometimes the alarm is redundant, if my 7-year-old keeps to his bio-rhythmic schedule: Sun up, Louie up, and climbing in my bed, silently but urgently, his feet pummelling me. It's quite a wake-up call.

Up now, out of bed, after a run-down of his dreams and night-mares the night before, or his request to go on the computer, usually denied, because it's a school day and we barely make it in time for playground play before the bells ring at 8:45.

Louie is reading the back of the cereal box while sitting at the plastic folding table in the kitchen. Vitamin D is squeezed from a dropper into their plastic cups of cold water. Now to Sadie's room: open shutters, kiss her forehead, thereby allowing a gradual awakening and the eventual arrival of her 9-year-old butt onto the plastic folding chair in the kitchen. I'm ripping shells off a boiled egg, chewing on raw almonds, gulping espresso, and making sandwiches while scouring for the small lids to fit the small tubs that look so neat on the grocery shelf but end up overpopulating a refugee camp of plastic in your cupboard.

It's a galley kitchen, the only thing in my apartment I wish were otherwise. The kids' rooms are slightly larger than their rooms at the ex-matrimonial home, literally two minutes away. That room size was enough to take the apartment on the spot, for the living room was massive and able to house the Guilty Father TV (Sharp Quattro 50-inch LED) and Elte white sectional couch (yes, snow white, as in "clean slate"), and a dining-room table made out of wood from an old bowling lane, rebuilt onto cast-iron painted roughly green, all with plenty of room to spare. I didn't care that my bedroom would be in the old dining room, with old-fashioned sconces and wainscotting that made it always look like a ... dining room. A veranda big enough for one 45-year-old to smoke a cigar was as much a bonus as the real fireplace.

But the kitchen is cramped and far away from the dining room table, so I got the folding table and chairs from Costco to be with the kids while they eat breakfast and Dad makes lunches. None of the foregoing activities took place at the house when married, for reasons I can't explain. In fact, despite my assumption that I was a great hands-on dad, I would have no idea what it was like to be a mom until I became a single dad.

After breakfast, I finish making lunches and getting their homework in their backpacks, occasionally completing the uncompleted homework assignment in the morning. French immersion for them means French immersion for me, too, and my vocabulary is increasing daily, with theirs. Sadie was soon so proficient and bilingual that she became our living, breathing Google Translate, which I resorted to often. Shoes re-tied, jackets re-located, jackets zipped up, and in the winter, scarves and hats assembled, matching gloves remembered. Backpacks on, and then the elevator door button gets pushed. Wait—sign the homework, return it to the backpack. Wait—it's library today, find the books. Push the elevator button again. In this building, there are only three units per floor, and the elevator is inches from our front door. The kids think it their own.

Then we walk to school together, a two-minute trek, at most. I had found Question Period at Queen's Park much less stressful than getting my kids to school on time. This was especially so after I found out that for the first four months of single dad-hood, I'd been delivering them to school ten minutes late, every day I had them. An 8:50, not a 9 a.m., start, I learned. Who knew?!

Well, Susan knew, but she delivered the news without rancour. Our relationship was always, and remains, as amicable and trans-actional as two partners in a highly successful dentist practice. No resentment, no envy, nothing negative. We swallow any of that when it burbles up, for the kids. It's easy, somehow, even if it was impossible when we were married.

With my newfound single dad-hood I learned many things: do not starve or over-sugar, find shoes, stop saying "shit," smell milk before pouring, get them to Tae Kwon Do or dancing or piano or Hebrew School, or a play date, or a birthday party, or the paediatri-cian, on time.

As time passed, my Bay Street job became less important to me. Most of my work at Norton Rose Canada (formerly Ogilvy Renault) was with my former classmate Richard King, some with Phil Fontaine, former national chief of the Assembly of First Nations, whom I had lured over to the firm. Basically, we helped companies do business with First Nations. It was less law than commercial matchmaking. But it was gratifying work, nonethe-less, in the field of aboriginal affairs, which was no longer my job description but still a vocation.

So, there was I, no longer living under the threat of criminal charges. But I was also no longer a cabinet minister, no longer a politician, no longer the president and CEO of anything, no longer a husband, still mourning a beloved sibling, and ever adjusting to a life led sober. I'd led a charmed life, and now I was leading a changed life.

SOME CHANGES WERE PROFOUND, others pedestrian. When the news media came calling, as they occasionally did, for comment on public-policy issues that I'd had lots to say about in a previous life, I ignored them or politely declined. The only exceptions were issues involving aboriginal peoples (now the mainstay of my law practice) and anything about gun control.

If a friend wanted me to speak at a political fundraiser, I did so, but they were always modest affairs. Some charities asked me to speak at events as well, and I happily obliged, but my performances were no longer the self-indulgent Michael-fests of old.

For a time that year, along with working at the law firm, I worked with my former neighbour, Michael Scot-Smith, from Gordon Head, in Victoria, who, among other things, owned Slimband, the gastric banding operation of notable success. Michael was a great entrepreneur, who had made his first million while I was still in high school. He asked me to run one of his new companies, which I did for a few months.

During those early months being a single dad, without a vehicle to transport the kids, Michael kindly let me borrow the Hyundai compact cars driven by his nurses to visit Slimband patients during after-care.

These two cars were utilized as much for advertising as transportation. Painted onto the deep blue Hyundais, which we called the Slimband-mobiles, were before-and-after photos of successful Slimband patients: typically, obese before, and leopard-skin bikini-ed afterwards. On the side door, it read, in huge, bold letters: "I lost 200 Pounds!"

Initially, the kids thought these cars were hilarious. And Louie enjoyed the gigantic breasts pictured on the car's hood. But soon enough they were suitably mortified, and asked that I pick them up a block away from wherever they were coming from. Plus, when I parked the car in the Whole Foods parking lot, the Porsche and Maserati owners literally sniffed at me. I needed to get a real car, one suitable for transporting two children.

So I bought the second largest mini-van on the market, the mammoth Honda Odyssey. The kids could sit in the second or *third* row and catch the DVD lowered from the ceiling, with enough cup holders to excite anyone under age 12.

With me at the wheel of a grey mini-van, whatever else I wasn't any longer, one thing was now official. I was, first and foremost, a single dad.

IN THE SPRING OF 2011, I was sharing the stage with some local celebrities for GetLit, a charity promoting literacy for underprivileged kids. We were all to read from a book that had a huge impact upon us in our younger days. After I read from John Irving's *A Prayer for Owen Meany,* and admitted the book brought me closer to God, I was approached by *Globe and Mail* columnist Margaret Wente (who'd read from A. A. Milne), while everyone was mingling around.

"Oh, my God! Michael Bryant! You have completely transformed!! What happened!?" Wente said.

The people standing around me stopped chatting to see what this was all about.

"Oh! ... Ok!" I said. "Wow. Er ... r ... thank you?"

"Yes, no—I mean: you're completely different? What did you do?"

I was wearing Peter Parker–esque glasses and sporting a beard, which someone told me was slimming, but I suspected that her observation was more about my character than my appearance.

I'd never try to finesse Margaret Wente, for fear of ending up in her column as a phony. So I just answered the question as bluntly as she asked it.

"I found humility, Margaret. My experiences over the last couple years have brought me humility, and that inevitable sweet surrender lends a certain—"

I stopped short when her face twisted up into something that conveyed incomprehension, maybe disapproval. She laughed nervously and said to me: "Michael, that's Too-Much-Information, dear. I just meant you look different with the facial hair."

Then, she winked at me. "Humility looks good on you."

But not everyone saw this as a change, or what feels like a change, in me.

"Actually, you remind me now of when I first met you, just before you first went into politics," my good friend Sandra D'Ambrosio said to me over lunch. "You were soooo idealistic, and so shocked that anyone would actually support you. It made people want to support you."

There are indeed moments where present changes feel like a return to a much younger, maybe more innocent past, more than a rebirth. I suspect it's probably too soon to risk any generalizations about such things. All I know is what it feels like.

It feels like I broke a giant string of Sadie's beads, and I'm finding them all over the place. Sometimes one is discovered under a bare foot, and it's surprising how much that can hurt. Sometimes the discovery is a marvel. At first it's a big mess, then tidied up with some help from others, and everything looks better than ever. Then you rediscover that it's not so tidy. You don't realize how fragile is that string, and how big a mess it will make, until it breaks.

That busted string of beautiful beads is gone for good, it seems, and I don't really want it back. My universe changed in a half-minute, then I learned that misfortune never arrives alone. I learned that it gets better, sometimes quickly, sometimes slowly, even when it doesn't always feel that way. And I learned how to do it on the sunny side of the street, away from those shadows of intemperance and pride, that dark, narcissistic mania; away from those shadows where Darcy Sheppard lived and died; and where I join so many who help, even as we are helped by, those deprived of light, soaked in a merciless night.

His death has awoken something in me. I know there are many people in my life who'd like me to "put all this behind" me. But I can't. Not won't, or shan't, but can't. I won't forget him, his life, his death, and I won't let you forget it either. How could I?

ACKNOWLEDGMENTS

Life is full of joy and suffering, spikes and lulls. The two people who always bring me to the best place are my kids Sadie and Louie. Thanks to them and their mom, Susan Abramovitch, for having them, for being a brave passenger during our 28 seconds, and for an epic and eternal partnership.

Thank you Nikki Holland for being Nikki Holland. Thanks to mentors Beverley McLachlin, Frank Iacobucci, Rosalie Abella, Roy McMurtry, Jim MacPherson, Dalton McGuinty, Les Scheininger, Tom Heintzman, Jan Innes, and John West. For saving my life, thanks to Susan, Marie Henein, Margaret Bojanowska, Jordan Glick, Matthew Gourlay, and Danielle Robitaille.

The book would not have happened without a lunch with my daughter's friend's dad, Doug Pepper, who encouraged me to write something down early and often. Nor would it have happened without Amanda Lang introducing me to her agent, Rick Broadhead (now mine too), who then introduced me to Diane Turbide, Publishing Director at Penguin. Thanks to Diane's extraordinary team at Penguin; I'm especially grateful for Diane's great compassion, editing, direction, and mentorship. Thanks to my high school English teacher, Mrs. Simpson (retired) of Mount Douglas Senior Secondary, for making me think I could write a book one day.

Nor would the book have happened without my family: Ray and Margaret Bryant, Janine Bryant Roy, Bob Roy, Matthew and

Hailey Roy, my brother Alan, Sadie and Louie Bryant, and their mom, Susan Abramovitch.

Nor would it have happened without friends with poignant words of encouragement: Phoebe Alix, Denise Brunsdon, Jim C. (again), Cynthia Dann-Beardsley, Marie Henein (again), Michael Ignatieff, and Sam Nutt.

Thanks for spiritual support from Mel, MB, Kyra, Janet, Dan, Dionne, Greg, Ron, Kim, Brandon, Billy, Kelly, Anne, Gail, Mary, Bruce, Wayne, Michael, and everyone at my home group. Thanks also to Dr. Bruce Sutton and Dr. Eliana Cohen.

The aftermath of the 28 seconds saw heroic efforts of friendship and support from countless people, including many already referenced here and in the book, plus Brent Belzberg, Barry Campbell, Earl Cherniak, Max Cohen, Ian Delaney, Peter Dotsikas, Mike Eizenga, Andrew Evangelista, Joanne Ferstman, Neil and Marie Finkelstein, Sandy Forbes, Linda Frum, Stephen Granovsky, Stephen Grant, Mohammed Hamoodi, Julia Hanigsberg, Graham Henderson and Margo Timmins, Richard King, John Keefe, Gary Kissack, Amanda and Adrian Lang (Junior and Senior!), Michael McMillan, Will McDowell, Mihnea Moldoveanu, Paul Morrison, Ralph Palumbo, Robert Prichard, Linda Rothstein, Joe and Sandy Rotman, Gerry Sadvari, David Scott, Lorne Sossin, Fab Stanghierei, Harvey Strosberg, Louise Summerhill, John Tory, Jaime Watt, Ann Wilson, and Ben Zarnett.

There is no political journey to tell without Nikki, Jan, Les, Joe Ragusa, David Caplan (and the entire clan), Tom Allison, Mitch Frazer, Doug Frith (deceased), Dave Pretlove, Emily Bullock, Melissa Rola, Erika Moses, Debora Steggles, Catherine Bruder, Cara O'Hagan, Sarah Robers, Elaine Mintz, Betsy Hall, Joanna Furse, Chris May, Glen Brown, Howard Brown, Michael Joliffe, Kelly Legris, Kinsella, Mohammed Al Zaibek, Vera, Paul and Gord Brookes, Rod Elliot, Graham Kechnie, Kate Julien, Danielle Kotras,

Nancy Medeiros, Katherine King, Andrea Bird, Alicia McFadden, Jason Murray, Lisa Gold, Joe Halicki, Daniel Infante, Alexis Levine, Beth Hirshfeld, Chris Holcroft, Stephen Delduca, Greg Crone, Natasha Holland, Adam Dodek, Linda Shin, Rod MacDonald, Paul Martin, Allan Rock, Terry O'Leary, David Hurley, David MacNaughton, John and Beth Webster, Tony Ianno, Christine Innes, Jeanette Harris, Keith Brennenstuhl, Senator David Smith, John Duffy, Tom and Mary Jane Heintzman, Mike Barrack, Will McDowell, Frank McKenna, David Peterson, Senator Grafstein, Peter O'Brien and Carolyn Bennett, but especially Carolyn and Peter. There are too many colleagues from the Legislature to mention.

Lastly, to friends who persevered amidst my dysfunctional Mr. Magoo moments, thank you. I was tardy, MIA and AWOL too often. Enough of all that.

INDEX

Note: Quotation marks around a name indicate a pseudonym. For simplicity, the following abbreviations are used in most main headings and in all subheadings: DS: Darcy Allan Sheppard; MB: Michael Bryant; SA: Susan Abramovitch. Unless otherwise specified, a relationship in parentheses after a proper name refers to that person's relationship with Michael Bryant.